D0872040

Just Getting Started

Edmonton Public Library's First 100 Years, 1913–2013

November 2013

Ghalib and Derek –
Reading the city into being.

TODD BABIAK

Just Getting Started

Edmonton Public Library's First 100 Years, 1913–2013

Gutteridge
BOOKS
An Imprint of The University of Alberta Press

epl.ca EDMONTON PUBLIC LIBRARY

Published by

The University of Alberta Press
Ring House 2
Edmonton, Alberta, Canada T6G 2E1
www.uap.ualberta.ca

and

Edmonton Public Library
Stanley A. Milner Library
7 Sir Winston Churchill Square
Edmonton, Alberta, Canada T5J 2V4
www.epl.ca

LIBRARY AND ARCHIVES CANADA
CATALOGUING IN PUBLICATION

Babiak, Todd, 1972–, author
Just getting started : Edmonton Public Library's first 100 years, 1913–2013 / Todd Babiak.

Includes bibliographical references and index.
Issued in print and electronic formats.
ISBN 978–0–88864–729–0 (bound).—
ISBN 978–0–88864–728–3 (pbk.).—
ISBN 978–0–88864–746–7 (epub).—
ISBN 978–0–88864–747–4
(Amazon kindle)

1. Edmonton Public Library—History.
2. Edmonton Public Library—Anecdotes.
3. Public libraries—Alberta—Edmonton—History. I. Title.

Z736.E36B32 2013
027.47123'34 C2013–904960–6
C2013–904961–4

First edition, first printing, 2013.
Printed and bound in Canada by Friesens, Altona, Manitoba.
Copyediting by Linda Goyette.
Proofreading by Linda Goyette.
Indexing by Judy Dunlop.

The University of Alberta Press is committed to protecting our natural environment. As part of our efforts, this book is printed on Enviro Paper: it contains 100% post-consumer recycled fibres and is acid- and chlorine-free.

The University of Alberta Press gratefully acknowledges the support received for its publishing program from The Canada Council for the Arts. The University of Alberta Press also gratefully acknowledges the financial support of the Government of Canada through the Canada Book Fund (CBF) and the Government of Alberta through the Alberta Multimedia Development Fund (AMDF) for its publishing activities.

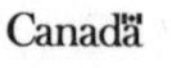

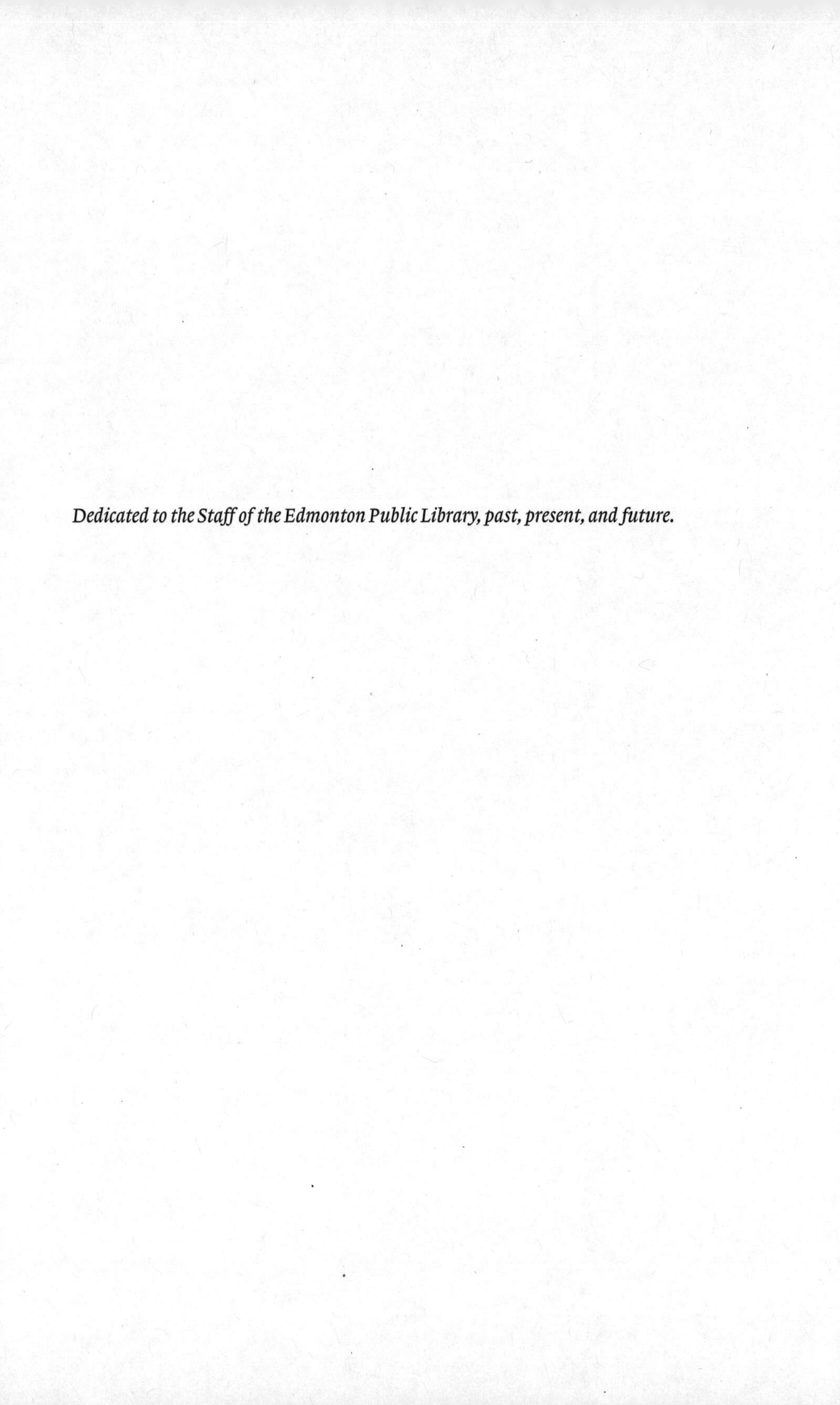

Dedicated to the Staff of the Edmonton Public Library, past, present, and future.

"...the contribution made by the Edmonton libraries to the sanity and support of the citizens cannot be estimated. No Annual Report can gauge things of this sort."

—ANNUAL REPORT OF THE EDMONTON PUBLIC LIBRARY, 1931

Contents

Acknowledgements

LIKE A LIBRARY, a book about a library is a team effort. This team came together quickly and elegantly, and always in good humour.

We would like to thank the Friends of the Edmonton Public Library for their generous financial support of this project.

Librarian Anne Marquis is the stage manager of this book: a researcher, editor, fact-checker, curator, critic, and international negotiator. Chris Bezovie was the photographic Sherlock Holmes, finding the unfindable in the Edmonton Public Library (EPL) archives. Yvonne Brown, heritage librarian at EPL, researched and prepared a lovely timeline. Anna-Marie Klassen hunted down and captured a writer for the project. EPL's Marketing and Fund Development department helped tremendously.

Professionals at the City of Edmonton Archives, the University of Alberta's Peel's Prairie Provinces collection, and the Provincial Archives of Alberta moved quickly and kindly to help a frantic team illustrate one hundred years of history.

Thank you to Edmontonians who allowed the writer to intrude upon their lives for an hour or two, with no reward but a lunch or a coffee.

Many of them, like Stanley Milner, insisted on picking up the cheque at the end of the conversation.

Edmonton Public Library CEO Linda Cook encouraged the writer to "try something a little bit different" with this book, and she was a wonderful editor of the hasty first draft. Linda Cameron and her team from the University of Alberta Press were equally encouraging. Several librarians, in branches across the city, told stories and helped the writer find things he could not have discovered on his own.

Every error in this book is entirely his fault, no matter what he tries to tell you.

Foreword

IT WAS A FOREGONE CONCLUSION that one of the major projects the Edmonton Public Library would undertake to celebrate its Centennial during 2013 was the writing of its history. Other than a few timelines highlighting various events that have occurred over the years, nothing of significance or of a lasting nature has ever been written to document the library's incredible journey. Between its somewhat controversial beginning in 1913 and becoming one of Canada's most successful public libraries in 2013, many interesting and oddball occurrences have taken place that need to be preserved and remembered.

As CEO of the library, I wanted to ensure that our history book would not end up as a simple keepsake relegated to the top shelf of a person's bookcase, to be taken down for dusting once every few months. How does one go about ensuring that a comprehensive history book describing the first hundred years of such a visionary library system as the Edmonton Public Library is written in a highly readable and entertaining style? Key to this goal, is selecting the right author. I had been aware of Todd Babiak for a long time—first from the thirteen years he spent writing for the *Edmonton Journal*, and then as the successful author of several prize-winning novels, three of which took place in Edmonton. However, it was a description of him in *Avenue Magazine* as one of their "Top 40 Under 40" that caught my attention:

> *When Babiak gets excited about Edmonton, its faults and glories, he can't be muzzled. Though wanderlust has pulled him away from the city, he always finds his way back to it, and it almost always finds its way into his work.*[1]

I felt he would be the perfect author to write our history with the care, attention, and passion it deserved. Upon approaching him, he initially declined, having just begun a new business venture called Story Engine. However, with the help of EPL Board Trustee Vice-Chair John MacDonald III, who had worked with Todd at the *Journal*, we were able to convince him to take on the project.

The final result is everything I hoped it would be—informative, funny, sad at times, and as much a history of our great city as it is of the library system. When I received the first draft to review, I found that, like a really good novel, I could not put it down. We learn about the politics, personalities and events that helped shape Edmonton Public Library over ten decades. Todd has done a tremendous job of enticing the reader with true and, at times, humorous anecdotes sprinkled throughout the book.

Edmonton Public Library has so much to be proud of and *Just Getting Started* is a wonderful story that will ensure the memories made over the first 100 years will not be forgotten.

LINDA C. COOK
Chief Executive Officer
Edmonton Public Library

1 Without a library, is a city a city?

BY THE TIME I WAS OLD ENOUGH for a genuine conversation with him, my grandfather was a dreamy widower. With a glass or two of rye he was a constant storyteller. He would talk about growing up in an Edmonton of the imagination, a place he could only see when he closed his eyes.

His wife had died young of cancer and he was not the kind to remarry. He learned to cook and retreated into his memories. The place and the early evening he often described on these retreats was somewhere in the 1950s across the street from the Hotel Macdonald, on a bit of grass. He is in his thirties, a young father, married to a tall and sarcastic woman. The kids are with a babysitter. They have just visited the downtown branch of the Edmonton Public Library, the Carnegie Library, in its original location on Macdonald Drive, and my grandmother wants a cigarette. They go down the stairs with the sun on their faces and enter the square park, a bowling green. It is May and just warm enough to leave jackets at home. Flowers are up and blooming on the borders of the grass. It smells of lilac and dusk is coming. My grandfather takes the novel his wife has borrowed, to carry it for her. The limestone of the library, in this

The Carnegie Library (far right) at "the top of the hill," built with Indiana limestone and a red Spanish tile roof with copper accents. It opened August 30, 1923. [EPL]

light, goes well with the grand hotel behind it. South is the river valley. They walk to the edge and the sun is shining off the water so powerfully my grandfather wishes for his sunglasses. Later they will go for dinner, maybe dance afterward. But first they'll stand here on Macdonald Drive, in a suit and in a dress, on a patch of pretty grass near the library and the hotel and the shining river, with the book they have borrowed.

"Just before I go to sleep at night," my grandfather once said, after more than two rye and waters, "that's where I am."

When I was in university, one of my professors told us to use something she called the universal present tense when we wrote about literature. Hamlet did not stab Polonius behind the arras at some specific point in history—not when Shakespeare wrote the play and certainly not in the Kingdom of Denmark in the thirteenth century. Hamlet is always stabbing Polonius behind the arras. He's doing it right now.

Right now, my grandfather—who is as dead as Shakespeare and, I suppose, Polonius—stands on Macdonald Drive in May, in the late afternoon Edmonton sunshine, with a novel his wife has just borrowed from the Carnegie Library.

Every city is a city of ghosts, even the young ones.

Of course, Edmonton is only young to students of architecture.

For thousands of years we have lived on the banks of the North Saskatchewan River, in a place we learned to call Rossdale Flats, storytellers if not architects. We disturb the bones when we dig holes for our bridges, and we lack the vocabulary for figuring out what to do about it. They say that Anthony Henday, whose name graces our ring road, entered the shining valley of my grandfather's imagination in the middle of the eighteenth century. He began trading with the Aboriginal people who had chosen this crossing, this gathering place for water and wildlife and wood.

Soon, they were building a fort—Edmonton House or Fort Edmonton, named after a borough east of London. The fort was not a literary society but it was a place of tales. Alberta author Fred Stenson's well-loved novel, *The Trade*, describes the way the Cree, Nakoda and Blackfoot people, the Métis, and the Europeans entertained themselves on the North Saskatchewan. They talked of where they had come from and where they were going, often in angry shouts. There were private libraries and book-lovers among them. Chief Factor John Rowand, who shouted the loudest, may not have been a reader but he collected literature for his massive house on the river—the first in the west to have windows.

Lewis Cardinal calls Edmonton a site of celebration and wonder, a "Pehonan," the location and its spirit a "great mystery."[1] He wants to build a story place, at the site of the original Fort Edmonton, to honour the mystery and its people.

The population remained relatively stable for nearly a hundred years. Then, very quickly, instability came. In 1891 the railway arrived in the district, bringing settlers from all over the world. Land was cheap and fertile, and a growing population meant entrepreneurs could set up easily. This has always been an eerily good place to make something, to prosper. The North Saskatchewan wasn't the most elegant route to the Yukon but the Klondike Gold Rush in 1898 attracted men and women to the most obvious, most northerly stop on the railway. Dawson City, at the end of the 1890s, was the most populous city in the west after San Francisco. The route north from Edmonton was marketed as the inside track.[2] You can see some of the newcomers arriving in Edmonton, looking at a map, the 1,600 miles that remained before them, and closing their eyes—imagining themselves into their own dream places.

Some of these travellers and farmers and entrepreneurs were just passing through, but many decided to stay, setting up a pattern that would continue for the next hundred and twenty years or so. You come to Edmonton to make some money and leave.

But you never leave.

Fort Edmonton—before the city. [City of Edmonton Archives EA-10-104]

The first boom in the boomtown: men outfit themselves for a long trek up to the Klondike.

[City of Edmonton Archives EA-10–2766]

Near the elevators in the Stanley Milner Branch of the Edmonton Public Library, on Sir Winston Churchill Square, is a watercolour painting of the original Carnegie Library on Macdonald Drive—a most attractive ghost. The painting was a gift to the library by its architect, George Heath Mac Donald. Elevators tend to be slow and there's nothing else to look at as you wait for a car. There are nine windows in the front of the building and four Doric columns. At the top of the stairs there is a carving of an open book, oak leaves and the words FREE TO ALL, which you can nearly make out in the painting. The Hotel Macdonald looms behind the library. The building offers a sense of architectural grandeur rare in Edmonton after the great boom in precast concrete towers that started in the 1960s.

One windy afternoon I studied a photo from the archives of the Stanley Milner Branch and stood at the spot where it would have been taken. In the 1950s, when my grandfather fell in love with it, it was a leafy and welcoming place. As my grandfather remembered, it was a gentle destination oriented around and toward the river. The little circle of stone buildings had turned its back on the commerce of Jasper Avenue to become something else. The need for a library, in Edmonton, was predicated on confidence—or a lack of it, another eternal city struggle. A city is not a city until it has a library, a building worthy of the intellectual and creative aspirations of its people, free to all.

In the spring of 2012, on the day I took the photograph, it was a deserted platform of concrete; cars and SUVs idled on Macdonald Drive while drivers texted, waiting for their husbands and wives to flee the Telus Towers.

It is fashionable to mock the city builders of the 1960s and 1970s who felt it necessary to knock down limestone Edmonton to make way for modernity: the miracle of concrete. Today, we're keen to take down all of this detestable concrete and replace it with glass. By 2060 the glass may seem as ridiculous as brutalism in 2013.

We can agree with the builders of 1913 and the builders of Canada's centennial year, 1967, that a city is not a city without a library. Once it was a cornerstone of the public square. Today, perhaps, as newspapers decline and the Internet goes borderless, the city library may be the public square.

E. L. HILL,
LIBRARIAN

2

Permanence and maturity and pride

THE NOTION that a people should have a library is not new. We carry romantic notions about the first of these institutions and its marvellous intention: to hold all the wisdom of the world, all the stories and all the poetry, in one building. There are no watercolour paintings of the library of ancient Alexandria. No one thought to sketch it before it was destroyed, maybe in a fire, maybe not. We're not sure when it was built and when it burned down; the margins of error, for construction and destruction, are hundreds of years. None of the written accounts of the library are particularly trustworthy. But as mythology and legend, the library of Alexandria is solid. It represents the birth of an idea.[1]

Reading and writing, studying, concentrating on a problem or a great mystery—all are solitary and private. The idea that we should share this activity with others, take it into the public realm, sit among the parchments and scrolls and books with other people, alone together, sounds as odd today as it might have in 300 BC. But it doesn't *feel* odd. Any scholar, amateur or obsessive, from the teenager to the PHD on the verge of retirement, knows the feeling of settling into a public library with a pile of books and papers. The sound and the smell of it. We learn better together, even if no one says a word.

Whether we are sharing tales around a fire, or sitting in a grand hall at a long table reading with our fellow citizens, storytelling is a marker of civilization. To learn, to grow, to change together, to share what would otherwise remain secret, is the work of a mature community.

Shortly after the Klondike Gold Rush ended, at the turn of the century, Edmonton's population was just over 2,000. It incorporated as a city in November 1904, in the midst of the first of many extraordinary booms. By 1909 23,000 people lived in Edmonton.[2]

A year earlier, in 1908, city leaders had decided there were enough people of ambition to warrant a library—proof of something. In 1907 the provincial government had passed the Public Libraries Act, which stipulated that the first step was a petition. If ten per cent of Edmonton men were passionate about a library, they could sign their names to a petition and force city council to enact a bylaw to start the process. A petition was circulated, but failed. Many of the men who had been attracted to the city, to make their fortunes or change their lives in some other way, were illiterate. They were itinerant, here to earn some money and move on, even if they later decided to stay.

More importantly, it was a cause without a leader.

"There were two things I missed when I first came to Edmonton in 1902," said John E. Lundy, who eventually became a city councillor. "One was a good fruit and the other a library. I decided there was no remedy for the first situation, but set out to remedy the library situation."[3]

Lundy and a new Edmontonian, Ethelbert Lincoln (E.L.) Hill, who had just taken the job of inspector of schools for the Strathcona district, schemed up a new petition in 1909. Hill had been on the library board in Guelph and in Calgary. In Calgary, where he had been master of science for high schools, he formed a board, found land for a building, and successfully lobbied the Carnegie Corporation for funds to build the city's first public library—all in the space of a year and a half.

The Edmonton Public Library's first director, Ethelbert Lincoln (E.L.) Hill arrived via Ontario and Calgary. [EPL]

This modest but driven social entrepreneur would come to be an early hero in the Edmonton Public Library story. By the time he arrived in Edmonton, Hill was in his early forties. His hair had receded far from his forehead and what remained was going grey. He wore a trim moustache and looked about in a perpetual squint, as though everything and everyone around him were part of a fascinating research project. He was a curler, a Baptist, and a Liberal.

Hill was born in Oxford County, Ontario, on September 29, 1863. He graduated from the University of Toronto with a BA in 1888 and married Jennie Stork in Balfour, Ontario in 1893. Jennie was a published poet and fiction writer, and a graduate of the first female class at University College in Toronto. Their daughter, Esther Marjorie, was born in Guelph in 1895. To prove the Hill family's hunger for self-improvement, E.L. Hill later sought a Master of Science degree from the University of Alberta; he was one of the first five graduate students at the U of A in

1911. Jennie graduated with an MA and Esther Marjorie would turn out to be a pioneer as well.[4]

Happily for Edmonton, Hill proved to be the right man for the position largely due to his influence on both sides of the river. In 1909, "a petition was again circulated, and this time with marked success."[5]

Edmonton historian Tony Cashman remembers Hill as "kind of a fussy Englishman. He was very quiet. He sort of kept to himself, despite everything he accomplished. He wasn't much of a joiner and, frankly, I don't think he had much fun. A lot of people wouldn't have recognized or even noticed him, as he was rather self-effacing. I never wrote about him, you know, because I'm always happier to find slightly more dishonourable people to write about."[6]

The argument for a library in Canada, and more broadly in the British Commonwealth, was familiar. A library was a symbol of permanence and maturity and pride. What made the petition drive difficult, in Edmonton, was the temporary nature of the place. The age and sophistication of the settlement on Rossdale Flats were not visible to the thousands of men and women arriving every year from Eastern Canada, the United States, and Europe. The place looked and smelled and operated as a new city in the midst of invention or self-destruction. It was not uncommon for a boomtown—such as Dawson City—to explode and disappear in the course of five or ten years.

At the same time, Edmonton was the capital city. The sandstone and granite Beaux-Arts legislature building was already under construction. There were plans to build a vast bridge, linking Edmonton with the town of Strathcona on the south side of the river, and rumours about a majestic railway hotel. The endless rivalry with that city three hundred kilometres to the south had already begun, and Calgary had applied successfully to an American philanthropist to build a library; Hill had been on the board of trustees and he had some experience negotiating with philanthropists.

In 1909 city council passed a bylaw to strike a library board. Calgary was already well into the process so the Edmontonians had to act quickly.

The first Edmonton Public Library board was appointed, and included Mayor Robert Lee and Alderman J. E. Lundy, who continued to search for a decent fruit in this northern town. The board purchased a site known as the Wilson Property overlooking the river valley on College Avenue—today known as Macdonald Drive—100 Avenue and 100 Street.

At the same time, on the south side of the river in Strathcona, a petition was presented to city council: give us a library. The board formed in October 1910, and Hill accepted the role of chair. This idea went back to 1897 when the Strathcona Literary Society had determined that any community worth living in needed a proper library.

The boards of the Edmonton and Strathcona Public Libraries did what you had to do in 1910 if you wanted to build a public library: they sent a letter to a man named Andrew Carnegie.

Andrew Carnegie, who grew up poor, always attributed his success to access to free books. He funded the construction of over 2,500 public libraries around the world, including 125 in Canada and one in Edmonton.

[Library of Congress LC-USZ62-101767]

The richest man in the world

ANDREW CARNEGIE grew up far from Edmonton in a one-room cottage in Dunfermline, Scotland. His father, William Carnegie, was a hand-loom weaver who helped to start a communal library for his fellows. Young Andrew found books in this little library and through his uncle, who encouraged him to read the heroic literature of Scotland. When things got worse for William Carnegie he borrowed money to move to Allegheny, Pennsylvania in 1848 when Andrew was thirteen.

The boy went straight to work as a weaver's helper.

Two years later he joined the Ohio Telegraph Company. Even though he was not a bonded apprentice, he was granted access to a private library that a local philanthropist, Colonel James Anderson, had opened to the boys of the city one day a week: the Mechanics and Apprentices Library.

Carnegie borrowed heavily from the library, and made up for what he lacked in formal education.

"I became fond of reading," said Carnegie. "I reveled week after week in the books. My toil was light, for I got up at six o'clock in the morning, contented to work until six in the evening if there was then a book for me to read."[1]

When the colonel's staff changed the rules of the library so it was no longer free to unbonded apprentices, Carnegie wrote a letter to the editor of the *Pittsburgh Dispatch* questioning the decision. His arguments were clear and forceful, and through his prose Carnegie, the unbonded apprentice, was operating proof of the library's success. The letter worked. The library was open to him again.

"It was also his first literary success," writes Joseph Frazier Wall, one of Carnegie's many biographers. "[A]nd for Andrew nothing else that he had known in the way of recognition by others had been quite as exhilarating as this experience of seeing his own words in print. It fed his vanity and at the same time increased his appetite for more such food."[2]

Soon, Carnegie was in the railroad business. His communication skills and the wisdom he had gleaned from his informal education, through the colonel's library, aided him in a career that would make him the richest man in the world. He earned his money in steel and sought friends and correspondents who happened to be writers and journalists and orators. Instead of holding on to his vast fortune he decided to replicate his own success—financial, literary and spiritual—by building free and public libraries all over the English-speaking world.

Of course, he did not make his fortune as a soft-hearted pushover. These were ideologically playful times. Some critics complained that Carnegie sought to make greedy little capitalists by building certain kinds of libraries filled with certain kinds of books, but these were silly and baseless critiques. He may not have been the kindest employer from the point of view of a steel worker, but he did not punish the curious by censoring the collections in his libraries.

The rules for a Carnegie library were simple. A city would buy the land and promise to operate the library. Carnegie's office in New York would be involved in the design of the building because he detested faddish extravagance. Smoking rooms for men were not allowed. Greek façades were ridiculous and a waste of money, according to Carnegie, and fireplaces were dangerous. The typical design of a Carnegie library was simple and elegant.

"To his detractors, the libraries he funded were merely stepping stones to personal glorification," writes Alberto Manguel in *The Library At Night*. "He very rarely gave money for books, only for the building in which they were to be lodged, and even then he stipulated that the town provide the site and the cash to run the library."[3]

These criticisms seem quite feeble in the hyper-logo'd, super-sponsored world of today. Carnegie helped build 3,000 libraries. He inspired people and municipalities all over the world to see value in libraries by his personal example, his advocacy, and his money.

But his office's relations with Edmonton were not altogether smooth.

In Strathcona, Mayor J.J. Duggan was on the library board. Across the river, Edmonton Mayor Robert Lee was on the library board.

Duggan, with the experienced Hill in the room, composed a letter to Carnegie's office in New York City asking for assistance. They asked for $25,000. Carnegie's secretary, James Bertram, thought they were asking for too much. Strathcona had a relatively small population. Why would the city need a grand library? The board responded that the city had grown and would continue to grow exponentially; they sent the architectural drawings, from the firm of Wilson and Herald, to New York.

Bertram didn't like the plans. He offered $15,000 and indicated this was as much as the Carnegie Corporation was interested in providing, for a much smaller building.

This was a significant amount of money for Strathcona—for any city in 1911. The board had a difficult decision to make. They were committed to building a library for their citizens: not a fancy and ostentatious building but the building they believed their growing city needed and deserved. Accepting $15,000 from the Carnegie Corporation meant ceding control of the building to the whims of a wonderful but strict philanthropist who knew nothing of Strathcona. Hill felt it was a poor deal and the mayor supported him.

They declined the money and decided to raise the funds in their community, to build the library they wanted without help from Andrew Carnegie. There was one small problem: the Carnegie Corporation had lost the architectural drawings for the Strathcona library.[4] Wilson and Herald, the architectural firm, worked from memory to put together another design—English renaissance without any Greek façades and without Carnegie's name on the front of the building or anywhere else. The local construction firm, W. Dietz, started work on the library in 1912, using orange brick with limestone details.

On the north side of the river, another mayor and another board negotiated with Andrew Carnegie. Edmonton was by far the larger city and the provincial capital. They had secured land across the street from what would be one of the finest hotels in Canada, the Hotel Macdonald. The provincial legislature was nearing completion. So was the High Level Bridge.

The Carnegie Corporation offered $60,000.

Like the members of the Strathcona board, the Edmontonians were distraught. They wanted a building worth about $200,000 and weren't keen on foregoing control for less than half the price. Again, this wasn't a simple decision. The money wasn't a gift but at the same time Carnegie's conditions were not onerous. Calgary—already an infamous rival—had opened its Carnegie-funded library in January 1912. The smaller city across the river would soon have a building. Every month that Edmonton delayed meant another anxious board meeting.

The cities on a river merged in February 1912: Edmonton, Alberta now had a neighbourhood on the south side called Strathcona.

In the end, the Edmonton Public Library board decided "it is undesirable that the City should accept any sum which it would be necessary for the City to supplement with the consequence that the library erected only partly at Mr. Carnegie's expense should bear his name and be subject to his conditions...therefore this Board is of opinion that further negotiations with Mr. Carnegie be dropped."[5]

If the people of Strathcona could raise the money on the south side, certainly central Edmonton could do the same with more people and more capital. This new feeling of independence was pleasing to the board. And now that the cities were one, there seemed no point in having two literary fiefdoms, two library systems. The boards merged and Hill became head librarian of the Edmonton Public Library and the Strathcona Public Library.

Here was a growing city with a university and three colleges, twenty-four public schools, four theatres, forty places of worship and, so far, no finished library.

George M. Hall, in the first annual report of the Edmonton Public Library and the Strathcona Public Library in 1913, points out the ridiculousness of this idea. Edmonton, he writes, in an admirably long sentence, "is now a city of over 70,000 population, with wide streets, boulevards that stretch, green and grassy, for miles, fine restaurants, substantial buildings and excellent shops and stores, banks, hotels and theatres, parks and public playgrounds, churches, colleges, and an excellent public school system; railroads, streetcars and automobiles in hundreds; in short a city with all the advantages and conveniences of modern life has burst forth from the trading post that stood on the banks of the North Saskatchewan for so many decades, a rendezvous for trappers and Indians, an abiding place in the wilderness of the west for the few white men who lived here and carried on the business of the great trading company into whose hands King Charles II gave the whole country of western Canada as a thing scarcely worth the while to give or take, and without a thought of the vast capacity for usefulness contained within the grant."[6]

The Strathcona Library was set to open March 14, 1913. Chief Librarian Hill and the board had invited dignitaries from both sides of the river and had hired a band. It was a spacious and attractive two-storey building, built for $30,000 by the community, and the community hummed with excitement for it.

The first public library to open in Edmonton was the Strathcona Library on the south side of the newly amalgamated city. Of course, some people on the north side of the river would argue about official opening dates. [EPL]

Leaders on the north side of the river weren't so sure. It was miserable enough that Calgary had opened its Carnegie library: now the junior partner in amalgamation, Strathcona, was going to open a library before the provincial capital. For a lot of powerful people on the north side of the river, this would not do.

Accounts vary, but either a few hours before the party in Strathcona on March 14, 1913, or a day earlier, the Edmonton Public Library opened in temporary quarters above a meat and liquor store in the Chisholm Block at the corner of 104 Street and Jasper Avenue.

"One of the problems we had in starting this library was the purchase of a safe," wrote John E. Lundy, city councillor. "It was not so much the price, but whether the floors and stairway of the Chisholm Block would stand the weight of the safe and the books."

It was a less-than-dignified solution to a problem of pride and perception. For the sake of history and correctness, downtown Edmonton beat Strathcona by a few hours.

Of course, a temporary space above a meat and liquor store didn't feel like the stately building in Strathcona on 104 Street at 84 Avenue. The new Strathcona Library had electric lighting and comfortable seating areas. The building was spacious but not cavernous; it fit.

A small band played upstairs on opening day. Mayor William Short made a speech. So did the ex-premier and Strathcona resident Alexander Rutherford. The former mayor of what had been the city of Strathcona, J.J. Duggan, officially opened the library. He said it might be a lovely idea to have a smoking room for the men, a mild insult to Carnegie-ism that inspired long and rowdy applause—at least from the men.

"The good things said cannot be hinted at in this sketch," wrote Anne Newall, "but one note was sounded again and again, recognizing the fact that while many had done valiantly, the main spring of the library movement centred in the untiring enthusiasm and skilled activity of Librarian Hill."[7]

The Strathcona Library had details a Carnegie-built building would not allow, like a fireplace and smoking rooms. This is the men's reading room. [EPL]

On the first floor there was a reading room and a "ladies and children's room," a vestibule. In the basement were the men's reading room and the furnace room. Upstairs, an auditorium.

From the beginning, it was an open-access library system. A borrower's card was free to all.[8] The fine for an overdue book when the two libraries opened was two pennies a day. The inventory was 4,827 books at opening. There were twenty-three daily newspapers, thirty-seven monthly magazines and seventeen weeklies. Circulation figures were, from the first days, astonishing to Hill and his team. Newall was not modest about reporting all of this. "The success of both libraries has been phenomenal. Only a year old and yet the figures outstrip all but a very few libraries in the Dominion!"

Downtown Edmonton's first library was in temporary quarters above a meat and liquor store in the Chisholm Block. It opened March 13, 1913, a day before the Strathcona Library. [EPL]

4

A repository for Edmonton-ness?

CARNEGIE BELIEVED THAT THE LIBRARY, more than any other institution, made what we now call the American Dream possible. Without access to a library, his trajectory from a poor and powerless boy to a poor and powerless man would have proceeded uninterrupted. If all people had access to knowledge and wisdom, no matter where they were born or what schools they attended, the old-world tyranny of class would become irrelevant.

In Britain, an Italian led the argument for public libraries. Antonio Panizzi was a lawyer who, as a young man, joined a secret society in Italy devoted to uniting the country. This did not go well with the authorities and he was forced to flee—first to Switzerland and then to England, where he found work teaching Italian. He had good luck meeting and helping men who would eventually do quite well in society and government, such as fellow lawyer Henry Brougham, who became Lord Chancellor of England and found a post for Panizzi in the library of the British Museum.

The assistant librarian post led to the contemporary-sounding position, keeper of printed books, in 1837. He was made head librarian in

1856 but by then he had already inspired and led a massive expansion—architecturally and otherwise. The British Museum's library became the largest in the world.

Like Carnegie, Panizzi was a democrat.

"I want a poor student to have the same means of indulging his learned curiosity, of following his rational pursuits, of consulting the same authorities, of fathoming the most intricate inquiry, as the richest man in the Kingdom, as far as books go, and I contend that Government is bound to give him the most liberal and unlimited assistance in this respect."[1]

Panizzi, an Italian patriot who became a British patriot, felt it was essential for a library—through its holdings—to build and sustain a national mythology. The largest and most important library in London, he felt, should privilege British writers, British history, British values, and *Britishness.*

Is the Edmonton Public Library, then, a repository for Edmonton-ness?

Jared Tkachuk, library outreach worker, and a client. [EPL]

5

A big city negotiation

THE STANLEY A. MILNER BRANCH of the Edmonton Public Library faces Sir Winston Churchill Square from the south. It is the core of the core of downtown, facing the pyramid of city hall and the changing landscape of the concrete plaza before it. The confidence and beauty of city hall, designed by Edmonton architect Gene Dub, sits next to the whimsical Northern Lights-inspired Art Gallery of Alberta. A few doors south of that, one of the finest concert halls in Canada—the Winspear Centre—stands across the street from the largest Canadian theatre complex west of Stratford, Ontario, the Citadel Theatre.

Only one of these institutions has a crowd on its sidewalk, all day. Walking into the library through its front doors is nearly always a big-city negotiation, weaving through smokers and texters and seniors and hustlers and mothers with babies, waiting for a bus or just standing and staring. Young men gather in circles. It is an odd place, sometimes a little threatening if you make eye contact incorrectly. But you don't. To keep the sidewalk free of cigarette butts a sweeper would have to walk it all day long, 100 Street to 99 Street, with a push broom.

Buses stop in front of the library and soon a tram will move back and forth on 102 Avenue. Edmonton has long been a place for people to stop and rest forever, or to make a bit of money on their way to somewhere else, and the front of the downtown branch of the library is a mini-Edmonton—a place of transition.

On a brisk springtime day a businesswoman stands next to a very young new mother in pink sweatpants, bouncing her baby. A teenage girl sits on the concrete, finishing a newspaper crossword. Some have just renewed their library cards and have received an Edmonton Public Library shopping bag in bright blue or pink. A group of men of a certain age are drunk but harmless: odd shouts and metallic cackles. Seniors on the transit benches read novels plucked from the stacks. New Canadians, from Africa and Asia and the Middle East, speak quietly in the languages they arrived speaking, and I wonder if their accents are already shifting with the English. They carry full bags, the sort of white plastic sacks now endangered by progress: empty lunch containers, a sweater, a book or two inside. A car pulls up and a woman in a fine black dress and fresh make-up steps out. The hatchback pops and she pulls out a black viola case. One of the security guards comes out of the library and it seems at first he wants to escort her into the building—needlessly protect her from something, like a concierge. He says a few words to her and taps on the passenger-side door of the car, a Subaru.

"This isn't a parking lot. A bus is always coming, always. If you want to park there's lots of room under the building. Just continue and turn right. You'll see, on your left, *Library Parkade*."

The driver pretends to ignore the security guard. "Break a leg!" he shouts, to his wife or his sister or his friend, and drives east toward Chinatown.

On cold days some of these people wait inside the library, close enough to the doors that they can spot their bus and run if they must. It frustrates the security guard, who wants people coming in or going out to have a route of entrance or exit. No one has told the guard it is against the rules to kick the people out. All he can do is manage the tension of the place, a busy public institution: managed by someone, owned by everyone. This is the library, free to all, and that spirit extends to the grubby sidewalk and to the vestibule, so narrow that a jangle of people have to negotiate steps and an operating lift for wheelchairs every time someone new enters or exits. Sorry. Excuse me. Sorry. Can I just? Thank you.

Inside, another security guard greets me as I enter. He says hello and gives us all a quick scan as we pass. What are we carrying? Can we walk straight? The check-out is automated now but there are greeter and ambassador librarians at the customer service desk. A woman with a staff card on a lanyard, her hands clasped peacefully before her, stands next to the short customer service line-up.

"Can I help you with anything?"

I tell her I am wandering through the library, studying it.

"Anything in particular you're looking for?"

"Everything."

She unclasps her hands and moves her arms like a conductor, just for a moment. "Curiosity! Well then, you've come to the right place."

At the tables and in the comfortable chairs, on each side of the stacks of books, young people tap away on late-model Apple laptops with white ear buds plugged in. A few metres away from them, men and women in layers of clothing sprawl on chairs sleeping, some of them snoring. Readers, regular recreational readers with a paperback in hand, are a minority here. On the other side of the south windows, one of the strangest places in downtown Edmonton: Centennial Plaza. It is a flat expanse of concrete before an outdoor amphitheatre that almost no one uses. There is a statue of two men in the process of negotiation, one an Aboriginal hunter and the other a fur trader. The men stand side by side, posing, as though they are dressed up as an Aboriginal hunter and a European Canadian fur trader and someone is taking their photograph.

Not far away, a bust of Gandhi. From time to time, in the warm months, a Zumba class or a basketball game breaks out on the concrete.

A man with an enormous and full backpack wanders about, asks where he might find a computer.

Computers are everywhere. I tell him as gently as I can manage.

"But those computers need a library card number."

"You don't have one? All you have to do is go over to the customer service desk and—"

"I don't want a library card! I just gotta get on Facebook."

"At the customer service desk they'll—"

"Ah, forget it," he says, and sits defeated on his long fat stuffed tube of a backpack. He smells of campfire.

The public computers are busy: YouTube and Facebook, webmail. It is difficult, on the main floor, to find a dedicated researcher with some writing paper and a pile of books. There are, at this moment in the mid-afternoon, precisely none. This has been a criticism of the urban library: that it has in some way betrayed its purpose. Where it was once a place of scholarship, or at least—according to Carnegie—an institution dedicated to personal transformation, improvement and democracy *through reading*, it is now a wired community centre.

This is not at all a new criticism. When Antonio Panizzi was keeper of printed books in the British Museum Library, he found himself in a feud with the writer Thomas Carlyle. Carlyle did not believe in the sort of social progress most of his literary peers celebrated. Old values were being sluiced away, a byproduct of the Industrial Revolution. The idea that libraries were engines of democracy was distasteful to him; the mob could not be changed, certainly not by literature.

Not that he was anti-library.

What we become, Carlyle said, in one of his most famous speeches, "depends on what we read after all manner of Professors have done their best for us. The true University of these days is a Collection of Books."[1]

Carlyle adored Collections of Books: a library of serious and already well-read men, leaders and captains, heroes. He disliked the notion of the free place where all patrons were equal, that a state-run institution should be in the business of creating equal opportunity. To a Tory satirist, these progressive ideas were somewhere between hilarious and distasteful.

Even so, Carlyle's issues with Panizzi were not philosophical. They were personal. On more than one occasion, Panizzi had denied the great essayist and orator special access to books and private rooms. Carlyle helped launch a rival institution, the London Library, in 1841. He spoke for a constituency of thinkers in England at the time and started a debate that continues today.

"I believe," Thomas Carlyle wrote, "there are several people in a state of imbecility who come to read in the British Museum. I have been informed that there are several in that state who are sent there by their friends to pass away the time."[2]

It is no longer controversial to consider that some people, in any number of states, would be attracted to the library to "pass away the time." Edmonton's city hall is an open space, a bright and pleasant one. So is the atrium of the Citadel Theatre, with greenery and water trickling in its fountains. A few Edmontonians will pass away the time in these places but the library is altogether different. Of the three institutions it has the least to offer, architecturally. The light is fluorescent, unnatural. While the main floor of city hall is empty unless an event is underway, and the Citadel atrium is only busy before a performance and at lunchtime in the winter, it can be difficult to find a seat in the Stanley A. Milner Branch of the Edmonton Public Library. It almost never feels crowded but there is always a crowd.

For everyone, whatever state they may be in, the library is a curiously warm and friendly home. Linda Cook, the current president and CEO of Edmonton Public Library, calls it the civic living room. She is a modest woman. It's much more than that.

In November 2011 a man named Douglas Myers entered the downtown branch to use a computer. Myers had sold his own computer and was coming off a session of detox for a crack addiction—the latest in a series of forays into drugs and crime. He walked into the library, as we all do, past the security guard and up to the customer service desks.

"Basically, my whole life I've been a non-member of society," said Myers. "I wasn't aware of what to do or where to go."[3]

Two things might have happened here. Myers might have been asked to leave, which often happens to men and women in his situation when they enter a mall or a café. Instead, the librarian referred Myers to Jared Tkachuk, an outreach worker the library hired in the summer of 2011.

Myers told an Edmonton newspaper that the librarian who greeted him and Tkachuk had showed "basic humanity." The outreach program in the library, he said, helped him stay sober.

"For the first time in my life I have I.D. I have a family doctor. I love this building. Without this building, I don't think I'd be halfway to where I am right now."[4]

Is this the business of the library today?

In early 2012 Professor Gavin Renwick of the University of Alberta's Department of Art and Design opened his Theory and Research in Design Studies class to innovative projects. "When we started working together," his students wrote, "the first thing we did was throw the proposed class outline away. We immediately discovered that we were all from somewhere else and were new to both Alberta and Canada...the class therefore became about 'being here,' being Edmontonian and our evolving collective neo-identities."

There were many ways to express and explore all of this neo-identification. The students in Renwick's class considered it and decided the library was a hub for these sorts of evolutions. So they put up a wide easel in the Stanley A. Milner Branch of the Edmonton Public Library and slapped a board on it.

They asked a simple question: "Why are you here?"

The students furnished patrons with sticky notes and a pen. Responses, by the month of March, made for an unscientific but charming survey:

- *To read Hemingway, eat Kraft Dinner, and nap.*
- *Because I believe in democratic intellectualism.*
- *To browse, play chess, make friends. Maybe find a wife.*
- *I'm here to always learn, and to share the gift of hope. I'm homeless.*
- *To hang with my bestie and nerd out on books.*
- *Poetry, people, chess, books, and all the treasures hidden in plain sight.*
- *Cause Nicole.*
- *It's on the way to Yellowknife.*
- *Romance. Actually, schoolwork, knowledge, community and to pass time.*
- *I'm homeless.*
- *Here in the library? Because I'm a bookworm with no money. Here on the planet? Still trying to figure that out.*

A minority of the respondents spoke of books but nearly all of them referenced learning, growing, expanding and improving their lives in some way. Taken together, this social and cultural function of a city centre library—as a crucible of transformation—would constitute a poignant nightmare for Thomas Carlyle. In the Edmonton Public Library, men and women sprawl out sleeping on the chairs, a paperback on their chests. No one taps them on the shoulder to wake them up, to send them to their home chesterfields.

For more than a week I watched a man in a changing series of business suits sit at a west-facing window alternately reading and napping. His hair was neat, thinning on top and at his temples. Someone took care of the back of his neck. Even in the middle of the morning he looked exhausted; there were dark little sausages under each eye. He read popular business books: *Good to Great* and *The 7 Habits of Highly Successful People*. Since I was in a library, a story place, and thinking of libraries and its characters, I decided not to interview the man. Instead I imagined him as a character. He has lost his job and he lacks the courage to speak to his wife and family. Every morning he walks out of the house with his briefcase, turns and waves to his children at the window, and sits in the most comfortable place in the city—a place of subtle honour—for men and women who either can't stay at home or don't have one.

A library can fight this natural magnetism, and for a time the Edmonton Public Library did fight it. The *idea* of the library has transformed over the years, according to the prevailing culture, the board, the management, city council and the mayor, whose effects on the primacy and financial health of the library can be either marvellous or devastating.

Despite his fervour for the country of his birth, which actually saw him sentenced to death *in absentia,* Antonio Panizzi understood the library as a keeper of culture.

"The attention of the emphatically British library ought to be directed most particularly to British works and to works relating to the British Empire," he said in a report to the House of Commons in 1836. "Its religious, political and literary as well as scientific history; its laws, institutions, descriptions, commerce, arts, etc."[5]

While this has not been a stated goal of the Edmonton Public Library, in any of its annual reports or mission statements, the library has become a keeper and a reflector of local culture. As a novelist I can say with experience that the library is keen to support books by Edmontonians. It runs a successful Writer in Residence program, sponsors and houses a Writer-in-Exile, places books by Edmonton authors on display shelves, asks us in to read from our work and speak about our artistic process, our work, our opinions. But more importantly, the library is an engine of local curiosity. It dignifies everyone who comes through its doors. The art and design students were clever to choose the Stanley A. Milner Branch to document the evolution of the city and its citizens because, more than any other institution in the city, it is Edmonton: the past, the present, the future.

Reference Dep't
YOUNG PEO
DEPARTMENT

6

Above the liquor store and meat shop

TODAY DOWNTOWN EDMONTON'S HEALTHIEST CORNER is Jasper Avenue and 104 Street. The north side is a meeting of old and new, in rare harmony—the new Sobey's grocery store and, across the street, the rounded and stately Birk's Building. Neither are high-rises and together they form a gentle entry point to Edmonton's most successful downtown street; the sidewalks are wide enough to invite safe jaywalking. Walkers are privileged here, not cars. The warehouses and high-rises up the street are full of lofts and apartments. Cafés and restaurants, a wine store, fashion and food mingle with office space that invites new enterprises. Farther up in the Mercer Block warehouse, Startup Edmonton, a home for early-stage creative and technology companies, is a beehive of young men and women with iPads. In the warm months an outdoor farmers' market crowds 104 Street every Saturday. In the winter this is one of the best places to huddle over a coffee or a glass of wine.

The south side of Jasper Avenue is altogether different. If a downtown resident isn't standing on the southeast corner, she would have trouble recalling what is on it. The building is five storeys tall, concrete and glass, stealth architecture with no consideration of beauty or spirit of invitation: it is all business, drive in and drive out. There is a bright 7-11 on the ground floor, a sign that more and more people live downtown.

On a warm but drizzly afternoon, the corner of 104 Street and Jasper Avenue is a study in urban planning and development. Opposite the 7-11, the "urban anywhere" quality transforms into a more particular feeling. Thanks to thoughtful and historically sensitive design, pedestrians walk slower between the Birk's Building and the Sobey's grocery. They stop. They walk up 104 Street to, perhaps, make an impulse purchase in deVine Wines or the organic living shop, Carbon, farther up the street.

It wasn't always so.

One hundred years ago the first home of the downtown branch of the Edmonton Public Library was housed here in a modest but welcoming three-storey building owned by A.R. Chisholm, a pioneer who had arrived in Edmonton by Red River cart in 1880.[1] On the main floor were a liquor store and a meat shop. The Grand Café was a couple of doors away. The library up the stairs consisted of several shelves in the middle of a long room and, at the front, a circulation desk.

In decades to come this building would become a celebrated candy shop, the Palace of Sweets, "Canada's Outstanding Confectionary Store." Lawrence Herzog, a beloved writer of Edmonton's heritage buildings, recalls February 2, 1966, when a fire started in the basement of the Chisholm Block—under the Palace of Sweets. It was early afternoon on a cold day.

"We figured they would get it out," Herzog's mother recalled, "but in a matter of minutes it spread, and soon we were running for the exits. I grabbed my purse and $200 from the till, and that was it. We were all standing in the freezing air, watching the fire crews rushing in. When they broke through the big front display window with their axes, we knew it was over."[2]

In 1913, Edmonton's readers entered the front door of this building for the first time and climbed the stairs, eager for the new books on the shelves.

The site of Edmonton's first downtown library, one hundred years later. [EPL]

Inside the Chisholm Block location of the Edmonton Public Library. [City of Edmonton Archives EA-10-650]

The stately Carnegie-built Calgary Public Library opened in 1912 and taunted Edmontonians for years. *[Bruce Peel Special Collections Library 5665]*

In every way it was a temporary library. Even under the leadership of the unbeatable Hill the notion of designing and building a new library on 100 Street and 100 Avenue now seemed daunting.

Between city incorporation in 1904 and 1912, the population had grown from 8,000 to more than 50,000. The development boom and cultural transformation began to move even faster when, on May 13, 1912, the Hudson's Bay Company put its block of city land up for sale. The day itself recalled the Klondike Gold Rush. Real estate speculators knew the land would hit the market at exactly 2 P.M. but the Hudson's Bay Company had tried to keep it a secret. This strategy failed. Shortly after lunch, more than 2,000 people had lined up at the Little Gospel Mission Hall. The wild real estate market became even wilder, with 1,543 new lots ready for development.[3]

Shortly after the two branches of the Edmonton Public Library opened, the first in the city's series of booms ended. Money markets collapsed and speculators who had not sold everything lost everything—or a lot of it.

A week and a half after the libraries' first birthdays, at the end of March 1913, Arthur Sifton became Alberta's second premier. This was a third majority government for the Liberals but urban issues could not have been among the premier's driving concerns. Rural populism was on the rise even before the recession hit. A big city library was not a wise political risk. The City of Edmonton could not raise $200,000 on its own and it seemed the library board and the Carnegie Corporation had exchanged their last correspondence.

The temporary library was a success in one vital respect: people came in, signed up, and borrowed books. In his annual report for 1914, Hill broke down the good news:

Volumes Issued for Home Use, 1913

Calgary	(including branch)	181,669
Winnipeg	(Main Library)	232, 866
Toronto	(College Street Library)	131,773
	(Church Street Library)	112,353
Edmonton 1914	(Central Library)	189,696
	(Strathcona Library)	89,696
Edmonton 1914 Total		279,392

Sure, Calgary had its luxurious downtown library. But even in its dark location above the meat and liquor vendors, Edmonton's library was lending more books. Its numbers, blended with Strathcona's, were extraordinary. In the second year of operations, the number of borrowers increased thirty per cent. Between fifty and sixty children showed up for Story Hour at the Strathcona Library. The slogan for the Edmonton Public Library: "Neither books nor bathtubs should be considered as luxuries—both are among the necessities of life."

Still, leaders on the north side of the river wanted a building, a marker of civilization and importance and progress. In a pattern that would remain for the next one hundred years, the city struggled with notions of greatness. The mayor and council wanted to attract business to the city, not just itinerant workers. Architecture and ambition were aligned in 1913 as they would be in 2013; a handsome and busy library was a symbolic victory in the early years of the twentieth century. The city manager couldn't put circulation figures on giant signs at the city limits.

A confidence problem is in the city's DNA. It is part of Edmonton's charm, source of its civic sense of humour, and a virtual boiler room for its novelists and filmmakers. There is, of course, a significant downside. A city can build a thrilling vision for its future that no one quite believes. In 2013, whenever a leader uses the phrase "world-class," Edmontonians cringe—at least the Edmontonians who have travelled. The greatness of the city, a century ago and today, lives in the circulation numbers of the library much more than in any building. In 1913, we were reading and participating at rates that suggested a much larger population. The trouble was—and is today—how do we see and feel and share and activate that energy?

The First World War began on July 28, 1914. If there had been any hope of building a new library during a recession, with municipal and provincial governments that were not entirely sympathetic, the goal was now entirely decimated. The downtown branch moved, in October 1914, to slightly larger space in the Roberts Block on 102 Avenue and 102 Street. Books were needed desperately, as the stock was getting low. Hill told the board in 1914 that the need for French and Scandinavian books was urgent. There was no money to buy a flagpole; happily, a wealthy citizen, John Walter Esq., provided one as a gift to the library.

There is no trace of the Roberts Block today. Here the City Centre Mall meets the northwest corner of Manulife Place—a Second Cup coffee shop—and the Don Wheaton Family YMCA. The First World War was not a time of growth for the downtown or the Strathcona Branch. Edmontonians borrowed books and the two libraries remained open, but quietly. They were community hubs for families whose men had gone

The Edmonton Public Library's second temporary location was in the Roberts Block at 102 Avenue and 102 Street. Visible directly behind the church steeple, it is the building with the advertising on the side.

[City of Edmonton Archives EA-24-26]

Where the Roberts Block once stood is, one hundred years later, the western portion of the City Centre Mall. [EPL]

overseas to fight the war or who had already been killed. Young men demanded books on engineering and aircraft, on military strategy and history, for context and perhaps to prepare themselves.

The library provided books to the military camps around Edmonton during the war but the stock—all stock—was meagre: 30,000 books in total. Hill used the libraries as a depository for citizens who might donate books of their own to the soldiers at Sarcee Camp. It seemed that *having libraries* was not enough. It was a sensitive time. The Canadian government had assembled a list of books by communists and socialists; RCMP officers were sent out to remove them from private and then public shelves. It was an uncomfortable time to be a librarian, although this police action did not greatly unnerve Hill—at least not enough for him to complain. Hill needed friends in politics. He needed a budget, even in times of scarcity, to hire good people and buy good books. The board advised him to write a letter to the Calgary librarian; they had to ask the province, together, to allow municipal governments to fund libraries more creatively. The board asked Hill to make "a list of the most necessary books bearing on the present crisis in the Empire and the Allies, and that the finance committee have power to authorize the purchase of such books from this as it may deem expedient."[4]

In 1916 the Hills' daughter Esther Marjorie entered the architecture program at the University of Alberta, the first of many courageous and difficult choices in her career. She later transferred to the University of Toronto and became, in 1920, the first female architecture graduate in Canada. She was mocked and jeered from the first day, and would endure this sort of treatment for much of her career. As lifelong students, community leaders and writers, her parents had prepared her for this challenge. Esther Marjorie was, for her father, a model Edmontonian: someone who would seek truth and surprise everyone.

Edmonton's Russian population presented a petition to Hill demanding some Russian literature in the library. Hill, as ever, was having trouble buying any literature, but the board found $50 for some Russian books.

The First World War brought austerity to the city and, inevitably, a smaller temporary Edmonton Public Library in the Civic Block. [City of Edmonton Archives EA-10-205]

To save public money during the increasingly lean war years, Hill was forced to move the library from the Roberts Block in September 1917 to a much smaller space on the main and second floors of the Civic Block on 99 Street and 102 Avenue.

The Civic Block stood where the Winspear Centre is today, on what was then called Market Square. It was not a beautiful building. Since it was designed and built in 1912 for government workers in a city that was already known for finding economic efficiencies wherever possible, there were few attractive touches in the six-storey tower. Of course, if it were still around today, we would bow before all of this Edwardian-influenced brick and stone. Unlike many heritage buildings downtown, the one consolation with the Civic Block is that it wasn't replaced with a devastatingly ugly precast concrete business tower in the 1970s. And there were efforts to save it.

In 1989, city administration recommended that the new concert hall, which had already received $12 million in funding guarantees from the Winspear family and others, be built behind the historically significant Civic Block. One alderman, Patricia Mackenzie, argued Sir Winston Churchill Square should be a cultural hub rather than an office ghetto for bureaucrats. One of her colleagues on council, Lillian Staroszik, damned the Civic Block.

"I can't think of anything worse than a world-class concert hall stuck behind this warehouse," she said.

Alderman Jan Reimer, who would eventually become mayor, voted with two others to keep the building—a minority view.

"In other cities, old buildings are preserved, renovated, and restored," she said. "In Edmonton, we rip 'em down." She argued the Civic Block could be something marvellous "if we dream a bit about what we could do."[5]

The timeline for the Winspear Centre, in 1989, was two years. It was completed in 1997.

Rent in the Civic Block during the First World War, for the Edmonton Public Library, was $4,250 per year. The culture of the downtown library and the Strathcona Branch began to change at the end of the war years. Soldiers returning from battle were keen to restart or remake their lives, and the library was a place to do it.

"More and more the libraries must become the General Information Bureau for the community," wrote Hill in the 1918 annual report, as he watched the city change. "The cosmopolitan character of our population makes this task more difficult, and at the same time, more important—difficult because of the wide variety of information sought, and important because of the futility of looking elsewhere between Winnipeg and the North Pole, for a source of information."[6]

Money remained tight, so expansion was not an option, let alone a new building. Paying staff was barely possible.

The Spanish flu began to spread in January 1918, and as soldiers returned to their hometowns they carried it with them. Soldiers' living

The Civic Block was torn down to make way for the Winspear Centre. [EPL]

conditions in Europe had been miserable. They were malnourished and often sleepless in the muddy trenches; their immune systems were depressed. The end of the war was also the beginning of the age of travel. It was easier than ever to go overseas. Media blackouts in Canada at the time make it difficult for present-day researchers to determine where early cases originated but the pandemic hit Edmonton in October 1918.

The flu killed between ten and twenty per cent of those infected, and the virus was unusually severe for young people—from teenagers to men and women in their forties. The library closed on October 18 and circulation was suspended until early December. The Young People's Department remained closed until January.

The population of the city was about 60,000 at the time. More than 600 Edmontonians died of Spanish flu in just a couple of months. Undertakers had to hire extra staff, including a small platoon of carpenters to build

Veterans of the 49th Battalion return to Edmonton in 1919. [City of Edmonton Archives EA-63-5]

coffins. The dead had to be buried, as the city did not yet have a crematorium. Albertans were ordered by law to wear masks whenever they went outside their homes, "except when it is necessary to partially remove the mask for the purpose of eating."[7]

At the eleventh hour on the eleventh day of the eleventh month of 1918, the Allies gathered with German officials at the western front in Compiègne, France, to put an official end to the war. The 49th Battalion, the Loyal Edmonton Regiment, had participated in the capture of Vimy Ridge in 1917 and the Battle of Passchendaele. The surviving soldiers returned to their families in Edmonton en masse in March 1919, and disbanded.

The economy didn't remake itself in a few months. The results of the economic crash of 1913 remained powerful in Edmonton, particularly in real estate. Credit, after the war, remained difficult to obtain. After the most devastating war in world history and an influenza pandemic, Hill and his library board were buoyed by the feeling that the outlook for Edmonton could only improve. They returned to their grand plan: an iconic downtown library.

In 1921 Hill and members of the board wondered if there might be a way to restart a conversation with the Carnegie Corporation. They had been exchanging letters with James Bertram in the Manhattan office since 1917 but the end of the war brought illness, confusion and, finally, a new focus. Carnegie had died in 1919 at the age of eighty-three. Officially, the charitable foundation had decided to move on from its original focus. They had stopped building libraries in 1917. Bertram remembered Hill from their negotiations over the Calgary Public Library and from the efforts to build Carnegie libraries on both sides of the North Saskatchewan River.

The city had grown substantially since then. It now had a glorious legislature, a great bridge and the limestone, château-style Hotel Macdonald. There were deposit libraries all over the city, in houses and community halls: Westmount, West Edmonton, North Edmonton,

H. Allen Gray School, and the Highlands Drugstore. Bertram was not entirely opposed to the idea of a new Carnegie library in Edmonton despite the fact that it broke the foundation's rules. In early 1922 Mayor David Milwyn Duggan and library board chair L.T. Barclay travelled to New York City to meet—and they hoped charm—him in person.

It worked, or it sort of worked. Bertram had a pot of money to distribute before the end of the 1922 funding season. He could theoretically make a special arrangement for Edmonton since they had begun negotiations before 1917. There would be no time for the usual process: no quibbling over money for months on end, no arguments over rules and regulations, no architectural competition.

Was Edmonton interested?

Ethelbert and Jennie Hill's daughter Esther Marjorie Hill was Canada's first female architecture graduate and first woman architect. She worked on Edmonton's Carnegie Library.

[UTA Esther Marjorie Hill B1986-0106/005P, Acc IB004]

7

Edmonton's acropolis

AT ESTHER MARJORIE HILL'S GRADUATION from architecture school at the University of Toronto in 1920, the chair of the department—a man named C.H.C. Wright—refused to participate, in protest. No one would hire her in Toronto so she came back to her hometown, where she registered as an architect.

The professional association denied her application.

Edmonton happened to be one of the most progressive cities in Canada at the time, and it was obsessed with reform. New ideas were at work here: the labour movement, protesting farmers, political reform and, of course, the temperance movement. During the war, some of the strongest advocates had been women. They had demanded that the city shut down the brothels and gambling houses, as there were more than one hundred of them at the start of the war. The battle ended up in city council, where Mayor William McNamara and Alderman Joseph Clarke—former allies in the fight against temperance—stood up from their chairs and threatened each other over the issue.

"I'll mop the earth with you!" shouted Clarke.

"You haven't the courage of a rat!" said the mayor.

It turned out they both had courage enough to move from words to fists. Their scrap began in council chambers and ended up on the street; both showed up for work the next morning with black eyes.[1]

More than 10,000 men, women and children for temperance had marched through the city on July 19, 1915. In the ensuing plebiscite, men voted 58,295 to 37,509 for prohibition.[2] Bootleggers would thrive in the city for eight years.

The most enduring and important sign of Edmonton's political transformation in this period was in the achievements of its women. They entered the workforce and volunteered. The first female police officer in Canada, Annie Jackson, was an Edmontonian. The first woman elected in Canadian municipal politics: Bessie Nichols, school trustee. The Edmonton Grads, a spectacularly good all-female basketball team, rose out of McDougall Commercial High School to become enduring world champions.[3] When a couple of hundred women marched into the legislature demanding the right to vote, Premier Arthur Sifton "told them to go home and wash their dishes."[4] Still, something irreversible was happening in Edmonton. The first female magistrate in the British Empire, Emily Murphy, lived and worked and fought for women's rights in the city. In 1916, women in Alberta were the first in Canada to vote in a provincial election. Roberta MacAdams, a nurse from Edmonton serving in the war effort overseas, and Louise McKinney, were elected to the legislature: a first for women in the British Empire.

By the time the library board was speaking to James Bertram in New York City, Irene Parlby and Nellie McClung had just been elected to the Alberta legislature. McKinney had narrowly lost her seat. These four, with activist Henrietta Edwards, were later known as the "Famous Five" for ensuring that women were legally considered persons in 1927.

Despite all these successes, Esther Marjorie's career proves that women continued to have trouble in Edmonton. But politicians—including Parlby and McClung—argued that the Architecture Act was unfair. In response, the government amended the legislation so "any graduate of any school of architecture in His Majesty's Dominion" would be accepted and registered.

Finally, in 1922, the daughter of a librarian and a poet—the first female architecture graduate in Canada—was ready to work. That same year, James Bertram of the Carnegie Corporation offered the library board $75,000. It was a substantial increase from the original offer, years earlier, but still insufficient to build a new library. Hill, Mayor Duggan and board chair Barclay continued to lobby Bertram—though there wasn't much time. Convinced that Edmonton was a city with a future, Bertram raised the donation to $122,500. The City of Edmonton, keen to take advantage of the donation before the offer expired, was prepared to contribute $37,500.

The members of the special committee of the library board decided they were "in favour of the erection of a building oblong in form, comprising one storey and high basement, with lantern lighting, to be built in stone and brick and conforming as nearly as may be to the elevations of the Library erected by the City of Washington, D.C."[5]

Since an architectural competition would take as long as the board had to complete the library, the committee appointed Magoon and MacDonald, one of the top architecture firms in the city. The architects had designed public and commercial buildings, churches and campus halls, simply and elegantly. You can still see their work in McDougall United Church, on the corner of 101 Street and 100 Avenue, the McKenney Building on 104 Street north of Jasper Avenue, and the attractive H.V. Shaw Building at 10229 105 Street. It may not have been a coincidence that Magoon and MacDonald happened to be the only architecture firm in the city willing to hire Esther Marjorie Hill.

Herbert Alton Magoon was from Quebec. He had been lured to Alberta, like the Hill family and everyone else, by feelings of hope and expansion. While he was a successful architect, his great skill was networking: meeting and convincing the men who wanted to build

George Heath MacDonald of the Edmonton architecture firm Magoon and MacDonald: the designers of the first freestanding library on the north side of the river.

[City of Edmonton Archives EA-234-1]

something. His younger colleague, George Heath MacDonald, had come to Edmonton from Prince Edward Island. His role in the partnership was to design lovely buildings.

MacDonald, twenty years younger than his senior partner, was not a salesman. He was too busy. When he wasn't designing buildings, he was writing for pleasure and rolling around with his friends on the football field and baseball diamond. Or perhaps drawing and painting; he was a founding member of the Edmonton Art Club. MacDonald took every free moment to travel across the continent, to visit the latest beautiful buildings and art collections. In 1913 he married Dorothea Enid Huestis and, for a wedding present, built her a white colonial home on Connaught Drive in Glenora that is on Edmonton's register of historic resources today.[6]

His work on Edmonton's downtown library was unusual in many ways. All Carnegie libraries had certain rules and regulations attached to them. Some of these, in 1922, remained as crucial as they had been in 1909, when Carnegie was still alive: no damned Greek façades and no miserable smoking rooms. Other rules were less rigorous, especially since Bertram and the foundation were rushing MacDonald along. It was supposed to look a little like the library in Washington, D.C., a little like the library in Somerville, Massachusetts.

What did that mean?

One of the most difficult aspects of the job, for MacDonald, was the prospect of not only pleasing his client but physically working with him. Hill had particular ideas about the library, and insisted—through Marjorie and through his own interventions—they be implemented.

The Edmonton Public Library would be rectangular, as per Carnegie's rules, with a hint of French renaissance about it. The main floor was one large and airy room, with a high ceiling. The loan desk would be on the western wall, to take advantage of natural light in the afternoons and early evenings. MacDonald, like many architects of his generation, had trained in the Beaux-Arts tradition; he planned four Doric columns in the front and Italian details. To meld with its larger cousin on the other side of 100 Street, the library would be built with Indiana limestone and cream, terra cotta brick—the roof with red Spanish tile and copper accents.[7]

It was normal for the Carnegie Corporation to spend some time with plans, to debate and criticize them, to find errors and outright abominations where designers and library boards found none. Not in this case. Bertram and his team approved and returned the drawings immediately.

Poole Construction, which would become one of Edmonton's most iconic businesses, was appointed general contractor—its first job in Ernest C. Poole's new hometown. Some of the problems that arose were avoidable and, it turned out, philosophical.

They might have selected a local supplier for the decorative face brick, although there was some disagreement at the time over whether or not a local company could produce the quantity and quality of bricks

EDMONTON PUBLIC LIBRARY

OPENING

OF THE NEW BUILDING
Macdonald Drive

AUGUST 30th, 1923

A PUBLIC LIBRARY

Here rests the wisdom-treasure of mankind:
The stalwart souls who this great wealth amassed
Sought not to bear it with them as they passed
To future worlds, nor ventured it to bind
In tombs of rock as kings of old enshrined
Their valued store, with spells and curses cast
Upon the ravisher, but free at last
From self, they left for men their wealth of mind.

So freely take and use and gladly share
The high companionship of those who lead
The upward march of man's dim-seeing host;
With them is found a guild of friendship rare,
Their standard bears the legend plain to read—
To scatter, yet increase is wisdom's boast.

JENNIE STORK HILL.

Jennie Hill wrote a poem to mark the opening of the main branch of the Edmonton Public Library.

[EPL]

that MacDonald had envisioned. Then, as now, there was a feeling that if something originated in Edmonton it lacked a certain worldliness and sophistication. So the builders went with the Kittaning Brick and Fireclay Company of St. Louis for the brick and soon regretted it. The bricks arrived uneven and ugly.[8]

In a letter to Kittaning, MacDonald wrote, "[t]hey are emphatically the worst I have ever seen."[9]

The library was not designed or constructed as a community hub, like its neighbour in Strathcona. It was a library and an administration centre for a library system, a signature piece of architecture in one of the most beautiful spots in the city—Edmonton's acropolis, despite Carnegie's warnings against Greek façades. The grand new building opened on August 30, 1923, fourteen years after its board first met to decide how they might build it. The front page of the program featured an original poem by Jennie Hill:

Here rests the wisdom-treasure of mankind:
The stalwart souls who this great wealth amassed
Sought not to bear it with them as they passed
To future worlds, nor ventured it to bind
In tombs of rock as kings of old enshrined
Their valued store, with spells and curses cast
Upon the ravisher, but free at last
From self, they left for men their wealth of mind.

So freely take and use and gladly share
The high companionship of those who lead
The upward march of man's dim-seeing host;
With them is found a guild of friendship rare,
Their standard bears a legend plain to read—
To scatter, yet increase is wisdom's boast.

Premier Herbert Greenfield and Mayor Duggan opened the new building, formally, at 3 P.M. Duggan was a pro-business mayor desperately if not always charmingly proud of his city. The first radio station in the province started operation when Duggan was in city hall and he was invited to speak for its first broadcast.

"Edmonton leads the way in all Alberta," said Mayor Duggan into the CJCA microphone. "Calgary and others follow. That is all. Goodnight."[10]

Premier Greenfield was a reluctant leader of a strange political party—the United Farmers of Alberta. Shortly after taking power, he appointed Irene Parlby the first female cabinet minister but he lacked courage in other matters. The death of his wife in 1922 haunted him and he neither engaged opposition members nor controlled the whims of his own backbenchers. He was comfortable, however, in the Edmonton Public Library.

Tea was served after the speeches in the assembly room, seared by the sun thanks to the high and wide windows on every side, and enormous skylights. A band played all afternoon. There was a lecture room and a children's library on the basement level, essentially the ground floor. A set of stairs at the front of the building led to the main floor, one vast room—120 feet by 60 feet wide—with white classical ionic columns, battleship linoleum, and terrazzo floors over marble. The stairs were also marble and terrazzo. Light fixtures were created by Macbeth-Evans Glass, one of the finest and dearest lantern-makers before and during the Great Depression. The trim was oak and matched the bookshelves, tables, and chairs.

The evening program included speeches from the chair of the board, L.T. Barclay, who had travelled to New York to press the Carnegie Corporation for funds just a year and a half earlier. Hill spoke triumphantly, and the keynote address was by Dr. George H. Locke, chief librarian of the Toronto Public Library and a leader of the North American library movement.

"Edmonton is fortunate in having a sculptor of wide experience and varied skill," the program for opening day noted. "A slight recognition of the generous Carnegie gift is the artistic Caen stone panel carved by Major Norbury, showing the profile of the great builder of public libraries and bearing as an inscription this sentence from Mr. Carnegie's address delivered upon the opening of the Carnegie Institute: "The taste of reading is one of the most precious possessions of life."[11]

The politicians and business leaders and artists came. So did mothers and fathers and children, in great numbers. As much as Hill wanted a building worthy of Edmonton's ambition, he also wanted a culture of reading and reflection and self-betterment in the city. Then, as now, there was only one good reason to leave your life behind in Ireland or Quebec or India or Poland or Somalia or China to come to the northernmost major city on the continent: to change your life. For those without the means or the time to go to university, the city's most powerful instrument for life changing was the elegant new building on Macdonald Drive.

Not everyone in the city agreed the new library—or any library—was a worthwhile public investment.

Edmonton in 1923 was as conflicted as Edmonton in 1913 and 2013. We want a great city, and great cities are filled with fine architecture and beautiful proportions, pleasing public spaces. At the same time we want a relentlessly frugal city council; we would rather spend our own money than have the government spend it for us. We don't want extravagance yet we know that beauty, in some calculation, is always an extravagance. No one wants to live in an ugly city yet, unchecked, public and private development oriented around cost savings and profit alone will turn out ugly.

The library was at the eastern edge of a pleasant circle, just north of Macdonald Drive, that surrounded the pitch of grass where my grandfather and grandmother stood when they were a young couple at sundown. Others enjoyed lawn bowling here, or sat with recently borrowed books on a sunny afternoon and entered an adventure.

Today this is Telus Plaza, a platform of concrete at the base of two office towers. On warm days, you can hear but not see children playing

Lawn bowling in the elegant green space out the front doors of the Carnegie Library.

[Bruce Peel Special Collections Library 6715]

The site of the Carnegie Library would transform into the AGT Towers; in 2013, the plaza of the Telus Towers and the Williams Engineering Building at 100 Avenue and 100 Street. [EPL]

in a high-fenced outdoor corridor—a daycare centre. Office workers will stand out here and smoke. When they finish their cigarettes, even on the most beautiful days, they go back inside the concourse, which is oriented like an indoor mall. There is no street-level retail, no invitation, no gathering places, no integration between the plaza and the bus stop on 100 Street. If you want to stand in a crowd, you have to go downstairs during the cigarette breaks, where between twenty and forty people will huddle together near some underutilized patio furniture.

The Legion was at the top of the circle, where the Telus Towers stand today. Next to the library was the Edmonton Club.

"It really was a beautiful circle," says Edmonton historian Tony Cashman. "The library was on the east side, the legion was on the north and Alberta College was on the west side. The Edmonton Club was right beside the library. It was *the club* at the time, certainly an old boys' club. It gradually lost relevance because the younger guns wanted to go to the places where women were allowed."[12]

Today, the concrete platform at the south end of Telus Plaza meets an underground parkade and then the entrance to a surface parking lot, this one for Alberta College. A few feet away, a man is planting flowers and clipping hedges in the sunshine along the southern wall of McDougall United Church—built by Magoon and MacDonald. He wears a grey hat and says hello to everyone who passes. Three others stand to talk nearby. It is comfortable here, even a little spectacular. To have a conversation about gardens or politics or books or God, with this view of the North Saskatchewan river valley, next to a well-preserved building: this is Edmonton, or an Edmonton.

8

“We’re bigger than our buildings”

ETHELBERT LINCOLN HILL had helped build two libraries in Edmonton. Now he turned his attention to creating a city of readers.

“It is a highly gratifying fact that the demand for literature of the more substantial character has shown a steady increase,” he wrote, reflecting on the excitement that grew with the improved Edmonton Public Library. “Books of biography, travel and poetry have been in constant demand. Strachey’s *Queen Victoria* has had over 100 issues. *The Life of Roosevelt* has had even more. Browning’s poems have been issued scores of times during the year. Our several copies of the poems of Robert Service are very well-worn by constant service.”[1]

Hill was not a blushing fan of popular culture. For generations, librarians of taste have smuggled smutty crime novels out of the building in their briefcases, careful not to reveal their pop desires. Hill was equally concerned about the dangers—political, social and cultural—of elitism. From the board minutes and from the annual reports it is easy to detect a considerable streak of sensitivity in his writing; Hill constantly argued that libraries were for everyone, not just a highly educated, refined class of Edmontonians with grand houses in the correct neighbourhoods.

He wanted city managers and politicians to understand that this "substantial literature" was moving through every apartment and house in the city, and changing lives. University graduates were taking books from the library but so were plumbers and bricklayers.

"The proportion of registered borrowers, with regard to occupation, for example, is closely parallel to the proportion as determined from the city directory. For example, the proportion of mechanics on the library register is about the same as the proportion of mechanics in the directory. This distribution ought to be gratifying to the Board as proving the general usefulness of the institution entrusted to their care. No one class of the community is being favoured at the expense of any other class."[2]

Carnegie's critics often argued he bought naming rights to libraries without providing the funds to fill them with crucial assets like books and librarians. It was enormously expensive to staff a library and maintain a steady collection of books, magazines, newspapers and reference material. The fact is, James Bertram was rigorous in finding assurances from cities they were willing and financially prepared to operate a library before any money left the Carnegie Corporation. City budgets are difficult beasts to manage; Edmonton can only raise so much money from property taxes. The problem, then as now, is that it can seem a battle between the necessary, the life-and-death, and intellectual extravagance. Children need safe water to drink. Can we trade one drop of it for a book?

More crudely, since the end of the Second World War, the argument has been between potholes and books. There will always be citizens who will fight tirelessly to be sure every pothole is filled before the city spends a nickel on a book. These core arguments about the role of government, at city hall and in the newspapers' letters pages, were as vigorous in the 1920s as they are today. One of Hill's most important jobs was to prepare for this criticism, and counter it, and to align the aspirations of the Edmonton Public Library with the aspirations of Edmontonians.

"It should be strongly emphasized that the relative cost of maintaining the library has been too frequently exaggerated by a few people who are opposed to the principle of a free public library. It should be remembered that out of forty-three dollars and thirty-five cents contributed by the tax-payer the library received only seventy-four cents with which to pay debentures on two libraries and meet all other capital and maintenance charges on the Edmonton Library, the Strathcona Library and four deposit stations, one at least of which (the North Edmonton unit) is really a branch library."[3]

The North Edmonton Community League was moving from a book deposit to a mini-library, at a cost of $10 per month. The cosmopolitan character of the city was changing anew. The Ukrainian population collected book donations in their language, for the library, and Hill found a bit of money to buy some more. But, as always during his leadership of the library system, there wasn't much money at all.

According to the Libraries Act, the system received $1 million—a fixed sum, dependent on property assessments. In 1925, money was so tight for the library that Hill and his staff had to take pay cuts. When the Strathcona Library required new lighting fixtures, the board asked Hill to sell the old fixtures, including the opalescent globes from the temporary homes of the downtown branch. In 1927, salaries returned to what they had been three years earlier. This was, according to the board minutes, a victory for everyone.

The Strathcona Library was in the process of becoming a horticultural marvel, with trees and shrubs, perennials and seasonal flowers surrounding the building. Inside, it was a meeting place for the neighbourhood and a resource for workers along Edmonton's second main street—Whyte Avenue.

A determined walk from the Stanley A. Milner Branch of the Edmonton Public Library to the Strathcona Branch takes about forty minutes. You walk south down 100 Street, past the Westin Hotel and the World Trade Centre to the generous grounds of the Hotel Macdonald. Inevitably,

In October 1902, the first train crossed North Saskatchewan River and entered Edmonton.

[Provincial Archives of Alberta A15485]

young people and exercise enthusiasts will be on the vast set of stairs next to the hotel, leading down into the river valley. The kids are smoking something-or-other and drinking something-or-other and the men and women in running gear are a generation older, seeking to undo some of the damage of their youth. Everyone is polite. At the bottom of the stairs you cross one of the oldest pieces of infrastructure in Edmonton—the Low Level Bridge, completed in 1900. The first train into Edmonton crossed this bridge on October 20, 1902. There is a photograph of the event in the provincial archives, with a few spindly and leafless trees along the muddy banks. Men in suits and hats have piled on to the train to commemorate the occasion. Most of the development was at the top of the hill so it's difficult to imagine—until the High Level Bridge was completed eleven years later—how anything heavier than a man made it downtown.

On the other side of the Low Level Bridge you put your hand out to stop traffic and cross Connors Road. Under the 98 Avenue overpass, an inhospitable place for a pedestrian, you enter its contrary: a calm pocket park with a blooming fruit tree. You say hello to other walkers who have discovered this place, and enter the shadow of one last overpass. Edmonton's river valley is today one of the largest urban parks in the world. One hundred years ago, when the Edmonton Public Library was born, it was the core of city industry.

At that time, writes historian Lawrence Herzog, "Emily Murphy described the buzz of the sawmills in the North Saskatchewan river valley as the typical sound of the Edmonton summer. In Edmonton's formative years, industry—not recreation—was the dominant force that shaped the valley. Coal mining, lumber, brick making, ice harvesting and gold mining all played a role in the development of the valley."[4]

Today, Mill Creek moves underground before any of its water enters the river system. In the early years of the last century, the creek flowed along the flats where today we walk on paved trails, and entered the river more naturally. The creek "was named after a grist mill established by William Bird in 1878, making it one of the first flour mills in all of western Canada. It operated until 1881 and was closed because there wasn't enough water in the creek to keep the wheel turning."[5]

Today, there are no mills or meat packing plants in the Mill Creek ravine: only cyclists and dog walkers and skateboarders and lovers and, when there is enough snow, cross-country skiers. We have barbecues and frisbee afternoons in the ravine. One of the finest winter festivals is an evening adventure walk where children carry homemade lanterns and move through pieces of Edmonton history and magic and nature—including men and women dressed as beavers and magpies.

Climb out of the ravine at 87 Avenue and walk west through Old Strathcona, between bakeries and cafés, a wine bar and a tattoo parlour. Here single-family homes, many of them more than one hundred years old, mingle with luxury condominiums and churches and plain apartment blocks. North of Whyte Avenue, an industrial area centred on the south side service garage for Edmonton Transit has transformed into a theatre and cultural district—home of the oldest and largest Fringe Theatre Festival in North America. One of the Fringe venues, where I have seen historical plays about Edmonton, nude stand-up comedy, dirty clowns, and British monologues about the transformative power of vegetable gardening, is in the amphitheatre on the second floor of the Strathcona Branch of the Edmonton Public Library.

If you stand across the street, when the buds are out and the flowers are up and the children are playing in the park, this is one of the most successful pieces of urban design in Edmonton. The Knox Church, built in 1907, is the library's spiritual sibling. Behind the library, the old bus barns have been rebuilt as Fringe Theatre Adventures. For ten days in August, an estimated half a million people walk through here to watch buskers from around the world and line up for beautiful, strange and occasionally horrifying theatre. A plaque next to the front doors of the English renaissance library reads, in typically Edmonton language, "The Carnegie Foundation offered to build a library of a specified size and shape; this did not meet the requirements of the citizens of Strathcona, who refused the offer and instead financed their own larger building."

Take that, good Mr. Carnegie.

Today we walk into the library and our small children can sit at the bench in the vestibule while we read the bulletins for upcoming literary readings and yoga nights and video games for retired people. This is Edmonton, so we nearly always have coats to remove. Through windows with oak trim, the librarians are working behind and on the other side of the square waist-high circulation desk. They aren't checking out books and DVDs: a computerized radio frequency system does that. Instead, they speak to readers and guide them to the stacks. Gentle period lamps hang from the ceiling, on each side of pretty arches.

In 2013, the renovated Strathcona Branch of the Edmonton Public Library is in one of the city's most vibrant social and cultural districts: home of the first and largest Fringe Theatre Festival on the continent and a marvellous farmers' market. [EPL]

"Is there something in particular you're looking for?" a young man asks. It's such a peculiar question, outside a retail setting, I worry that I am ill-dressed for the occasion. There is something so fine about the proportions inside the old library it does feel incorrect to wear anything less than a suit and leather-soled shoes. To the right there is a teen area and that controversial fireplace. Carnegie hated fireplaces in libraries.

I ask at the desk if the fireplace still works.

"Oh, good question." One of the librarians stares at it a moment. "I have no idea."

One of his colleagues turns around. "It does, of course. Would you like me to turn it on?"

There is a sign, part of the library's award-winning marketing campaign, that states, "We're bigger than our buildings." While this is evident downtown, where the building serves a number of social functions, the Strathcona Branch—thanks to its age and architectural details—still feels like an old-fashioned Canadian library. There are books, of course, but there are also computers. Here in Old Strathcona, where the clientele is different, the computers are not the most popular items in the room. Most computer users here are parents whose children are in the back of the library, in the 2006 expansion. The former back wall of the library has opened into a rounded new room—large enough for a children's library and a bright and quiet reading area overlooking the park to the south.

There is no one in the Strathcona library in, as Thomas Carlyle so gently put it, "a state of imbecility." No one is sleeping or cackling troublingly to himself. Two little girls sit side by side in a wooden train, arguing loudly about snakes instead of reading, and—when they think no adults are looking—terrorizing smaller children by sticking out their tongues and making monster poses. This is all Strathcona can manage for imbecility on a cloudy weekday afternoon. It is quiet and sober apart from the little girls and two others, their cries muffled and tears dried by their parents' legs.

Originally, there was a piece of art on this floor, on the south side of the room at the base of one of the arches. It was dear enough to warrant a paragraph in the first annual report of the fused library system in 1913.

"In the Entrance Hall, facing the loan desk, stands 'The Prayer of Faith,' a beautiful bronze statue by F. Fleming Baxter, presented to the Library by the sculptor as an expression of his interest and faith in this far western metropolis. It was previously exhibited at the International Exhibition, Graffton Galleries, London England, in 1910. Through the interest of J.M. Douglas, M.P., and O. Bush, Esq., the customs charges were refunded, making it possible to obtain this valuable addition to the Library, free of duty. Mr. F. Fleming Baxter has exhibited several other

"The Prayer of Faith," a sculpture by F. Fleming Baxter, was an important feature in the Strathcona Library until it was removed by someone. Staff are still looking for it, and offer amnesty to anyone who wants to return it. [EPL]

notable pieces of sculpture, and is now at work on a memorial tablet to be placed in Guy's Hospital, London, England, in honor of Sir Samuel Wilks."[6]

The sculpture was mysteriously removed.

Today, on the Edmonton Public Library website, there is an offer of amnesty and immunity for anyone who provides information about "The Prayer of Faith." Photos of the statue, from afar and close up, accompany the plea. Who took it? Where has it lived since that day? As fascinating as the answers to these questions might be, all the library really wants is a piece of its history back.

"A landmark of the Strathcona Library for many years, 'The Prayer of Faith' seems to have vanished from the face of the earth. Where is it? The statue is out there, somebody knows...Call 496-1855. All we want is the truth."[7]

The Strathcona Branch is our family's local library. On cold days and rainy days we have spent hours there, hunting for books or reading them on the train or in a chair or on the floor. When we visit the downtown branch, my daughters—seven and five—are more social. They talk at full volume. In the Strathcona library they whisper and, curiously, ignore the computers. The room is haunted by its past, by the thousands of people who have sat and read and dreamed between its brick walls.

I do have a romantic view of certain eras, especially when I'm sitting in a space like the Strathcona library. But men and women in the 1920s misbehaved from time to time

Halloween night in 1927 was an unhappy one for the old library. The front of the building was beginning to win landscape design awards. The library was not only a gathering place but a place of beauty for residents of the near south side, including the Hill family.

"The urns in front of the Strathcona building were thrown down and the bases destroyed by a gang of young men," wrote Hill, in that year's otherwise subdued annual report. "The police have made no report as to the culprits. It will be necessary to have these structures rebuilt."[8]

Hill had them rebuilt in time for the summer of 1929, when the library took second prize from the horticultural society in the category of public buildings. The downtown branch, despite its novelty and grandeur, only managed to snag a special mention.[9] Indignities were perpetrated downtown as well. In 1929 the board reported a burglary in the Carnegie building, in the children's department facing the grand Edmonton Club.

The catch on the window was exposed and released, enabling the miscreant to raise the sash and enter. After ineffectual attempts to break into the safe

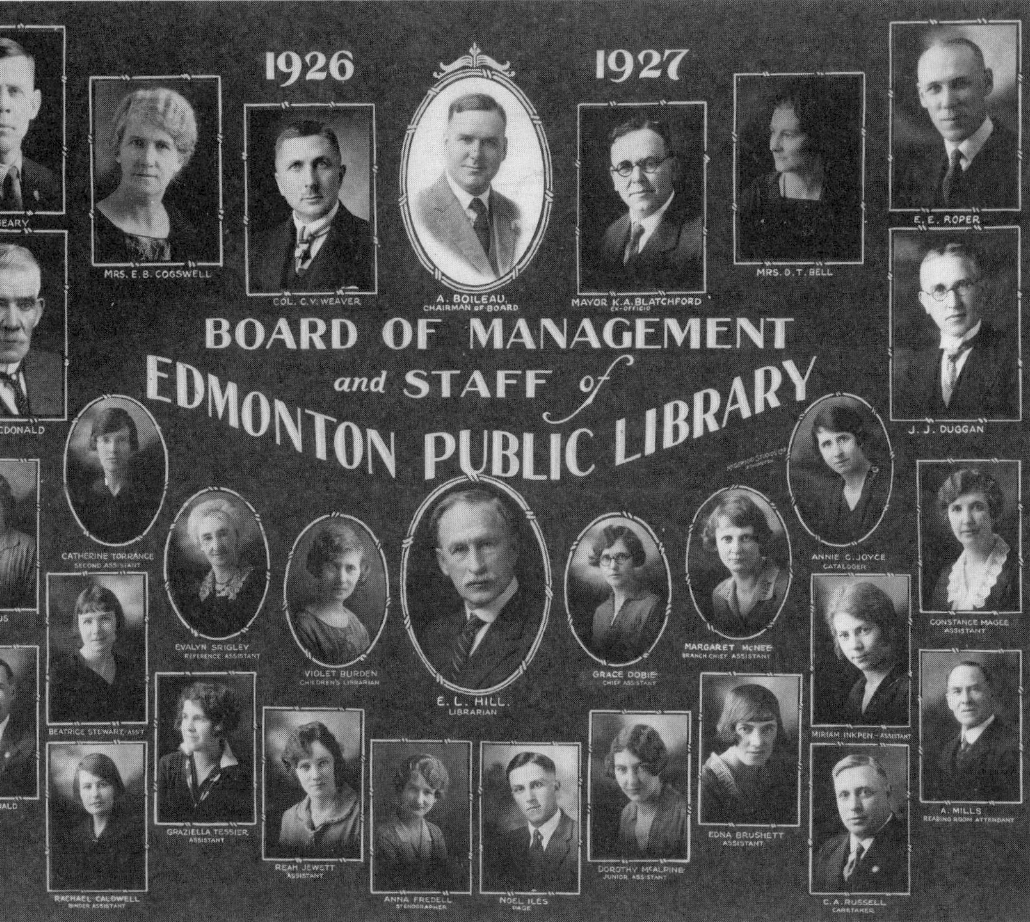

The board and staff of the Edmonton Public Library in 1926 and 1927. [EPL]

from the front after breaking off the dial, he turned the safe on its face and proceeded to chisel through the back. After cutting through the back plate, he removed a portion of the fire-proofing composition and exposed the steel lining. He cut through this sufficiently to allow removal of cash boxes, etc. He appears to have brought with him a new hammer and stout wrought steel nail-puller. In order to operate on the back of the safe, he brought up from the basement a chisel, the heavy gate-shaker and a piece of gas pipe. He entered the vestibule at some time during his operations and failed to notice that *the vestibule door had the night-latch set. He was thus trapped in the vestibule. In order to get back into the library he broke a pane of plate glass in the partition, apparently using a broom handle for the purpose. It is evident that he must have worked for some hours. He rejected the copper and nickel coins, leaving these on the counter and on the librarian's desk. The librarian's desk was also broken open and drawers rifled but nothing seems to have been stolen from this desk or elsewhere except money. The amounts stolen are calculated to be...$103.75. Fortunately no imprest fund money was on hand as this had been exhausted as per vouchers. The safe is so seriously damaged that repairs for practical use would be too costly to consider seriously. A temporary arrangement has been made with Robertson Safe Co. to have the use of a safe until the Board can take action. In addition to the loss set forth as per foregoing statement, the burglar secured $20.00 belonging to Miss. Dobie, chief assistant, and some $5.50 belonging to the staff's "flower fund"... In December the Board refunded this money.*[10]

These problems and competitions would come to seem quaint.

New ideas from literature swirled through Edmonton during the Depression. The Hunger March on December 20, 1932, started boisterously and ended in bloodshed. [Provincial Archives of Alberta A9215]

9

Tough times in the "Rome of the West"

OCTOBER 29, 1929 was the final day of an extraordinary transformation in North America and the world—a time of optimism, cultural experimentation, growth and, ultimately, dangerous nonsense. Edmonton had thrived on a foundation of commodities. The agriculture and mining industries that sustained the Alberta economy were caught up in the multi-billion-dollar collapse that expanded into the Great Depression. Brokers in Edmonton, as elsewhere, committed suicide. The misery was less immediate for other Edmontonians but the lives of every one of the city's 75,000 citizens would change over the coming decade. More than 10,000 new Edmontonians, most of them economic refugees from devastated rural communities, would struggle along with established city families.

Almost twenty per cent of Edmontonians would come to rely on direct government relief as a combination of high unemployment and low wages affected everyone from shop owners to banks. Companies that had entered the Depression with cash swooped in to buy up land and businesses at a discount. Small retailers along main streets like Jasper Avenue and Whyte Avenue were forced to close, including grocers who had helped local families. At the same time, Safeway, based in California, opened its first Edmonton store on 124 Street and 102 Avenue with lower prices and a rather distant sense of community.[1]

If it was difficult to argue for better library funding in 1928 and 1929, it was impossible during the Depression. The debate had little connection to books versus potholes. This was, quite visibly, books versus starving children.

Still Hill made his point. Even during hard economic times, perhaps especially during these rugged years, the library was our best hope for individual and social change. Education was the key to making it through these hard times.

"Any sane library policy must take cognizance of the fact that the public library is practically the only institution that provides educational material and opportunity and opportunities for the people at large," Hill wrote. "Once more it should be emphasized that, 'The Public Library is an integral part of Public Education.'

"The men and women being displaced by machines and mergers are being displaced faster than our economic structure can absorb them. These surplus unemployed will have to 'learn or perish.' There must be some provision for alternative training. The public library is a most important factor in this re-education."[2]

Re-education may have been a way out of the Depression, but that didn't prevent staff shortages and fewer book orders, fewer programs, fewer hours. One of the chief assistants of the Edmonton Public Library and, for a few years, acting chief librarian, Grace Dobie, looked back on the 1930s as a time of surprise and wonder.

"Our greatest circulation and our highest point in purchases were reached during the Depression years, particularly in 1932. It is remarkable how closely our circulation follows prosperity, in an inverse ratio."[3]

There was little evidence this was numerically true. Spiritually true, surely.

The Depression forced Edmontonians to live differently: backyards that had been devoted to leisure were now gardens and chicken coops. With less money to spend on recreation, free public spaces were more popular than ever, especially in the river valley. It was also a time of intellectual inspiration. The status quo was no longer in need of protection, as it had turned out so poorly for everyone.

Not all of the intellectual playfulness was positive. In 1929, a handsome and well-spoken man named John J. Maloney arrived in Edmonton. He had grown up Irish Catholic in Ontario and had studied to be a priest in Montreal. The vow of celibacy and other rules did not agree with him so he took a less priestly vocation within the church. When that failed him, he sued for wrongful dismissal. The church counter-sued and Maloney turned both Presbyterian and ferociously anti-Catholic.

When he arrived in Edmonton, Maloney was not impressed by the cultural diversity of the city. Too many people from other places, too much immigration in general, too much racial intermarriage, too much French spoken, too many Catholics. His reading and his recent experiences had drawn him to become a member of an American organization called the Ku Klux Klan—based on Anglo-Saxon purity and "moral virtue."[4] At a time of high unemployment, the idea that immigrants were both muddying up the ethnic mix and taking jobs from Edmonton's accent-less, British royalty-supporting, not-at-all-swarthy population was an abomination to him.

Dim economic times, and a boom in literature supporting the supremacy of the white race and the conspiracies against it, helped the charismatic new Edmontonian gain a following. The peak arrived in March 1932, when hundreds gathered in Memorial Hall to hear Imperial Wizard Maloney call them to "study the Klan's 'wholesome teaching and to morally profit thereby.'"[5]

This was not the sort of re-education Hill had imagined. Edmonton was a small market for the Klan, which had a membership in mostly rural Alberta of almost 7,000 in the early years of the Depression. The Klan's progress in the city was halted, some months after the rally in Memorial Hall, when the latest in Maloney's troubles with the law made the newspapers.

On New Year's Eve, Maloney drove his car into a snow bank at the Mayfair Golf and Country Club. In his efforts to extract the car, he broke into the toolshed and started a fire. Once he freed the car, he realized it had been damaged and filed an insurance claim—stating that the shed had been smashed by thieves who had stolen the car. He went to court on fraud charges and arrived for sentencing January 31, 1933.

"Please, please give me one more chance, just one more chance," the philosopher pleaded, tearfully. "I'll show the world what I can do. I was trapped. My parents are sick in Hamilton. Please give me a chance. I have Bright's disease."[6] He ended up in prison, and this was not the end of his legal woes. Even the Klan ended up pressing the Crown to charge him with theft for misappropriating funds.

Of course, none of this was Maloney's fault. He noted in his book, *Darkness, Dawn, and Daybreak* that he was up against the Liberal Party machine in Edmonton. He had no chance.

"In his autobiography, Maloney asserted that his court cases in Edmonton were 'pure frame-ups activated by forces whose wrath I had incurred through fighting for principle and right.' He claimed that new evidence was surfacing but that he would not disclose it prematurely and allow his enemies to turn it to their advantage. Claiming that he had suffered personally as a result of the litigation, Maloney characteristically added: 'But that's nothing; I knew what to expect when I entered Edmonton, the Rome of the West.'"[7]

As Maloney transformed in the public imagination from orator and leader to liar and criminal, another European intellectual movement was gaining supporters in and out of libraries, halls, and dining rooms.

William "Bible Bill" Aberhart, premier and radio personality, was progressive in economic matters and conservative in social and religious concerns.

[Provincial Archives of Alberta A2043]

10 From the library to the street—and the legislature

FOR CHILDREN, there wasn't a lot of good news in the early 1930s. But is was warm in the library, and safe. Hill was more than just a keeper of books and buildings. His ambition was to transform young Edmontonians into thoughtful, reflective, empathetic adults through reading.

> *In 1932, "116,767 volumes were loaned to the boys and girls of Edmonton. Much of this reading has been done in line with judicious (but not officious) advice by library attendants in the Department. Gratifying results have been obtained in developing a taste for reading. Once more it should be stated that the child borrower displays remarkable judgment in the selection of books. It may be easily conceded that the average child makes better use of biography, travel and history than the average adult does in the adult department."*[1]

Far away, a *fin-de-siècle* philosophical movement had helped take the idea of a natural ruling class, of racial and national superiority, of heroism into political parties and factions in Europe, the Middle East, Asia and South America. Italy, Spain and Lithuania had fascist regimes and Hitler's Nazi Party would rise to power in Germany in 1933. There was a spirit of curiosity and a longing for certainty in the early years of the Depression. A new idea, a way out of this mess, would be desperately welcome. Around the world, writers and libraries and readers unofficially conspired to build new ideologies and government policies. Some readers found Hitler's *Mein Kampf*, and books about militant nationalism and racial superiority; others turned to *The Communist Manifesto* by Karl Marx and Friedrich Engels, and to books about the 1917 October Revolution in Russia. Intellectually, communism was far more attractive to many families in Edmonton in 1932 than whatever Maloney was preaching. The Edmonton Public Library was a place to discover new ideas and to debate them.

Of the thousands of refugees who arrived in Edmonton from the rural west in those years, few found jobs. The municipal and provincial governments lacked the money to intervene in the economy in any meaningful way, with capital projects or even a bit of cash for destitute families to secure shelter and food. Shortly before Imperial Wizard Maloney crashed his car into a snowbank, the Communist League had organized a parade in downtown Edmonton to plead the cause of the proletariat.

The current Stanley A. Milner Branch of the Edmonton Public Library is on land that, in December 1932, was called Market Square. The Hunger March committee had several demands: "Non-contributory unemployment insurance (there was at this time no unemployment insurance of any kind); the closing of the 20-cents-a-day relief camps called "slave" camps by their inmates; cash relief instead of bags of groceries or scrip; relief for farmers; and an end to evictions and foreclosures in both city and country."[2]

The RCMP had warned farmers not to come into Edmonton for the march. They had raided the organizers' headquarters, the Ukrainian

Labour Temple, the night before the Hunger March. Mayor Dan Knott, who had run as a Labour candidate, and Premier John Edward Brownlee of the United Farmers of Alberta, might have been expected to support the march on ideological grounds. But together they denied a parade permit. Thousands arrived at Market Square on the afternoon of December 20, 1932. So did hundreds of RCMP officers on horseback and city police on foot, clubs drawn.

It started peacefully, with a dozen speakers. A committee ran across downtown to ask the premier, one last time, for permission to march. The premier denied it. Still, the speakers and the marchers convinced themselves they had a right to protest and to petition the legislature. Just as they prepared to march, the police rushed in with clubs and batons. Men tried to hide under a canopy of Christmas trees, and to defend themselves with branches. They received the worst beatings. The crowd dispersed without any march on the legislature and, the following day, known communist gathering places were raided. Police loaded organizers and leaders into paddy wagons, charged them with unlawful assembly, and took them to jail in Fort Saskatchewan.[3]

A third economic and political philosophy circulated through the city in the early 1930s. A British engineer and Cambridge University dropout named C.H. Douglas had observed, during the First World War, that the total cost of what workers produced was more than what they were being paid. This meant, fundamentally, that workers could not actually buy back what they had created. Douglas studied British corporations and found the system was consistent: the economy was designed to make owners rich at the expense of workers. Marx and Engels might have told him the same thing, but his analysis was based on contemporary data and his conclusions were far less radical. There had to be some way to bring powers of consumption, for workers, in line with the value of what they created. A new system would increase personal liberty and flatten economic shocks.

Fundamentally, Douglas believed profits should be distributed more equally across society. He called his theory Social Credit. The movement, which featured a streak of anti-Semitism, was curiously popular in the literary world. Poets such as Ezra Pound, William Carlos Williams, T.S. Eliot, Aldous Huxley and G.K. Chesterton were attracted to the theory.

One of the people reading Douglas in Alberta was a Calgary preacher and radio announcer named William Aberhart. Aberhart infused Social Credit theory with a fiery dose of religion instead of poetry, and promoted it on CFCN radio. When Premier Brownlee was forced to resign in 1934, accused of seducing one of his clerks, Aberhart was eloquent on the matter. Not only were the economic policies of the UFA government unfair; the government itself was morally bankrupt. Social Credit study groups had popped up all over the province, in and out of libraries.

The extremely young Social Credit Party of Alberta ran in the August 1935 provincial election and took more than fifty per cent of the popular vote. The party formed a majority government without a leader. Aberhart, who had not run in the election, agreed to take on the job as premier in September.

Alberta became the Social Credit testing ground for the world. The party was radically populist, especially in its early years, when the government issued Prosperity Certificates to help battle the effects of the Depression. Critics called the certificates, worth one dollar each and requiring one hundred stamps, "funny money." The glue on the stamps would dry up and the stamps would fall off.

"In Edmonton, the money could be cashed in only a few places—the ATB, Alberta liquor stores, the University of Alberta Tuck Shop and the Army and Navy Department Store. Nobody wanted cracked money, that had to be carried in a shoebox, or to give change in good Canadian coin. Finally the Supreme Court declared the monetary system illegal."[4]

These and other faintly ridiculous policies were attacked daily in the press. To counter the bad publicity, Premier Aberhart and his government created legislation called the Accurate News and Information

Act—which would create an office of censorship. Aberhart had special access to the hearts and minds of regular Albertans, through his radio show, and often attacked newspapers such as the *Edmonton Journal*. The idea that his good government could correct the malicious liberalism of the press was not broadly unpopular.

The bill was, of course, unpopular with librarians. If censorship can happen to newspapers it can and will happen in libraries: the wrong sorts of books, magazines and papers would vanish along with the freedom of the editorial department of the *Journal*.

> *The* Journal *responded with a front-page editorial and fought the bill all the way to the Supreme Court, which ruled the bill invalid on March 4, 1938. "If this bill should pass and stand where then would freedom of speech and liberty of the press—proud boasts of Britons for two centuries?" the* Journal *wrote. "Where then would be the liberty of the citizen to free expression of opinion? The press bill now before the legislature is a dictatorial challenge to every freedom-loving Canadian whose home is in Alberta."*[5]

Today, a block away from the original home of the downtown branch of the Edmonton Public Library, there is a bronze plaque in the atrium of the *Journal* building. On May 2, 1938, the newspaper won the first Pulitzer Prize citation awarded outside the United States.

The premier was not hunting the stacks of the Edmonton Public Library for offensive material, but as the middle of the Depression came and went, Hill was having trouble making his plea for support. The staff was thin, and thinning, and the budget for new books was minuscule.

"There was very little controversy," says historian Tony Cashman. "When Ethelbert Hill was running the library it did not get involved in moulding public opinion. The library, then, was very solemn. A bit more quiet than the church down the street. They were sort of like temples, which is maybe why so many were designed like temples."

Still, books and ideas were fuelling disquiet all over the world. Nazism was battling communism and communism was battling capitalism. In Alberta, all manner of populist silliness was bursting from the legislature. Hill had wanted a lively reading culture in Edmonton, where citizens decided these issues for themselves, democratically and ambitiously, where they transformed their lives—fulfilling the promise of this northern, "far western metropolis."

His arguments weren't so much unsuccessful as ignored. Neither the City of Edmonton nor the Government of Alberta had money to spend on books, and philanthropists in the city were actively supporting hunger initiatives. The libraries also lacked the political leadership Hill was looking for, abstract and emotional and certainly financial. Aberhart believed there was really only one book worth reading, so libraries were not on his list of key assets. Mayor Joseph Clarke, who ran for nearly every election during his adult life, losing most and winning a few, was more inclined to athleticism than reading. He built a football stadium that was named after him; after his fistfight in council chambers with his old friend Mayor McNamara, his fisticuffs continued. He was often connected to gambling and prostitution rings, the original inspiration for his famous and very public fistfight, and historical documents show scant, if any, connection to the Edmonton Public Library or its chief and founder—E.L. Hill. It was, in short, a frustrating time to be a librarian and a miserable way to exit twenty-four years of service to Edmontonians.

Circulation plummeted in the middle of the 1930s. The public was tiring of the same old books, it seems, and Hill didn't know what to do about it. He mentioned infantile paralysis, which swept through the city in the middle of the decade and inspired occasional closures. But in his reports, he hardly mentioned the steep drop in figures. The board had asked him to raise the profile of the library in the city, in the manner of the flamboyant chief librarian in Calgary. Perhaps he could host a radio broadcast.

Hill was not the sort to host a radio broadcast. He requested funds, in 1934, to attend the American Library Association annual general meeting in Montreal and the board—unsettled by the quality of his leadership—turned him down.

Elizabeth Sterling Haynes, a theatre director from Toronto who had lived in Edmonton since the early 1920s, was founding theatre companies, groups and schools in and out of the city during the Depression. The first mosque in Canada, Al-Rashid, opened on 101 Street and 108 Avenue. Something in the intellectual and cultural spirit of the city had changed. Instead of leading and instigating this change, the library remained a couple of pretty buildings full of books.

It was Hill's protégé and second-in-command, Grace Dobie, who first mentioned the circulation problems in the 1937 annual report, a problem that went back to 1934. Between Hill's retirement and the arrival of the new chief, Dobie ran the library. She blamed broader cultural forces for the decline, rather than anything the Edmonton Public Library had done or had not done.

"There seems no doubt but that the sophistication of much of the current popular writings which most libraries do not countenance, even though it means a lessening of popularity, makes a difference," Dobie wrote. "Another reason may well be the great output of sensational magazines flooding the country, from some sixty varieties of the Digest type for the more thoughtful readers to the even greater number of the pulp magazines of the trigger-finger type for our youth."[6]

In two of his annual reports before retiring, in 1934 and 1935, Hill quoted an American state governor—not by name—in a bid to convince his funders that libraries were more important than ever.

"'The richest asset and the final support of the state is the citizen. The best conservation is his continual growth in mental power, character and civic spirit. Public libraries are essential to a democratic state because reading and study promote these great ends. Libraries provide generous

Today, a sliver of green space in Old Strathcona is named after E.L. Hill. [EPL]

opportunities for all for richer understanding of contemporary life, for mastery of circumstance, and for greater social and civic usefulness."[7]

On November 1, 1936, Hill retired. He and his wife Jennie moved to Victoria with their ambitious daughter, Esther Marjorie, where she set up an architecture and design practice. Edmonton's founding librarian died in 1960 in Guelph at the age of ninety-six, largely forgotten in the city of his life's work.

There is a small park in Old Strathcona, near the railroad tracks where the Fringe festival streetcar runs in the summertime. It can be found at 105 Street and 86 Avenue, adjacent to the community garden. Nothing about the park suggests reading or self-improvement, and unless you've convinced yourself to be creative it doesn't feel much like a park. There are no benches. Tony Cashman, who likes to tour Edmonton's parks with his son Paul, a retired *Edmonton Journal* editor, suggests bringing a folding chair to E.L. Hill Park if you would like to visit.

On a warm but windy spring day in 2012 I visited E.L. Hill Park with my daughters. We didn't bring folding chairs but we did bring a soccer ball so we might play, and we played, and I told them what I had learned about the chief librarian. I showed them a photo of him on my iPhone and we talked about his great achievements: the libraries, of course, and in collaboration with his wife Jennie, the raising and nurturing of a courageous and accomplished daughter—the first woman to graduate from architecture school in Canadian history.

Alexander Calhoun, Calgary's founding librarian, had a branch named after him in 1954. The University of Alberta gave Calhoun an honourary doctor of laws, calling him "a pioneer in a pioneering province."

In 2006 the municipal affairs department of the Alberta Government compiled a list of "100 Legends in Alberta's Public Library Service." Eighteen Edmontonians made the list but Hill was not one of them. He remains mysterious, the quiet man Cashman describes, a slow-motion advocate. A kind of sadness lives in his final reports as chief librarian. It was as though he had tried and failed to create, for all Edmontonians, the spirit of inquiry and attainment his daughter had carried so well.

Edmonton's second library director, Hugh Cameron Gourlay, was a youthful and energetic Ontarian filled with new ideas. [EPL]

11

A firecracker of a man

FOR NEW ARRIVALS TO EDMONTON, in the 1930s, the library system would have seemed a dusty and appealing bit of northern antebellum. Neither Hill nor his staff was educated in the latest theories. When Hill was in graduate school, library science was not a science at all. A library was a place for books, where citizens gathered to read and borrow them.

What was so complicated about that?

Hill was not an aggressive lobbyist or fundraiser. His political skills were weak. By the time of his retirement the city's two libraries had settled into a period of nostalgia. There was no money to hire a replacement but the board wasn't concerned about that. Grace Dobie, the assistant librarian, had worked closely with Hill. Books were on the shelves and the doors were open.

Of course, some members of the library board travelled. They had seen libraries in New York and Boston and Toronto and San Francisco. Libraries in these cities seemed different somehow. Shinier and with more and better books, but they were bigger cities. It was a library chair's business trip to Calgary in 1938 that changed everything. The Calgary

The Calgary Public Library's founding director, Alexander Calhoun, was a courageous civic leader and public intellectual. [Courtesy of Calgary Public Library, Community Heritage and Family History Collection CPL_103-03-01]

Public Library was not bigger than Edmonton's, but it felt different: more energy, better signs, new furniture and bookshelves and *books*, more people, a proper reference library. This was embarrassing. It would not do.

Instead of becoming defensive, the Edmonton Public Library Board gathered its courage and asked Alexander Calhoun, of the Calgary Public Library, to travel a few hours north and make a frank assessment. Calhoun had been everything Hill was not. When the federal government removed books by communist and socialist writers from the shelves, Calhoun—out of the country at the time—wrote a Calgary newspaper, sickened: "Soon we will have no liberties left."

From his arrival in Calgary, at the age of thirty-one, Calhoun had been a vocal booster, a community organizer, a volunteer city planner and advocate for beautification. The Calgary Public Library was distinct because Calhoun had designed it to be a lively intellectual meeting place: Silence signs were forbidden in his building. He was a mountain climber and a debater. In 1925, he co-founded a group of learned men called Knights of the Round Table and, in 1932, the Current Events Club. He was in the outreach business before most of his peers in the library world. The Calgary Public Library did not pretend that having books on shelves was enough to transform a population; he organized adult education classes in the humanities and social sciences. The federal government had a dossier on him and considered him a subversive, though he was always rather open about his socialist sympathies. Calhoun helped start the Co-operative Commonwealth Federation, which would eventually become the New Democratic Party.[1]

Calhoun was loud when Hill was quiet. Calhoun was creative when Hill was careful. Worse yet, he was a Calgarian. With the invitation, the Edmonton Public Library was admitting that Calhoun had done a better job of leading his institution and stirring his community.

The Calgarian was not shy. In his report, he used words like obsolete and inefficient, and phrases like "genteel shabbiness" and "pitiably inadequate from whatever angle."[2]

Edmonton in 1939 shared certain insecurities with Edmonton in 2013. If you want to see action, compare the city unfavourably to Calgary. Stomachs and brains and wallets will stir. Invite a Calgarian to town and ask him to look over a failed institution, and you can guarantee he will have plenty to say.

"In this hasty review, I have merely touched the fringes of your problem," Calhoun wrote to the board. "What is the cure?"

> *The answer is obvious, a directing head. A good librarian can iron out a great many of these problems in a very short time. If you can find the right person, he can save his salary in the second, if not the first year.*

What I have outlined should surely demonstrate that only a man thoroughly familiar with the best library practice is competent to reorganize your library. He must be able to re-organize but also to revitalize the library. To achieve this he must have the ability to rouse this community, to win its respect and support for the library. The day is gone when a library can depend entirely upon a good collection of books. It must be publicized.

Your task is to find that man.[3]

For years, city council and the board had kept funds from Hill, even asking him to take a large pay cut for three years in the middle of an economic boom in the city. If only he had visited Calgary with a camera and a notepad.

The library board placed a job advertisement in national newspapers. They received fifty applications from qualified candidates and from that list created a shortlist of seven. Many librarians were looking for work, but the board wanted precisely what Calhoun had advised them to want: a firecracker of a man.

Of the applicants, one was a more likely specimen than the others. He was young, just thirty-six, and he had trained in all the latest methods. The board offered the job to Hugh Cameron Gourlay, a man with rounded glasses and a crooked smile, on June 28, 1939. At the time, Gourlay was head librarian at McMaster University; he had also worked for the Carnegie Corporation in Ann Arbor, and as chief of circulation at the University of Missouri, one of the three universities in the education portion of his resume. The annual salary, starting at $3,000 with an eventual ceiling of $3,800, was a pay cut from what he had received at McMaster. But, he said at the time, he wanted an opportunity to transform something. Not only a library system, but a city.[4]

Gourlay arrived "somewhat unpressed in appearance and with a ready sense of humour," which fit well with Edmonton's business culture.[5] He set to work immediately, rearranging and redecorating the library according to the latest concepts and methods. Soon there were clear signs and large labels, telling patrons where to go. He created more open space, better lighting, and more adequate bookshelves. He made the children's library more fun and the adult areas more welcoming. The newspapers wrote glowing features about him and his entrepreneurial approach to the library. Gourlay set up a three-year plan to address the problems Calhoun had identified in his report—problems the board and city council had accepted with shame and resignation. Suddenly, business language like "realizing organizational objectives" appeared in library reports.

The new chief was not without philosophical flourish. "The recognition of the library's place in public education, second in importance only to the school, is the main reason for public support," he wrote, in the 1939 annual report, to help the board understand ways to better advocate for funds. "The library has always been a leader in adult education. It is often called the people's university—a university without formal courses, without a stadium or a campus but providing voluntary individual instruction."[6]

In a memo to the chair of the library board, Gourlay criticized the book-buying policy. It didn't make sense, he wrote. He was keen to differentiate himself from his predecessor. This was not entirely fair. "Almost since the beginning the library had gone from financial crisis to financial crisis," writes James Pilton, Gourlay's biographer, who would be inspired thirty years later to celebrate, apologize for, and figure out one of the most complex figures in the history of the Edmonton Public Library.

"Ethelbert Hill had operated on the philosophy that something on the shelves was better than nothing. He had been forced to bind and re-bind and put patches on top of patches in order to maintain a reasonable number of books on the shelves. It is ironic that Hugh Gourlay was to face a similar situation only a few years later, but in 1940 he was still the new broom."[7]

The new broom was not an apt metaphor. Gourlay dealt quickly with the past and set about focusing on the future: he was an idea machine in his early years and, possibly, the inventor of a culture that remains in the library today.

Reporters liked his sense of humour and his ambition. Hill had only showed up in the newspapers in lists of the library's new arrivals; he was not a personality. Gourlay courted community leaders and writers and editors down the street at the *Edmonton Journal*. "Circulation was increasing. In every way the library was moving forward. The city was very pleased with its new chief librarian."[8]

For years, Hill and Grace Dobie had expressed regret in annual reports and board minutes that children and adults in far-off corners of the city such as Calder and North Edmonton found it difficult to borrow books and participate in the life of the library and the life of the city. What bound all three of them, Hill and Dobie and Gourlay, was the sincere belief that a healthy democracy requires an engaged and knowledgeable citizenry. The example in Europe, and the reason so many young Edmontonians were rushing overseas to fight, demonstrated that ignorance is not only unfortunate—it is dangerous, deadly. Then as now, some children did not have attentive parents. Many adults had missed an opportunity to stay more than a few years in school.

For hard-working families living in industrial North Edmonton and Calder, with little time to travel to the core, there was—in 1940—no easy way to send children to the library. The board did not have the funds to build a new branch in these neighbourhoods or any other. The Carnegie Library downtown couldn't go to them.

Or could it?

In 2013, after over fifty years of car-based transportation and planning, the City of Edmonton is becoming a city of light rail transit and trams. This harkens back to the early 1940s, when this was a streetcar city. Most families could not afford a car, let alone two. They relied on cheap and efficient public transportation. Streetcars were so popular they wore out.

In 1938, one of those streetcars retired. No one else in Canada had thought of turning an old streetcar into a moving library. To Gourlay and

Top: One of director Gourlay's innovations was Canada's first streetcar library. It reached communities far from the core of the city. [EPL] Bottom: City leaders and city readers came out for the launch of the streetcar library, which was featured around the world on newsreels in movie theatres. [EPL]

his increasingly enthusiastic Edmonton Public Library board, this only made the idea more appealing.

The Christian Science Monitor was one of the international media outlets that covered one of the city's first library innovations.

> *This streetcar first went into service on Edmonton's municipally-owned street railway in 1909, and was "put out to pasture," or wherever honourably retired streetcars ultimately go, in 1938 after running 897,130 miles. Now this surprised old trolley car has had its seats removed, a new roof and ceiling added, and an excellent lighting system from 40 electrical lamps, and natural wood shelves, five rows high, installed to hold some 2,000 books.*
>
> *The streetcar is visiting the outlying districts, such as Calder and North Edmonton, once a week, where it is parked on new spur tracks out of the way of regular street-railway traffic from 3 P.M. to 9 P.M. This brings the library service within reach of many families who would not be able to come into town regularly to the two public libraries.*
>
> *And how this rejuvenated old trolley must pinch itself with surprise and say: "Surely this is none of I!" For inside, the walls are completely filled with shelves containing a well chosen selection of novels, travel, biography, and non-fiction. Nor are the juvenile readers forgotten. A clever arrangement of "knee-high" sloping shelves have been filled with the gay and absorbing illustrated books guaranteed to be of interest to the children of grades 1, 2 and 3.*[9]

Newspapers carried the syndicated stories of the strange city in western Canada that made a travelling library out of an old streetcar. It inspired library buses, even library burros, in cities around the world. In 1941, when the royal blue and cream streetcar library launched, short features preceded Hollywood films in the theatres. A film crew arrived in Edmonton to shoot a vignette about the streetcar library for a series called "Unusual Occupations" and the short was soon broadcast around the world.

A former Edmontonian named W.H. Porter, writing from Cairo, Egypt, sent a letter to the library board. "I had a real touch of home last night," he wrote. "I went to the movies and one of the shorts was entitled 'Unusual Occupations' and there on the screen was the library streetcar rolling down Jasper Avenue and out to the edge of town. Boy! Was I tickled. It didn't last long enough to suit me."[10]

For a city with a confidence problem, Gourlay and his re-imagined Edmonton Public Library were a solution. Suddenly, Edmonton was associated with new-ness, with charming and creative solutions, with youth and vigour and education. It was rare for the city to show up in the international press, and rarer still to appear an innovator.

In his 1941 annual report, Gourlay coolly presented the streetcar library statistics and began pressing for his ultimate goal: true expansion. "The response to this service is indicated by 1,563 borrowers joining the library and through the circulation of 17,000 books in the first two and a half months of operation. The car has demonstrated the need of extending library facilities within the city. To provide adequate library service, some branch or other agency should be within one mile of every resident."[11]

The world continued to discover and rediscover the streetcar library, and Gourlay did not let his board or city council forget it. By 1945, the moving library served Calder and North Edmonton, Westglen and Parkdale. The library "continues to get publicity for the City of Edmonton throughout the world in magazines, newspapers and newsreels," Gourlay wrote in his 1945 annual report. "The publicity value of the car to the city has never been fully recognized. It is estimated that 45 million people saw the pictures of the car in the Paramount Short Coloured Feature alone."[12]

Unlike his predecessor, Gourlay did not resent or fight populism. As long as Edmontonians were reading something—anything—he was happy. The war overseas was often the main topic of conversation in this military town so he tried to facilitate those conversations.

> *Naturally the demand for technical books in relation to war time activities is very prominent in these days. Airmen, soldiers, sailors, students at the Youth*

Training Schools—all want books on navigation, aircraft engines, machine tools, radio, sheet metal work and kindred topics...geography, history, biography...Although the main trend is toward more serious reading, the library must meet the need for relaxing in troubled times. Others keep themselves well balanced by some hobby or avocation. The requests for something 'humourous' are legion...Through its educational as well as recreational features, we feel that the Public Library is making a direct and valuable contribution to the war effort.[13]

By the end of the war, popular topics had shifted to reconstruction and rehabilitation, roughing it in the bush, beekeeping and rabbit breeding, housing, the United Nations and strikes. Soon, as a prosperous sort of calm settled over the growing city, these interests shifted to hobbies and houseplants. In a city of ambition and progress, librarians weren't just keepers of books. They were community leaders, sociologists, producers. When Gourlay arrived he discovered his staff members, like their former chief, had loved their jobs without demonstrating a lot of curiosity about the field of library science.

Fresh out of university, as a student and as a librarian, Gourlay encouraged his staff in methods of professional development: tours of libraries in other cities, first. He restarted the defunct Alberta Library Association and served as its president. He published articles for his staff and in library journals—even in *Maclean's* magazine—in an effort to advance the conversation about libraries in Edmonton, in Alberta, and in Canada. He became the first treasurer of the Canadian Library Association.

McGill University ran a summer program in Montreal to train librarians. Gourlay met with senior administrators at McGill and convinced them to extend a summer program in Alberta to serve western Canadians. It was called the McGill University Library School Summer Institute and it ran for three weeks in August 1941. Several of his staff attended and returned full of vigour and new ideas.

In every way, it seemed, the Edmonton Public Library had found its man.

Writing in 1971, only a few years after the opening of Edmonton's state-of-the-art Centennial Library, Gourlay's biographer was overwhelmed with admiration for his subject, and nostalgia for his era.

"In retrospect, the 1940s, especially the war years, were the golden age of the Edmonton Public Library," writes James Pilton. "Cultural and recreational facilities were limited in the prairie town that was Edmonton in those days. The public library filled the need to the best of its ability and with its limited financial resources. Both the chief librarian and the library board were especially responsive to the needs and requests of the community."[14]

Of course, enthusiasm and ambition—coupled with a dose of naïveté—could also be dangerous qualities in the prairie town that was Edmonton in those days.

Nicholas Alexeeff, janitor turned music director, Nancy Tighe, Clifford Lee, and Hugh Gourlay open the library's new music room on June 16, 1947. [EPL]

12

The violinist with a broom

HUGH GOURLAY was not always complimentary toward his staff, particularly those who had not been trained in the latest methods of library science. During the war years, when American contractors were hiring qualified Edmontonians for war work on the Alaska Highway, the chief librarian struggled to find men and women of the right calibre.

"Considerable planning had to be done to be sure that the library could be kept open due to the unusual situation then prevailing when all available help was being absorbed by American firms in the city," he wrote in 1943. "Since the majority of the positions in the library require professional training, and all demand a professional attitude, the problem of securing even part time help became acute."[1]

He spoke often of his struggles to maintain a proper library in conditions of scarcity: human resources, money, even sophistication. The job of making Edmonton more cosmopolitan, it seemed, had fallen to Gourlay—librarian and civic modernizer. "In spite of carrying on the daily work of the library under these conditions" is a phrase Gourlay repeats, in multiple forms, in his written reports.

Not everyone appreciates a cosmopolitan. Some of the long-time staff members, who had endured salary cuts and the Great Depression with Hill, resented the changes Gourlay brought to the workplace. Not everyone was bursting with new ideas, or felt comfortable in an atmosphere of risk, change, competition, and snide remarks. What had been so terrible, after all, about the quiet and comfortable library of the 1930s?

Gourlay was a curious man. He wanted to know as much as he could about his staff members, and not just the librarians. Shortly after he arrived in Edmonton, he met the janitor, a man named Nicholas Alexeeff. Not every leader, caught up in the business of utterly transforming an institution and the intellectual spirit of a city, has time to develop a relationship with the janitor, but Gourlay did.

This janitor had joined the library as a permanent staff member in 1928. There is no evidence that anyone had even noticed him until Gourlay arrived eleven years later. Oddly, in a place of stories, few people had asked Alexeeff for his story.

He was born in the capital of the Tatar people in Central Russia, Kazan, where the Volga meets the Kazanka River. It is a 1,000-year-old city, known for a peaceful history between large Christian and Muslim populations. The city was progressive, diverse and relatively autonomous when Alexeeff was a boy. He was a talented violinist and his parents had the means to see him trained by a professor from the Paris Conservatory. He was sent away to study and take the examinations at the Petrograd Conservatory. Finally, for one winter he lived with one of the greatest teachers of the century, the Hungarian violinist Leopold Auer, in Saint Petersburg. His career seemed set: he would become one of the greatest musicians of his generation.

One year before he could finish his studies at the conservatory, a Bosnian-Serb student assassinated Archduke Franz Ferdinand in Austria. Soon, like all young Russian men, Alexeeff was drawn into military service. In 1917 the October Revolution split the army in half. The young man joined the anti-communist, counter-revolutionary, White

The music room at the Carnegie Library: Helen Sinclair, behind the desk, and Gunter Kirschhoff.

Russian army in Siberia, fighting under Admiral Alexander Kolchak—the Supreme Ruler of Russia in the eyes of his followers. It was the right side for Alexeeff but history was not with him. Kolchak was captured and assassinated by firing squad. Alexeeff fled to Harbin, Manchuria, where his skills as a musician helped him find a position in an opera company.

In 1924, he arrived in Canada and started on his way to Edmonton.[2]

Gourlay was enchanted to discover a violinist and adventurer on staff, someone who had trained with the great Leopold Auer. Auer had taught Jascha Heifetz, who had played at Carnegie Hall. One of Gourlay's plans was to build a music department, to bring the Edmonton Public Library in line with what was happening in New York and San Francisco. This had thrilled some of the librarians on staff, who had an interest in music and hoped to lead the new department. One of them, Evelyn Baker, had also trained as a musician. She had been granted a leave of absence to train further, for two months in Los Angeles, to prepare for a career in music and in music education—that is, the director of the music department of a city library system.

Instead of encouraging Baker, Gourlay sent Alexeeff—the janitor!—on a buying tour of the west coast to begin building a viable music collection for the library.

"There are indications that some members of the staff did not approve of this appointment and perhaps never forgave their chief librarian for having made the recommendation to the library board," writes Pilton.[3]

Evelyn Baker quit, humiliated. In 1944, Gourlay made things official: Nicholas Alexeeff became director of music at an annual salary of $1,700, a significant raise from what he had made as janitor. Mary Donaldson, the only other person on staff with a degree in library science, also resigned.

The media adored the story of Nicholas Alexeeff, janitor turned music director. He was immediately popular. To help Edmontonians make it through the war in more-or-less jolly and exalted fashion, Alexeeff inaugurated a program called Music at Nine. At nine o'clock on Tuesdays, Thursdays, and Saturday nights, Alexeeff would lead a live or recorded evening of chamber, symphonic, and operatic selections.

Humiliation and transformation have a way of leading to resentment—and worse.

The columns, wood accents, large windows and skylights made the central branch of the Edmonton Public Library one of the finest rooms in the city. [EPL]

13

A centre of culture

THE PUBLIC LIBRARY WAS THE GOOGLE OF THE 1940S. If Edmontonians had a question no one nearby could answer, they would visit the reference desk downtown or in Strathcona. In 1943, Gourlay reported, certain topics of inquiry came up again and again.

- *Curing nervous tension.*
- *Should refugees be admitted to Canada*
- *Youth in the post-war world*
- *Diseases and internal parasites of wild animals injurious to man if their flesh is used as food.*
- *How to cook food to avoid loss of vitamin C and minerals*
- *The relation of Canada's transportation system to economics*
- *Dehydration of foods*
- *Japanese problem in Canada*
- *Fads and fancies as factors in demand for goods*
- *How to live off the country up north*
- *Discovery and development of the sulfa drugs*

- *Will war decimate the middle class*
- *Are Great Britain's colonies essential to her future*
- *Juvenile delinquency and its prevention*
- *Rehabilitation of service men*
- *Recreation for war workers*
- *Problems of a country school teacher*
- *Use of propaganda in wartime*
- *History of social insurance*[1]

The library was useful, but usefulness was not a word Gourlay would have used. Library science was still a new discipline, and its leading academics were not shy about its importance in civic life. One of Gourlay's favourite quotations, and one he internalized, was from his mentor at the University of Michigan in Ann Arbor, Professor C.B. Joeckel.

> *In the library the community has a force potent enough to render more good to the populace than any single force or body I know. Unlike the church, it serves people of all creeds; unlike the school, its doors are open to people of all ages; its shelves are open to one and all regardless of race or worldly possessions. It can do more to educate the people, young and old, to help keep a democratic, representative government alive and destroy hates and narrow thoughts more than any other means known.*[2]

Gourlay was in the life-changing business and in the city-changing business. Every problem could be solved on Macdonald Drive.

Hugh Cameron Gourlay had arrived in Edmonton in 1939 with his wife, Catherine Margaret Fraser, and their two sons: Hugh Cameron Jr. and Gordon Fraser. He had solid Ontario roots, international experience, and enough enthusiasm for ten libraries. He was both a golfer and a United Church man, highly acceptable things to be in 1940s Edmonton. The Carnegie Library was conveniently located next to the preferred gathering place of the city's political and financial elite—the Edmonton Club.

Music director Nicholas Alexeeff organized live and recorded concerts in the library at a time when live music—especially live classical music—was uncommon. [EPL]

"The Edmonton Public Library is not a building filled with musty books, read in an atmosphere bordering on graveyard silence," wrote the *Edmonton Journal* on August 31, 1946. "Under the progressive-minded Hugh C. Gourlay, with Nicholas Alexeeff, director of music, the library is rapidly becoming one of the city's cultural centres."[3]

It had been difficult for Edmontonians to accept that Calgary, in its early years, had profited from a more dynamic library and librarian—a man who seemed to capture the city's personality in the operation of one of its most important institutions. Hill had been a fine and fair manager but he had not led or challenged the city beyond the borders of the downtown and Strathcona buildings.

Gourlay was different.

He declared, in his 1946 and 1947 annual reports, that they were the most successful years in the history of the Edmonton Public Library: this

The oil discovery at Leduc No. 1 changed Edmonton and the Edmonton Public Library.

[Glenbow Museum NA-5470-5]

was a time of hope and expansion. The "university of the people" was doing precisely what he had hoped, and the media were lauding him for it. Study groups, music clubs, schools and colleges and associations used the space and requested speakers from the library. On mild evenings from spring to autumn, the library burst out its doors to deliver musical performances, lectures, debates and story hours on the lawn. Expansion and more partnerships were inevitable, if only there was a way to find more money.

When the new music room at the downtown branch opened in June 1947, 700 people showed up to celebrate. The band of the Northwest Air Command performed on the main floor for the adults while kids watched movies. Following the success of the streetcar library, the Edmonton Transit System agreed to repurpose an old bus as a travelling bookmobile. In the history of the Edmonton Public Library, the most successful directors have been the ones who have read most carefully the aspirations of Edmontonians. The dream of the library is the dream of the city, and who better to articulate it? Gourlay, with his knack for media attention, his courage and imagination, aligned the library's development with the development of the city after the Second World War.

On February 13, 1947, a massive oilfield was discovered south of Edmonton. That discovery, Leduc No. 1, had an immediate effect on the city: billions of dollars in new investment and thousands of enterprising young people on their way to Alberta.

What could go wrong?

Life inside the streetcar library. [EPL]

14

Gourlay's error

THE LIBRARY SUDDENLY HAD MORE IDEAS and more energy than it could fund. Since the opening ceremonies, in 1913, Hill had politely argued for a fairer funding arrangement. According to the most recent Libraries Act, from 1922, library boards could request one mill from the municipal tax assessment. While this ensured steady funding, it also ensured steadily meagre funding. It was never enough; the library could not grow with the city. The boards could beg for one-off grants from the provincial government, but they couldn't plan for the future with any feeling of certainty.

As every Albertan knows, economic booms are both exciting and absurd. No government ever seems prepared for a boom or the inevitable bust that follows. In 1947, as more and more people arrived in the city from rural communities, from the rest of Canada and the world, there weren't enough houses for them. Edmonton didn't even have a full-time city planner and wouldn't have one until 1949.

Gourlay called the *Edmonton Journal* and, as always, it printed his story: "The Edmonton Public Library Board will seek the support of other library boards in the province to obtain minor amendments to the present act passed in 1922 which would allow cities and towns to budget for library expenditures according to the wishes of their governing aldermanic boards."[1]

The city had reached a certain distinction, by the latter years of the 1940s, as a liberal and lively place, an unlikely cultural centre in the west. Gourlay took credit for much of this, and felt the library deserved a fairer investment. He had already achieved so much on the banks of the North Saskatchewan. If he were to have a free conversation with the mayor and city council, without being bound by the provincial act, he could make the case for more ideas, more progress, more publicity. That is, more money.

His partnership with the Calgary Public Library was only half successful. The province did not trust city governments to make these decisions entirely on their own. The ceiling for library funding would go up to $1.5 million, but not immediately.

Gourlay's needs were immediate, and his pleas were not subtle. "The library had somehow survived a depression and the war years," writes his biographer, James Pilton, "but its future was now in doubt."

Municipal governments in Alberta have only one stable source of funding. Cities cannot tax income; as their needs expand with the economy, all they can do is raise property taxes. Edmonton's housing and infrastructure needs were expanding with the economy and the population, and Gourlay was right to anticipate his own shortages.

The library board asked the city for $103,000 in 1948. What actually happened to this request will always be impossible to figure out, but it appeared to Gourlay that city council had only approved $93,000. His budget for books and for binding and repairing current books had been cut from $30,000 to $20,000.[2]

Gourlay was a star: young, intelligent, well-spoken, well-connected. In less than ten years he had read the city as well as any book, and he had helped to give Edmontonians—ever-lacking in confidence—a sense of pride and sophistication. This budget decision was an insult and he would not stand for it. He deserved better.

Another director might have requested a private audience with the mayor or key aldermen. He might have worked with his board to find a solution. This was, historically, how government relations worked in Edmonton. The chief librarian has many roles: lobbyist is among the most sensitive and important of them.

Instead, Gourlay went out into the community that so adored him.

He started with the *Edmonton Journal* in the middle of September 1948, to set the scene.

"[The] main financial problem confronting the board is that of a fund for purchase of books," a reporter wrote. "The amount of $20,000 for books and binding has been spent. If funds are not obtained, a period of book scarcity will develop during the winter, which is the busiest library season, the officials said."[3]

Gourlay was "the officials," the anonymous source in the story. Emboldened, he told his board he needed an extra $15,000 for books—not $10,000. Then, before the next library board meeting on September 20th, Gourlay contacted the principal of Forest Heights School and one of the best community organizers in the city, Stanley Churchill. Representatives from more than ninety groups, who believed in Gourlay and his plea, came to the meeting. When it was his turn to speak he said, "About $10,000 for new books is needed immediately, if the supply is to be procured before the winter season...the absolute minimum required for immediate use is $13,000 with an additional $2,000 to operate on."[4]

The board did not make a decision at the meeting. Some board members were incensed that Gourlay would invite or at least tip off other organizations about the desperate, seemingly life-or-death plea for $15,000. There was a feeling of entitlement and arrogance, to some board members, and they were not prepared to forgive Gourlay for making a private library matter so public. His response, of course, would have been that a public library is public. The $10,000 cut in his book budget would affect every one of the ninety organizations represented that night.

A couple of days later, the library board's finance committee met. Then they met with Gourlay. They came to some agreement and, together,

Top: When Edmonton's streetcar lines were torn up to make way for more space for automobiles, the bookmobile launched: this is Bookmobile Number One in 1947. [EPL] *Bottom: Only a certain number of children were allowed in the bookmobile at any one time. This photo is from 1951.* [EPL]

they revised their official request to the city from the $14,000 to $15,000 that had already been published in the *Edmonton Journal* as the precise minimum to...$5,000.

It had been clear enough, to his community supporters and to the readers of the newspaper, that the library needed $15,000. Now, according to the tamed chief librarian, the figure had always been $5,000. Trying to clarify the issue to the press, he said that "the $15,000 estimate would have carried beyond the fiscal year."[5]

Stanley Churchill, who had organized so much support for Gourlay, felt tricked. "I wish to go on record that I acted in good faith in contacting and calling together the delegation of prominent citizens representing the major organizations of this city, which met the board on Monday, September 20. I believed the librarian's assessment of library needs to be accurate....This is chaotic."[6]

In the political life of a city, there are always controversies. In Edmonton, there had always been plenty of them. But none of the controversies were library controversies. Front-page newspaper stories about an unfeeling city council gouging the library into ruin, followed up by a bizarre recanting by the head librarian, also in the *Journal*, would not do. The mayor and aldermen were accustomed to unhappy civil servants who wanted robust budgets. Negotiations, in the coziness and privacy of council chambers, were perfectly fine. Civilized. But ninety community organizations? High-profile media coverage?

Members of the library board and members of city council did what they had to do. They isolated Gourlay.

"Alderman Bissett reported that while the board had stated to the press that its 1948 estimates had been sliced by $10,000, this was not so," the *Journal* reported. "He claimed that the board, along with the finance committee had agreed to the budget slice earlier in the year on the understanding that if the library found itself short of funds later, it could ask for more money."[7]

City councillors shrugged their collective shoulders, feigning confusion. If the library needs extra money, they ought to ask for it. Properly, of course.

Gourlay, who had done so much to transform the library and build a new sense of identity in the city, who had earned the right to a fair budget, now seemed an imbecile. His friends in the Edmonton Club and on the golf course, in the community and in the media, now looked askance at him. The library board, once so supportive, was not planning to forgive Gourlay any time soon for his antics. What didn't make the *Journal* story about relations between city hall and the library was a stern warning, what James Pilton calls a slap on the wrist: keep your librarian in line, play by the rules.

The most damaging aspect of the story was that it made the Edmonton Public Library, a media sensation and an example of innovation to institutions around the world, seem fragile and mismanaged. In 1948, $10,000 was a lot of money. An immediate budgetary request that was off by $10,000 did not look good. The 1948 version of the Canadian Taxpayers Federation, angry writers of letters to the editor, attacked the library and city council in the press. When there were so many other needs in the booming city, all those grand arguments about education and democracy were torn up and forgotten. If a city institution is off by $10,000, it could easily be off by $50,000—and who is to say it hasn't been going on for years, this flushing away of public funds?

Board meetings of the Edmonton Public Library, in the autumn of 1948, were not happy affairs. The great leader of the library revolution was ruined, and in a relatively small town this misery was compounded and echoed by staff members who had felt slighted by Gourlay in the past. A new member of the library board, Allan McTavish, knew how to make all of the negative publicity and nasty rumours go away: an official inquiry, an audit. If it seemed the library was being mismanaged, it probably was.

Gourlay, at this time only forty-five years old, had a stroke.

Top: Rain, shine, or three feet of snow, the bookmobile was on the road. This is the second phase of the bookmobile, 1962. [EPL] *Bottom: Into the late 1960s and 1970s, bookmobiles started to lose the bus inspiration.* [EPL]

Hard times hit Edmonton, and EPL, in 1982. The bookmobile persevered, for a time. [EPL]

Even as the librarian recovered, McTavish called his policies "ridiculous" in the newspaper and questioned his leadership.[8] This inspired more letters to the editor, of course. Another board member, who sympathized with Gourlay, defended him in the press, claiming the numbers show that "on a per-book-put-out, the Edmonton Public Library was operating on a more economical basis than any other in Canada."[9]

It would take a lot more than that defence to change the narrative of Gourlay's management of the Edmonton Public Library. Annie Joyce, who ran the library as Gourlay recovered, asked the city commissioner to sell a car, quietly and cheaply, to her chief—to encourage him and help speed up his recovery. He was under the care of the Baker Clinic in February, March, April and May. The board paid his salary until the end of May and then cut it in half, until his return.

"Those who knew him say that Hugh Gourlay never fully recovered his health," writes James Pilton. "During the remaining five years that he was chief librarian, the going appears to have been uphill all the way for him. His absences from the library were frequent."[10]

Gourlay did return to his post. As it had been a decade earlier, at the start of the war, the city found itself at the beginning of a dramatic transformation. Gourlay had neither the confidence nor the imaginative power to be a part of it. His great achievements, in his last few years as director, include launching the bookmobile fleet of underutilized buses. The city was tearing up and paving over its streetcar tracks; at the same time, the city limits were expanding beyond the limits of the streetcars. Between 1948 and 1958, the population of the city would double—from 126,000 to 252,000.[11] Two libraries were not enough. Gourlay's last great appearance in the media would be for the opening of the first branch library, Sprucewood, in 1953.

All the verve was sucked out of his writing style in the annual reports. His participation in library board meetings—once aggressively positive, a burst of new initiatives—went dull and silent. Media coverage of the library changed from ideas to photo ops of retirements and lists of new book arrivals. One of Gourlay's former staff members, the head of the circulation department who had resigned under his leadership, was invited to join the board in 1951—another humiliation and a sign of his diminished power. Two years later his greatest friend Nicholas Alexeeff, janitor turned music director, left the library and the city for a post in San Francisco.[12]

One of Edmonton's strangest and most controversial stories is that of William Hawrelak. [City of Edmonton Archives EA-10-1600]

15

Call me Bill

SHORTLY AFTER chief librarian Hugh Cameron Gourlay returned to work, another man entered the public service in Edmonton. William Hawrelak—call him Bill—tried for the second time for a seat on city council.

On November 2, 1949, he became an alderman.

Hawrelak had grown up northeast of the city, near Smoky Lake, where hundreds of other Ukrainian immigrants had set up farms. His father, Wasyl Hawrelak, had expected his son Bill to take over the farm, and that one day his grandchildren would inherit the land. But Bill was born a city boy at heart. After high school, in the late 1930s, he had written letters to politicians and bureaucrats until one day he was rewarded with a job offer at the liquor control board in Edmonton. He started behind the counter and moved into the accounting department. And he might have remained a lifelong bureaucrat if his father had not developed a heart condition during the Depression. Hawrelak went back to the family farm.

Even on the farm he wasn't much of a farmer. Pearl, his wife, wasn't remotely interested in country life. He organized the Alberta Farmers'

Union in the district, served as a school trustee and, during the war, sold bonds.[1] The war ended and the Hawrelaks decided to rent out the farm. They borrowed a truck, loaded it with everything they owned, and in November 1945 found a little house on 86 Avenue east of 99 Street.[2] They put a $1,500 down payment on it. There was one bedroom for them and another for their seven-year-old daughter Jeannette.

At the time, the city's power brokers still considered Ukrainian-Canadians to be outsiders, and not political material. Hawrelak wasn't deterred. He bought a large share of Prairie Rose Manufacturing, a soft drink company that bottled Orange Crush in the city. He was an unusually active community league president, lobbying successfully for garbage collection and sewer lines. Politics came naturally to him and his neighbours noticed. They urged him to run for council. He did, and failed. He did again, and this time he succeeded.[3]

In 1949, Hawrelak was thirty-four.

The oil strike in Leduc had opened the city to the world, and Hawrelak represented a brash new generation of hustlers—many of them with unpronounceable names—showing up to build new lives. The Edmonton Public Library helped these newcomers to integrate. Certain phrases smell old-fashioned in the annual reports of this period, between 1949 and 1955, as a chastened Hugh Gourlay tried to adapt to a city in the midst of startling growth. But one phrase, a generous one, repeats itself throughout the board minutes and the annual reports: New Canadians.

Not foreigners but New Canadians. They often didn't understand how a library worked. They were awkward and occasionally impolite. Many of them couldn't speak English. But the library published with pride the number of people they had helped from around the world: Europe mostly but also Asia, Africa and the Middle East.

It is unclear whether Hawrelak had a genuine interest in libraries. Perhaps he was just constantly on the hunt for more supporters, more photo opportunities. New Canadians, after all, were voters-in-training, and if they spent time at the library he would spend time at the library. Edmonton had never seen a politician like him: he was loud, he was shameless, he was a populist and an elitist at once—transitioning quickly out of his little house in Mill Creek into a big house in Windsor Park, a neighbourhood west of the University of Alberta.

By the time he ran for mayor in 1951, he had become one of the most famous men in the city. In a pattern that would continue for the rest of his political and business careers, which were linked in unsavoury ways, Edmontonians either loved him or hated him. He was impossible to ignore.

"In some parts of Canada, his name would have been against him," said a Calgary editorial writer after Hawrelak had been elected mayor. "But in fast-growing, forward-looking and progressive Edmonton all that mattered was his ability."[4]

The interior of the Sprucewood Branch in its early days, with the circulation desk and the shiny tile of 1950s Edmonton. [EPL]

16

The first branch

SINCE THE EARLY 1940S, Gourlay, board members, and library staff had been begging for expansion—with statistics, quotations from the learned, and nods toward Calgary. Every Edmonton family deserved a library "within one mile" of its house, and Edmonton, a city of communities, was falling behind. New subdivisions were spreading in every direction by the early 1950s and the public transit system couldn't keep up.

How could a child living in the far south or the far north participate in the library?

Gourlay was no longer an effective advocate. He was too humiliated to walk down Macdonald Drive to the *Edmonton Journal* or to speak forcefully and poetically in front of city council. The library board was not as connected to the animated new mayor, the young Bill Hawrelak. As an alderman, his interests had been difficult to sum up. He had worked with the federal government to bring a Trans-Canada Highway through the city. Yet he had also served, while in office, as director of the Federation of Edmonton Community Leagues.

Economic booms are thrilling. If we're not prepared for them, they're also astonishingly ugly and expensive. In the early 1950s, there was so much infrastructure to create—roads and bridges and sewer and power—the city found it couldn't keep up. Property developers were becoming immensely wealthy; Hawrelak himself, who had moved from soft drinks into real estate, was already rich.

The City of Edmonton was going broke. In 1952, the city had the highest per capita debt in the country.[1]

Pressing for new branches was not going to be a simple affair. In 1947, before his error and fall, a confident and popular chief librarian had created a comprehensive list of branch libraries to build all over what we now know as Central Edmonton: from Bonnie Doon to King Edward Park and Garneau on the south side, to Calder, Westmount, and Glenora in the north. At the time, Mayor Harry Ainlay was on the board and encouraged the chief librarian.

Pressing for a new branch in 1952 was something else altogether. The city didn't have a spare nickel but its communities, growing exponentially, needed services. Hawrelak and much of city council at the time were susceptible to certain kinds of arguments, despite their inability to fund projects. Did Edmontonians want their city to be great? Yes. What do all great cities have? Libraries. What is the best way to integrate new Canadians and civilize the wild youth? Books and reading.

Oh, and how many libraries did Calgary have, by the early 1950s? Five, with another one set to open in 1954.

The plan had always been to build new branch libraries. No other building is quite like a library with its need for open space and an atmosphere of meditation. Except, perhaps, a church. Edmonton's post-war movement away from places of worship was well underway, and though the proposed new site wasn't ideally located in the centre of the neighbourhood the board found a compromise on Alberta Avenue.

St. Alphonsus Catholic church, on 118 Avenue and 85 Street, had more space than the parish needed at the time. The library board decided,

Branch libraries launched any way they could: the first Sprucewood Branch was in St. Alphonsus Church on Alberta Avenue. [City of Edmonton Archives EA596-18]

in the spring of 1953, to inspect the building. They imagined a space without pews: solid, one-storey, natural light. They took over the lease of a portion of the church in June and set to work renovating and redecorating. They bought what they had to buy and borrowed shelves and books from the Carnegie building downtown and the Strathcona Branch.

Four months later, the first non-locomotive extension of the Edmonton Public Library—the Sprucewood Branch—opened with a big community party. Mayor Hawrelak, who had approved the project, showed up for the photos and the handshakes. It was a mild October day and hundreds of people from the neighbourhood walked through the building and signed up for library cards.

Harbin Gate marks a route into Edmonton's past and its imagined future. [EPL]

The building process—from taking over the lease to opening the library branch—was short. Funds were so difficult to find and the stock of books and periodicals was meagre. For the first few months there were severe restrictions on borrowing. The busy core of the Sprucewood Branch, in its first months and in its early years, was the children's department. The reference librarians, without a lot of material for adults, became a community hub for helping kids with their homework.

Today, walk east from the Stanley A. Milner Branch, past the Citadel Theatre and Canada Place. On your left, you will see the Winspear Centre—the ghost of the Civic Building and therefore the Edmonton Public Library. Eventually a tram will run down this stretch of pavement, 102 Avenue, harkening back to the days of the streetcar library. Walk past the lions and under the ornate Harbin Gate, one of the finest pieces of street decoration in the city. Here we enter the third largest Chinatown in Canada, or at least what remains of it.

The original borders of Edmonton's Chinatown were closer to the library, but this part of the neighbourhood was destroyed to create Canada Place in 1988. The community had been founded by entrepreneurs who opened laundries and cafés, beginning with the first Chinese-Edmontonian, Chung Kee, in 1890. The newcomers endured years of racism and underemployment before becoming part of the city's leadership class. This same community invested nearly $100 million in Chinatown after Canada Place was built. Today, many of these people are disappointed that a tram will run through the middle of it, in front of the seniors' centre on 102 Avenue and 96 Street.[2]

Today, what remains of Chinatown is haunted by more contemporary ghosts: the east side of downtown Edmonton, one of the city's most historic neighbourhoods, is full of gravel parking lots, filthy taverns, and empty buildings. Now that almost all of its historical bones have been knocked down and carted away, it is one of the most desolate corners in Edmonton. The Hung Fung Athletic Club, next to the old and unloved Mount Royal Hotel, doesn't have a chance to be anything but sad, dusty, and dangerous. And everyone knows it. The Quarters, a master-planned solution to the problem, is a mixture of expensive and affordable housing, retail strips and parks, hotels and arts habitats.

Moving north past the police station, a concrete bunker, and past more parking lots and a few brick warehouses that demand to be repurposed, we move through the core of Edmonton's inner city. Here, a bright agency called the Bissell Centre does what it has been doing since 1910, three years before the two branches of the Edmonton Public Library opened: it helps people who need help.

It started as All People's Mission, founded by Reverend William Pike and his wife Florence. A few thousand immigrants, most of them Ukrainian, had landed in Edmonton's inner city. The Methodist mission helped integrate them for twenty years until the Great Depression hit. By this time, New Canadians from all over the world and old Canadians, too, were in desperate need. The Methodists had merged into the United Church and the outreach mission moved into a new building here in 1936. The mission was renamed the Bissell Institute, named after founding philanthropist Torrence Edward Bissell. Today its simple vision is to eliminate poverty in this community and the city that surrounds it.

The Boyle McCauley neighbourhood, to the north, is in the midst of transformation from one of the poorest in the city to one of the most hopeful. Young families are buying up historic homes at low prices and fixing them up. Old churches are shining. The Edmonton Homeless Commission, implementing a bold plan to help thousands of people find affordable housing, has been more successful than its original targets. All three levels of government team up with agencies and businesses to bring food, accommodation, and dignity to all Edmontonians. One of these partners is the Edmonton Public Library—providing computers, education and, of course, books.

Moving north we pass through immigration movements past and present, from Italian and Eastern European to Vietnamese and, more recently, some of the city's newest citizens from East Africa. Ethiopian and Eritrean restaurants and halal meat shops co-exist with Vietnamese storefronts, old Eastern Orthodox churches and Little Italy.

Stop at one of the best pizza parlours in town, Tony's, on 111 Avenue and continue north through lovely Norwood. Architecturally, it is one of the best-preserved neighbourhoods in Edmonton. In its founding era, property developers and city regulators did not mandate sameness and blandness. Craftsman and California bungalows sit next to barn-like houses infused with Dutch colonial influence or even Spanish revival. Mature elm trees line the boulevards. For many years these beautiful Norwood homes were either neglected or ruined by bizarre updates from the seventies and eighties. Today, the neighbourhood is reclaiming its grandeur as a family-friendly district twenty minutes—on foot—from the core of downtown.

Alberta Avenue was once a vibrant main street, with a frontier spirit. Small businesses lined the avenue: supermarkets and hairdressers, theatres, restaurants and cafés, shoe and clothing stores.

"Back in the 1930s, Alberta Avenue was a bit like Whyte Avenue is today," says Tony Cashman. "Athletic clubs were set up to keep young men away from a life of crime, and the Maple Leaf Athletic Club sort of defined Alberta Avenue. In the winter, the community rink was one of the social centres of town. It was very lively, full of young people. Skating was a great way to make yourself an introduction."[3]

The neighbourhood was a social centre in the city. Jazz star and future senator Tommy Banks would play The Paddock, a horse-themed club, in the early 1960s. But by then, families had already started moving out to the bigger houses of the inner suburbs and the neighbourhood began to decay. The latter years of the twentieth century were devastating for Alberta Avenue: the area gained a reputation for poverty and violence, and became one of the city's drug-and-prostitution playgrounds.

Some families and businesses never gave up on the neighbourhood, and quiet pockets of dignity and beauty remained north and south of Alberta Avenue. The City of Edmonton, without any real consideration of the soul and history of the area, called it "Avenue of Champions" and affixed sports cut-outs to light standards. One road did lead to the hockey arena on 75 Street—Wayne Gretzky Boulevard—but this seemed the thinnest of strategies. Avenue of Champions, much like City of Champions, had no lasting resonance.

In the last few years of the 1990s and into the 2000s, artists seeking bargains began moving into the Alberta Avenue neighbourhood. They started calling it Alberta Avenue again. Some bright, unstoppable men and women, led by theatre artist and community organizer Christy Morin, believed that culture, rather than nostalgia for the Oilers' good years, might be a better strategy to revive the neighbourhood.

In 2006, Morin launched Arts on the Ave, a modest first step. The new mayor, Stephen Mandel, heartily approved of arts-based revitalization.

By the end of the decade, thanks to Morin and her team of volunteers and entrepreneurs, Alberta Avenue was an exciting intersection of ethnic grocers and restaurants, theatre companies, and new developments such as the Nina Haggerty Centre for the Arts. At the nearby Carrot Community Arts Coffeehouse, there is a quotation on the wall from Paul Cézanne: "The day is coming when a single carrot, freshly observed, will set off a revolution."

Today, Arts on the Ave runs several arts-related festivals all year, including Deep Freeze in the winter and the Kaleido Family Arts Festival in the fall. By the summer of 2012, Kaleido was enormous. During the Edmonton International Fringe Festival every August, the neighbourhood hosts a mini-Fringe of its own, in two or three venues including the historic Avenue Theatre.

St. Alphonsus, with its maroon brick and blue doors, is a community hub. It faces the street in front of a park and a community hall, and was an ideal location for the original Sprucewood Branch even though the quarters were cramped and purpose-built for a small chapel. Thousands of kids moved through it, to borrow a book or to find the right dates for First and Second World War battles, or for the founding of Canada.

The Sprucewood Branch would not stay in an annex of St. Alphonsus for long. Five years after the grand opening, on another mild day in October, a purpose-built single-storey Sprucewood Library opened on 95 Street a few blocks south of Alberta Avenue, on a corner lot. The dedication tea was sponsored by the East End Businessman's Association. Today the branch is a five-minute walk from its spiritual sister, The Carrot, a café with a bookshelf of its own, full of paperbacks and games.

On a rainy Saturday in 2012, the Sprucewood Branch was full of parents and children from the neighbourhood. The library has an Aboriginal section, to reflect one of Alberta Avenue's dominant communities. For years, this has also been a destination for new immigrants, a fact reflected in the street fronts, from the Ethiopian and Eritrean café to Paraiso Tropical, one of the city's best Latin American groceries. The

The renovated exterior of the Sprucewood Branch, looking spry in its fifties. [EPL]

multicultural nature of the neighbourhood also surfaces on the shelves of the library and in its clientele on a Saturday: books in Somali and Portuguese, Arabic and Russian and Spanish and Chinese.

"Libraries do a lot for the city and they've changed a lot, in the way we think of them," says Edmonton's three-term mayor Stephen Mandel. "Today it's a community centre. New immigrants learn to read in their own language, in English, and they learn about our culture. Kids get used to the look and feel of books. We're a city of immigrants and the Edmonton Public Library plays an incredible role in integrating new Canadians. We want them to be comfortable here, to feel welcome. A big recreation centre, imagine: that can be confusing to someone from another country, another part of the world. No one is intimidated by a library."[4]

Sprucewood Branch, on a grey and wet day, feels like an extension of Alberta Avenue's living room, The Carrot—only quieter, and without the smell of coffee. It was renovated and updated in 2004, and feels today like a careful negotiation of past and present.

Back in 1953, when this neighbourhood first opened a library branch, director Hugh Gourlay helped choose the site and, to the best of his abilities, start operations. The board signed a three-year lease with St. Alphonsus and put up a sign. There weren't many books or other resources to fill the space, and no hope of them coming any time soon. The library, in the early 1950s, lacked a full-time advocate. Gourlay lacked the energy and affection for what had seemed his grandest ambition: to build a vibrant culture in the city using the library as its foundation. One spectacularly humiliating autumn had stretched into six years of cautious leadership. If not for the board and for a sympathetic mayor, Sprucewood likely would not have happened and the second extension, into the growing west of the city, would have stalled as well.

"It must have been discouraging for Hugh Gourlay to look at the book collection and realize that for lack of funds, it could be described as worn-out and obsolete, exactly as he had found it when he had arrived fifteen years before."[5]

In an emergency meeting on New Year's Eve, 1955, the board of the Edmonton Public Library board met to receive what many Edmontonians had been expecting for years: a letter of resignation from Hugh Cameron Gourlay.

The third director of the Edmonton Public Library, Morton Coburn, expanded the branch system and led the construction of what is now the Stanley A. Milner Branch. [EPL]

17

That tiny Carnegie library on the hill

ETHEL SYLVIA WILSON was in her fiftieth year when she ran for city council in Edmonton. To support her three children she had found work as a seamstress after her husband died in the middle of the Depression. Gaining a seat on city council in the 1950s did not mean quitting your job. After her election in 1952, Wilson was both an alderman and a seamstress. Like a lot of Edmontonians, her roots were rural. She was a tough woman who spoke the truth as she saw it, and entered politics through the labour movement. Hawrelak, the young mayor approved by a coalition of business leaders called the Citizens Committee and therefore no blushing fan of the labour movement, would come to trust Alderman Wilson like no one else on city council: she never said a word to please him.

When the second director of the Edmonton Public Library retired in 1955, Wilson was the city council representative on the board, and the chair. Applications came in from across Canada and the United States. Wilson was sent out to screen candidates and create a shortlist. In Detroit she met a Canadian PHD, then working in the United States, and another candidate: a young man who had spent most of his time in university libraries.

"I was working at the military library in Alabama," says Morton Coburn. "Being a northerner, I wasn't particularly interested in staying much longer in the south at that time. When I saw the advertisement for the job in Edmonton I thought, 'Why not?'"

Coburn was born and raised in Chicago, so cold weather wasn't a deterrent. Something about the northern character appealed to him. He was certainly not of an overly sensitive character. He had graduated from a prestigious high school in 1941, the Lane Technical Institute; it has produced more PHDs than any other school in the United States. In 1942, after some work for the military, he was drafted. Coburn went to Camp Stewart in Georgia, where he was chosen to train on the Bofors anti-aircraft gun. Before the end of the year, he and his unit were shipped to Australia. His role, for the rest of the war, was to guard American airfields in New Guinea and in the Philippines. Just before he was set to ship out for the invasion of Japan, the atomic bombs on Hiroshima and Nagasaki and subsequent Japanesee surrender brought his military career to an end.

With his twin brother, Coburn enrolled in the University of Illinois. He brought malaria with him, and he often suffered attacks as he worked his way to a Masters in Librarianship. He worked in university libraries in Kansas and Ohio before finding a job in Alabama. He was thirty-four when he met Ethel Wilson in Detroit for an interview.

"Something happened between us, I guess," he says. "We had a long and wonderful discussion about libraries and about Edmonton, and I remembered her saying, 'Mr. Coburn I believe we will continue this conversation.'"

The board of trustees invited Coburn to Edmonton, for a fuller interview. After the conversation, Wilson asked him to wait outside. Coburn found it unsettling and strange, to be asked to wait outside the door as they discussed him. A few minutes later, they opened the door.

"'You are the new librarian,' they said. And I was thrilled."

Today, Coburn lives in an apartment on Canal Street in the South Loop neighbourhood of his hometown, Chicago. His birthday is December 28 and his birth year is 1921, making him the oldest full-time librarian in the United States. He is director of library building programs with Chicago Public Library, a job he has held for over thirty-eight years. Everything he knows about building libraries he learned in Edmonton, where as a young man he built a pile of them.

Late in the summer of 1956 he arrived, not long after rock and roll arrived in Edmonton. I asked him about first impressions. Coburn paused, careful not to offend me. I begged him to be honest.

"Well, I remember looking at that tiny Carnegie library on the hill, where my office would be, and I thought: 'If my friends could see me now they would think I am a failure.'"

He was young for the job and only somewhat experienced in administration. He says, in the mid-1950s, the library world—like the political world—was managed in the east. Almost no one educated as a librarian in Montreal or Toronto or New York would have seen western Canada as a destination.

"For me, I loved it. The city was wide open. It was a chance for me to see what I could do, as an administrator, and to build. To build something. That's what I really wanted to do."

When I look at photographs of the Carnegie Library on that gentle circle on Macdonald Drive I am struck with romantic notions. I see my grandparents all dressed up, and beams of sunlight passing through the columns, the dark wood and ornamental windows, the chandeliers, the limestone and marble.

In 1956, Coburn saw only littleness and inefficiency.

Tony Cashman, who is about the same age, remembers the arrival of Coburn as something altogether novel in Edmonton.

"Mort brought a new way of thinking with him from Chicago," says Cashman. "He was a new age librarian. He had these very sad expressions. He used to call the library at the top of the hill 'tragic.' Tragic was his favourite word! He had all kinds of sad adjectives. He was often before city council. City council operated in those days as a board of directors, so it was not a full-time job. Everybody thought the library was fine, but Mort was new age."[1]

There is, even in Cashman's remembrance of Coburn, this vague feeling that he was an outsider who didn't really understand Edmonton or its culture. But when I spoke to Coburn, a ninety-one-year-old man with an ironic sense of humour and a fighting spirit, his summing-up of the city in 1956 was not so far from the city in 2013.

Edmonton is wide open. Edmonton is a place for builders.

The former director, Hugh Gourlay, was both respected and despised by the time Coburn arrived in Edmonton. His glory years, when the streetcar library was a sensation, were remembered well. But the unionized staff, much of the board, and the *Edmonton Journal* were critical. The dinner party circuit, in the mid-1950s, was not kind to Gourlay. They were glad to see this young man from Chicago—or so it seemed.

"What happened to Gourlay is the trustees took against him at some point," says Coburn. "He had his supporters and then, for whatever reason, he lost them. When that happens, you're finished. Members of the staff start talking to the trustees, behind your back. Your job, at that point, is finished."[2]

Coburn doesn't dispute the core of Cashman's criticism: he did not think the Carnegie Library at the top of the hill was big enough or modern enough for a city with a population of a quarter of a million people. In his first memos and presentations to the board, and in his first annual report, he suggested three main goals: to reorganize the administration of a growing library system, to create branches, and to design a new, modern library in downtown Edmonton.

The bookmobiles were doing an admirable job of extending library services to those communities without ready access to the Carnegie Library downtown, the Strathcona Branch, or the small Sprucewood Branch in St. Alphonsus Church. Old buses had been retired and the city had retained the services of the Wells Corporation, a car manufacturer in Windsor, to put together purpose-built bookmobiles. Even so, Edmonton clearly needed new libraries.

The Woodcroft Branch in the city's new west end, planned before Coburn's arrival, opened in 1956 at 134 Street and 114 Avenue. The building was a classic modernist design: a rectangular structure of one-and-a-half storeys with large windows in the front. The adult library was on the main floor and the children's library was upstairs. As much as the Sprucewood Branch expanded the reach of the library, the space was small and ill-suited to the demands of the community. The year of Coburn's arrival, 1956, was really year one for the spirit of expansion that would see the construction of seven branch libraries before Edmonton's centennial project—a new downtown library and the fulfillment of Coburn's dream—opened in 1967.

Another project would bedevil Coburn as he tried to realize his predecessor's goal. From his first annual report in 1939, Gourlay had tried to imagine a way to introduce more professionalism to the library staff.

Coburn had the support of Alderman Wilson and he always would. In 1959, she ran as a Social Credit candidate in Alberta's provincial election and won a seat in Edmonton North. Now she was, at the same time, an MLA, an alderman, a library board member, and a seamstress; it wasn't until 1962, when Premier Ernest Manning made her the second female cabinet minister in the history of Alberta, that Wilson gave up her side career as a seamstress.

Thanks to Wilson, Coburn also had the support of Hawrelak. In the 1950s and, oddly, for much of his strange political career, Hawrelak was able to achieve many of his ambitions in Edmonton. Depending on your memory and your politics, this was either through charm and skill or graft and nepotism. For the library director, little of this mattered as long as the mayor supported you. And Hawrelak supported Coburn.

New libraries meant new librarians, and they were hard to find. In the late 1950s, departments of library science were rare in Canada's universities and scarce in the west. "I'm sure I was hired because they were having trouble finding anyone else," says Coburn. "Back then, there were so few librarians in the west and no real way to lure them out here. They said about me, 'Oh, Coburn, he doesn't like librarians,' and 'He doesn't believe in a professional staff,' because we had devised a training program for people who had no formal training. But it wasn't that. It wasn't that at all! We were expanding the system and I needed staff. If I could have lured people from the east to come out to this isolated place in the west I certainly would have. But I couldn't!"[3]

The mall revolution begins: Westmount Shoppers' Park.

[City of Edmonton Archives EA-33-193]

18 The fight against the fleshpots

LIBRARIANS WERE RARE COMMODITIES in the late 1950s. The economic expansion demanded researchers: corporations needed librarians, law practices needed them, and so did all three levels of government. With so few graduates coming out of Canada's library science programs every year, the promise of luring a bright young man or woman from Toronto or Montreal to an actual library on the west side of Edmonton was somewhere in the range of faint to non-existent.

One fall day Coburn walked on to the University of Alberta campus for the first time to meet Bruce Peel, who had become its chief librarian in 1955. Peel was an early version of what is today a growing breed in the west: men and women who resist the urge to live in a mega-metropolis because they have fallen in love with this place. As a librarian, scholar, and bibliographer, Peel's great ambition was to inspire more literature about Edmonton and the west—particularly the prairies.

Coburn stood in front of what was then the central library on campus. It was a miniature version of a library he knew well, from his home state: the one at the University of Illinois at Urbana-Champaign. Peel

Bruce Peel was chief librarian at the University of Alberta when Morton Coburn was director of EPL. Together, they found a way to build a school of library science at the U of A. [UAA 057.90-36-001-1]

confirmed it. His predecessor had been an admirer of that library but had been unable to secure the funds to build an exact replica. So they had just made it a little bit smaller.

Like Coburn, Peel was devoted to building a cadre of professional librarians in the west. In the 1950s "[p]rairie students were recruited and sent elsewhere for professional education, only to be lured by the libraries and 'fleshpots' of the East."[1]

Coburn and Peel became immediate friends and allies. The first library school in western Canada opened in 1961 at the University of British Columbia. It was closer to home for young westerners keen to train as librarians. Unfortunately, spending time in Vancouver was somewhat detrimental to the library systems that desperately needed them in Edmonton and Calgary, Regina and Saskatoon, and Winnipeg. By the time they were ready to graduate from UBC, they refused to leave the coast. Those who did come back were, Coburn says, problematic.

"They arrived in Edmonton because their husbands had taken positions in our city. Some of our B.C. librarians turned out to be rather serious problems."[2]

Aleta Vikse, who had served as interim chief librarian in between the departure of Gourlay and the arrival of Coburn, had done a marvellous job of creating a sense of family among the librarians. With the assistance of a third librarian, James Pilton, Coburn and Vikse devised a training program for Edmontonians without formal library education.

It was rigorous and potentially brutal.

"We were given an opportunity to hire staff on a three-month probation period," says Coburn. "Recruits were brought through an intensive program of learning how to handle library jobs of various kinds. We usually sought applicants who had university backgrounds or held advanced positions in private industry. Written tests and evaluations by their peers either brought their stay with us to an end, or they were taken on the permanent staff."

This strategy worked for a while but it wouldn't work forever. Coburn, new to town, was developing a false reputation as someone who didn't value library science degrees.

"Oh that isn't true at all," says Heather-Belle Dowling, an Edmonton woman who received a $250 scholarship to attend McGill University in Montreal as long as she promised to come back for at least two years. "He was a true librarian and a fine manager. For my part, it was easy: I had fully intended to come back and work at the Edmonton Public Library. I was so fond of that Carnegie building and genuinely loved working there."[3]

Not everyone was as devoted to the city as Dowling. And the library wasn't downsizing. The only long-term solution was to establish another library school on the prairies. "The question was where. Winnipeg, Saskatoon, and Edmonton were all interested contenders."[4]

It may have been a rigged process, but Coburn chaired the committee to find a solution to this problem. Peel represented U of A. Coburn wrote a report and presented it to the presidents of the western Canadian universities. "The brief indicated the extent of, and anticipated need for professional librarians in the area, and evaluated the relative merits of the cities of Edmonton, Saskatoon and Winnipeg as 'library bases' for the projected school."[5]

The university presidents chose Edmonton. It took some time to get it running, as even then the processes of approval and government funding were labyrinthine. The campus was designated in 1965 and the first intake for the Bachelor of Library Science was in 1968. Coburn was poetic on the subject in his opening remarks for the 1963 annual report.

> *It is sometimes said that there are no more frontiers and that the day of the pioneer is over. It isn't true. The librarians and their assistants who keep the doors of the libraries on the Canadian prairies open are pioneers in every sense of the word, just as were the earlier arrivals who crossed in* Red River *carts. It requires courage and dedication to labour far beyond one's pay cheque simply because of the knowledge that the job is important and that one is building something good. The story is the same in every prairie province; the burden is heavy and too few are available to carry it.*
>
> *One of the facts of life is that not everyone is constituted to break new ground, to be a pioneer or a missionary. Perhaps to many, because of economic necessity, the dollar sign is of greatest importance. The emergency situation that exists in almost every prairie library can be resolved only if premium salaries are offered to lure librarians here from what they may consider more favourable geographical and intellectual climates, and to retain those that we already have who may be looking with longing toward the bright lights of Toronto, Montreal, or* New *York.*[6]

It would take a few years to realize Coburn's dream of a legitimate, made-in-the-prairies training system. In the meantime, there were more capital projects to consider.

For the moment, Coburn and the library board had the attention of Edmonton's mayor and aldermen. The Hawrelak years brought division and rancour but they also came with a spirit of ambition.

There were now two branches apart from the founding libraries, in Sprucewood and Woodcroft. In the twenty years after the oil discovery in Leduc in 1947, the city's population and its land mass more than doubled. More fundamentally, Edmontonians were in the midst of changing the way they lived their lives. The Sprucewood Branch, first in the church on Alberta Avenue and later on a corner lot in an old residential neighbourhood, spoke of pre-war living: main streets and pedestrian-oriented development. Woodcroft, when it opened in 1956, represented the future.

An economy based on oil and gas, when resource prices are rising, is a glorious thing. From entry-level workers to chief executive officers, everyone is making more money than they would elsewhere. There is always the threat of a bust. But the particular psychology of a petroleum economy is intoxicating: we live for the moment.

And in 1956 Edmontonians were living in a moment of consumption.

The city's first shopping mall, Westmount Shoppers' Park, opened in August 1955. Looking back, this was probably the most fundamental before-and-after project in Edmonton's history. It was explosively successful, with major department stores such as Kresge's and Woodward's anchoring another forty shops.

"Young families needed new appliances," writes historian Lawrence Herzog, "washers, driers, electric refrigerators, gas stoves and furniture. Land was plentiful and cheap and Westmount was the right idea at the right time. Huge newspaper ads proclaimed the new shopping complex as another first in Edmonton's phenomenal march of progress."[7]

Before the war, Edmontonians had walked to their main street to purchase food, appliances, and clothing. They consulted their local shopkeepers; they knew each other's names. After the war, gas was cheap and cars were suddenly affordable for just about everyone. Edmonton wasn't hemmed in by mountains or water. It could go on forever. The magic of Westmount was simple and delicious: three thousand parking stalls.

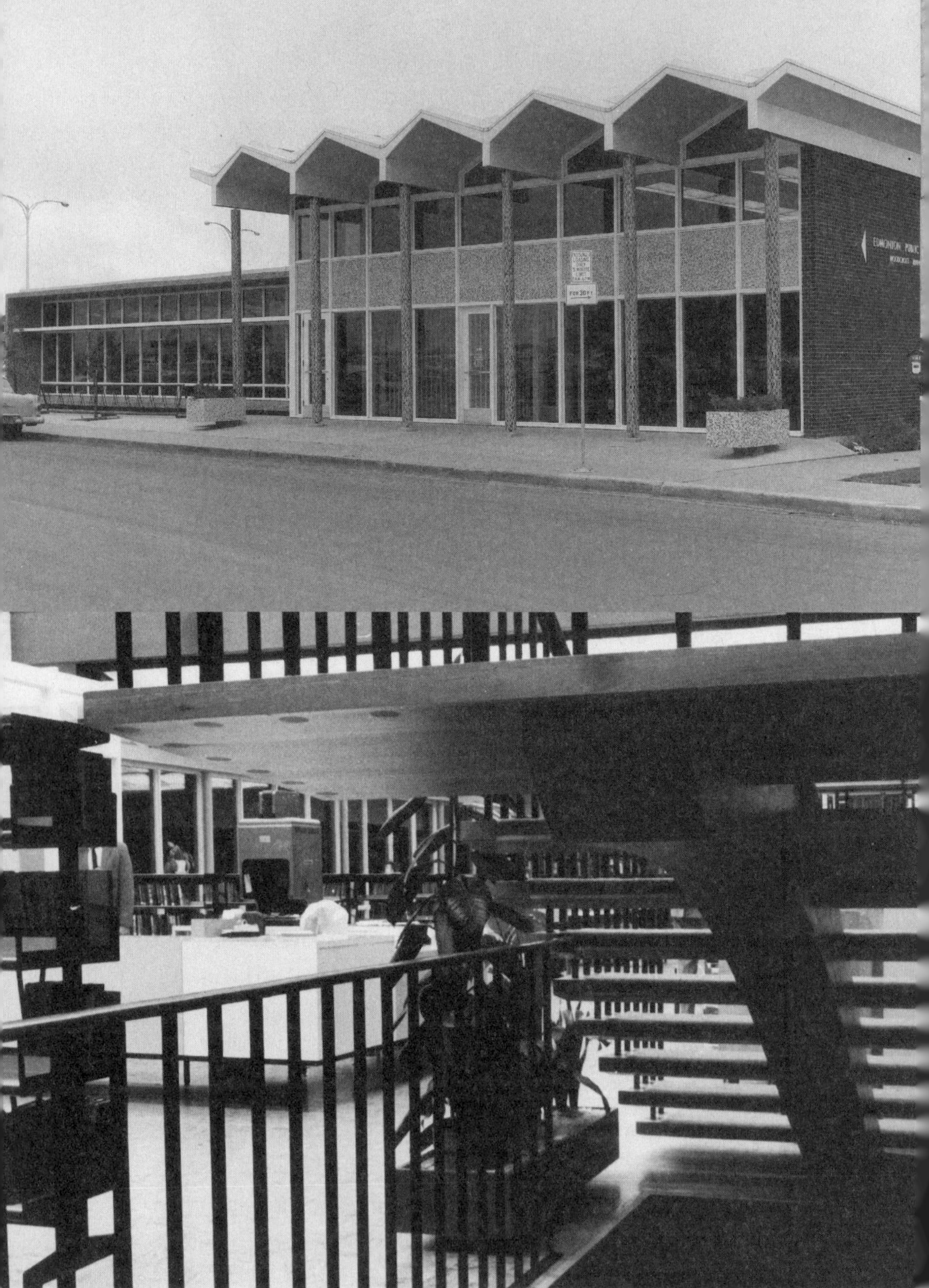

Top: Woodcroft Branch in Westmount was the first to tie its fortunes to a shopping mall, 1964. [Provincial Archives of Alberta PA 450/1] *Bottom: The interior stairway at the original Woodcroft Branch of EPL.* [EPL]

Members of the library board understood instinctively that if they wanted to attract Edmontonians to libraries, if they wanted citizens to mix a bit of reading into all of that buying, there was really only one place to build a library: in or very near a shopping mall.

Like the two previous directors, Coburn emphasized in his presentations to council the vital role of libraries in a democracy. New immigrants were arriving daily from around the world, and a strong city-wide library system was the smoothest way to integrate them into Edmonton and Canada. It seemed the quickest and smoothest transformation, for new Canadians, was from people who didn't understand malls to people who spent as much time as possible in malls. Building new libraries deep into neighbourhoods, where parking can be scarce, made no sense after 1955.

In 2013, Edmonton is in the midst of becoming a hybrid. In the inner city, families are choosing to live the way we lived before the grand opening of Westmount Shoppers' Park. Downtown, the city is tearing up Jasper Avenue to widen the sidewalks. This will make outdoor, street-level shopping and recreation more comfortable and more fun. West of 109 Street, condominium towers and inner-city redevelopments such as Railtown and Oliver Square are helping to create pockets of pedestrian-driven life. On the west side of 124 Street, the last main street and one of the borders of old Edmonton, we enter car city. Westmount Centre, the evolution of Shoppers' Park, is on the other side of several subdivisions: the mansions and glories of Glenora, the boulevards of North Glenora and Westmount itself. While this had once seemed the outer limits of suburban Edmonton, today Westmount counts as mature—part of the city's core.

The Woodcroft Branch stands at 13420 114 Avenue, across the street from the north parking lot of Westmount Centre. It has always been at this location, although the actual building has changed. In the 1990s, the library board decided the 1950s structure no longer worked. It had to come down. Since they were destroying the place, they decided to look at three options: remain in the current location, give up on compromise and go right inside the mall, or attach the library to the Edmonton Space and Science Centre down the road. Of the three options, the cheapest was to relocate to the Space and Science Centre; a private donor had expressed an interest in supporting the project financially if it were moved there. Apart from an expanded Woodcroft Branch, this building would include a special science-themed room as well. It fit with a long-held philosophy, to create multi-use facilities that serve a number of functions rather than stand-alone buildings.

Brian Mason, then a city councillor and board member, said in October 1996 that the city would be in danger of abandoning the actual point of a library if it moved to a science centre. "We need to be careful that, in our search for innovation, we don't lose sight of the fundamentals," he told the *Edmonton Journal*.[8]

Of course, whether a library attaches itself to a shopping mall or a science centre, the fundamentals are another conversation altogether. The members of the board had already decided that the 1950s rectangle no longer served its community. In the end, they chose to listen to the citizens.

Some people were excited by the idea of a library at a science centre with the potential for packaged activities. And it wasn't so far away from the original site: across a vast field surrounding a school and a swimming pool. Statistics showed well over forty per cent of Woodcroft Branch users, in the 1990s, either walked or used public transit to get there. The proposal to move farther away, over a park or down the freeway, was not popular in the community.

In January 1997 the board voted to build a new building at the original location. An *Edmonton Journal* editorial praised them for it. Library users in Westmount had "rightly pointed out to the Edmonton Public Library board that whatever the advantages of moving the library branch to the Edmonton Space and Science Centre, they were outweighed by the less-convenient location.... Getting a science library is not worth the price of alienating patrons of the Woodcroft Branch."[9]

After some controversy about a new location near the Space and Science Centre, a new and improved Woodcroft Branch launched in the original location in 1998. [EPL]

The grand opening was at the end of June 1998. Mayor Bill Smith and federal Justice Minister Anne McLellan, the Member of Parliament for the surrounding constituency, attended the event to launch the new branch. There isn't much of a local feel about the area today. The mall, across the street, has been repackaged as a combination of an indoor shopping centre and a power centre. There is a Home Depot. The ubiquitous Boston Pizza launched in Edmonton long ago, but there is little of Edmonton about it today. From the front lawn or looking out the windows of the Woodcroft Branch, the view is of a concrete box with discount jeans inside and the parking lot that launched the city's love affair with the mall.

Woodcroft is a light brick and beige building with a leafy adolescent tree in the front yard. Inside, it is bright and clean and busy. Its rounded front is a clear contrast to the sharp angles of the modernist original. It is a single-storey structure, and wheelchair accessible, and sings out: "functional."

The Jasper Place Branch at night. [EPL]

19

Mid-century modern

THERE IS A HANDSOME PEN set into a marble base on Coburn's desk in Chicago. It reads: "Awarded to Morton Coburn by the Jasper Place Library Board."

Jasper Place, in the 1950s, was a separate town on the western border of Edmonton—located between 149 Street and 170 Street. At the time it enticed newcomers for two reasons, one more permanent and the other temporary: municipal taxes were lower than in the big city and, in 1953, town council had passed a clever law to entice shoppers. In Edmonton, stores closed at 6 P.M. In Jasper Place they stayed open until 9 P.M. six days a week.

Before the Second World War, Jasper Place was for mavericks. Unlike the city next door, services weren't centralized. Residents had bits of land and raised chickens, grew food in their gardens, did their quiet business in outhouses. The war had changed life in Jasper Place as much as it had changed life in Edmonton. The oil strike in Leduc brought in many more residents: new families interested in buying large houses, without paying large taxes, while still working in downtown Edmonton.[1] These new Jasper Placians bumped against old-timers who saw the inevitable amalgamation with the big city as something like starting a construction business with Satan.

Coburn, the young director of the Edmonton Public Library, had a main branch and three others to manage. The board was planning a new branch, Idylwylde, in the expanding Bonnie Doon neighbourhood on the south side of the river. As with anything in Edmonton, these sorts of decisions took years. Layers of managers and experts were consulted. Most decisions ended up as compromises.

Woodcroft was a success. Turning to the Idyldwylde Branch, the board members decided they didn't want to build across the street from a mall. If they really wanted to attract modern, shopping-crazy Edmontonians, asking them to cross the street was perhaps too much. Idylwylde would share a parking lot with Bonnie Doon Shopping Centre, a twenty-two-acre island of shops surrounded by friendly asphalt that opened in 1958. The library itself would be the western half of a building that housed a medical clinic.

If you walk south from downtown, through the evolving river valley and into the Mill Creek Ravine, you will arrive at a cross path. Turn right and you climb westward toward the Strathcona Branch. Turn left and pass one of the few houses that remain in the ravine, surrounded at night by skunks and coyotes, the occasional deer, and groups of illegal campers taking shelter in the urban forest.

Campus Saint-Jean is the French-language campus of the University of Alberta. On a warm day, students toss Frisbees and flop on the grass, reading books—all in French. In the winter they build snowmen. Across rue Marie-Anne Gaboury is la cité francophone, a complex devoted to French-language businesses and services, a dance school, a bookstore, a theatre and a dance studio. This neighbourhood is, historically, Edmonton's French quarter.

In the early twentieth century, Father Giroux led a group of Quebec homesteaders across the country to northern Alberta, not far from the

Top: Idylwylde Branch opened in 1960 in the parking lot of Bonnie Doon Mall, attached to a clinic. [EPL]

Bottom: The check-out desk in 1960 at the new Idylwylde Branch of EPL. [EPL]

A bright new redesign of the Idylwylde Branch launched in 2008. [EPL]

Peace River—*Rivière de la Paix*. Not all of these Franco-Albertans, who developed their own unique traditions and their own accent, remained in the north. Like other rural Albertans, they were drawn to the city—and this is where they tended to cluster, replicating in an urban neighbourhood the feeling of a village.

Bonnie Doon Shopping Centre is ten blocks east. When my daughters were infants, this is where we took them to be immunized. It's one of the most miserable experiences in the life of a young parent, holding your baby's hand and looking in her eyes as a nurse pokes her with a needle. Today, as in 1960, the clinic is attached to a library. To calm ourselves down after the mini-horror of vaccination day we would walk through the entrance and into the Idylwylde Branch.

Its bones remain the same today, mostly because the clinic and the buildings west of it remain as they were in 1960 when the branch opened. Across the parking lot, well-populated with seagulls, are a Sears and a Kal-Tire. On a recent visit to the library I stopped in first to look at vacuum cleaners at Sears: the cavernous department store was nearly empty. But the library, originally built in a shopping mall parking lot to ensure its relevance, was full of people.

The branch was renovated in the 1990s and again in 2007. The latest renovation was finished in autumn 2008. The glass exterior is now decorated with the word "library" in several languages, and the interior is bright and busy with light wood accent and curves where, in 1960, all had been corners and rectangles. On a recent trip to Idylwylde Branch I returned a John le Carré novel using the new 3M radio frequency system that identifies a book and whisks it away on a conveyor belt.

Adults were sitting in the southeast corner of the space, at single desks and at shared tables, some with books and others with laptops. Women browsed the fiction stacks. Parents were at the back, where kids climbed on a boat attached to a large aquarium. All the computer stations were taken, just as they are downtown. You can imagine this aspect or some future manifestation of it growing as the bookshelves slowly disappear; the idea is only depressing if you allow it to be.

I watched an adolescent boy with messy red hair, sitting at a computer and thought of Andrew Carnegie: "There is not such a cradle of democracy upon the earth as the Free Public Library, this republic of letters, where neither rank, office, nor wealth receives the slightest consideration."[2]

The boy was playing a computer game called *Happy Wheels* on a website called Total Jerkface. It seemed the hero was in a wheelchair. The boy moved his avatar on a wheelchair around on the roof of an office tower and then plunged off. On the way down, the man in a wheelchair tried to wipe out as many other people as possible—from other office towers. The more people who fell to their death the better.

Of course, this scene is probably the modern version of a tension that has always existed in libraries: literature versus entertainment. As interim chief librarian Grace Dobie had put it in her 1937 annual report, no one concerned with a republic of letters is overjoyed with "the pulp magazines of the trigger-finger type for our youth."

It is a tension that remains on the display shelves of the library where Michael Ondaatje shares a rack with John Grisham, Margaret Atwood with Nora Roberts. The Ondaatje and Atwood of video games are in the midst of creation on the south side of Edmonton, where the writing team at BioWare build complex characters and storylines that make *Happy Wheels* seem utterly ridiculous.

Coburn was involved in developing the Idylwylde Branch in the late 1950s, but it was difficult for a man of ambition to see the personal challenge in attaching a library to a health clinic. The finished library at Idylwylde has always been successful, but its creation was a process of accommodation and compromise. The town of Jasper Place was more nimble. "Then an independent community, its citizens knew it was only a matter of time before Jasper Place would be a part of the city of Edmonton," says Coburn.

The nascent library board in Jasper Place also knew that the moment the town was amalgamated, it would be placed on a long list of Edmonton's suburban communities that needed a building. The community would end up waiting years, if not decades. The board contacted Coburn and he attended a meeting. Instead of lobbying politicians, climbing through layers of bureaucracy, the Jasper Place trustees offered Coburn an opportunity to do something extraordinary. The project would change the course of his life. They asked him to work with an architect and design a brand new building, taking everything he had learned and everything he would like to see in a library of the future.

Under budget, of course.

The Idylwylde branch opened a year before the Jasper Place Public Library, but the contrast between the two experiences was enormous. Building something in Edmonton required committees and approvals and, ultimately, political manoeuvring. Jasper Place simply wanted a damn fine library. Trustees told Coburn how much money they had and

Before it was annexed by the City of Edmonton, Jasper Place asked Morton Coburn to help design its library. The modern marvel, a highlight of his time in Edmonton, opened in 1961. [EPL]

said, "Go build it." Of course, Coburn had to ask his bosses first. At that time, the Edmonton Public Library board was thrilled with the ambitious young director and granted him the time to work with Jasper Place. "From its opening day," says Coburn, "it was designed to operate as another branch of the EPL system. The Jasper Place community funded its operation."

Most importantly for Coburn, nobody got in his way. He wanted a contemporary design, with as much zest and experimentation as he could afford. He didn't have to blend the library into a health clinic or any other public institution, so he studied libraries in the United States to find the latest fusions of library science and architectural design. "It was hailed at the time," writes historian Lawrence Herzog, "for its cutting-edge design, bright reading spaces, and undulating roof line."[3]

What I remember of the old building is the effect of the undulating roof lines at night. The building was a long, low rectangle with four arches in the front. My grandparents, who moved to Rio Terrace in the late 1950s, drove past the library almost every day. When I visited them as a boy, I would often stay in the library looking at books while they shopped for dinner. While Jasper Place Library wasn't attached to anything, the board wasn't crazy. No one, in 1961, opened a suburban library far from a mall: in this case, Meadowlark, which had the saddest shopping mall Santas in the world from the late 1970s to the early 1980s.

The library was one of the last pieces of public infrastructure Jasper Place would build. Three years later, the glorious library and everything else became the property of the City of Edmonton—which also assumed the town's budgetary problems. The headline on the front page of the *Journal* on August 17, 1964 wasn't subtle: "38,000 people, $8,177,000 in Debt and 'The Damndest Mud in the World' Becomes Part of Edmonton."[4]

In 1988, brick swallowed up modernism. A major library renovation closed off the windows, adding fluorescence to make up for the loss of natural light. The age of computers had made much of what was happening in the Jasper Place Branch obsolete, and the building itself was failing. The new design, unfortunately, made the place feel like a bunker—as though medical experiments, not storytelling, were happening inside the building.

It takes an hour and a half to walk from the Stanley A. Milner Branch of the Edmonton Public Library to Jasper Place—if you're willing to jaywalk from time to time. West of leafy Glenora, past the current location of the Royal Alberta Museum, 102 Avenue widens into a commuter road. Soon, if all goes well, the LRT will stop here and again, farther along Stony Plain Road, at the strip mall nexus and the old Jasper Place border: 149 Street.

Here, Stony Plain Road begins to mirror Alberta Avenue. It is an old main street calling out for a central theme: more local shops selling goods that people in this part of the city actually need and fewer pawn shops and quick-cash outlets, dodgy massage parlours and dim bars full of video lottery terminals. The road is punctuated at 156 Street with the strange orange arts building. For years it has been the western

A central figure in Edmonton, and the EPL: architect, city councillor and entrepreneur Gene Dub.

[City of Edmonton Archives EA-117-165]

campus of MacEwan University, formerly Grant MacEwan Community College, where actors and writers trained. Soon it will be a city arts institution of some kind and, potentially, an anchor for something new on Stony Plain Road. Ten or eleven blocks south, past more strip malls and some rectangular apartments, a few houses, we reach a curious place of transition.

Linda Cook, the current CEO of Edmonton Public Library, is like Coburn in 1961: a risk-taker. No one wept, in 2011, when the 1988 makeover of the Jasper Place Branch was demolished. The latest thinking on libraries and Cook's current obsession is contained in the question: "What is a library?"

"We don't know if there will be books in the library of the future," says Cook. "This is what we're preparing for today."[5]

Edmonton's best-known architect, Gene Dub, and his son Michael, worked with Hughes Condon Marler Architects from Vancouver, to

In 1988, the Jasper Place Branch went through an extensive renovation. [EPL]

The design of the new Jasper Place Library, by Dub Architects and Hughes Condon Marler Architects, has a roofline that hints at the curves of the original building. It opened in 2013. [EPL]

design the new Jasper Place Branch. This building is the opposite of the one it replaces: highly energy efficient and draped with glass. The design harkens back whimsically to Coburn's work on the original library, with undulating roof lines.

It is obvious that Dub and his team listened carefully to Linda Cook before sitting down to sketch the library of the future. Cook herself has been the architect of a new role for libraries, where they operate as community hubs. This is the place we go, in some sense, to become Edmontonians.

"No one knows exactly where libraries are going in the future, so they require that flexibility," Dub, most famous for his pyramid-shaped design of Edmonton's City Hall, told the *Journal* in 2010. "They're now looked at as being a focal point for community communication and not necessarily just for books...The library people really pushed us along and encouraged us to do something which was extraordinary in its spatial quality. The openness is far greater than the typical library—the openness of the common area. We were looking for a special quality of space and we think we've achieved something that we haven't seen before with the undulating concrete ceiling, so we're pretty excited by that."[6]

The new building opened in early 2013, in time for the Edmonton Public Library's centennial. It is the first project in a new building boom for city libraries, a mirror of Coburn's time as leader in the 1960s. Today, instead of attaching libraries to malls, Cook is imagining them as companions to community and recreation centres.

No one was thinking about libraries without books in 1961. Coburn, fresh off a thrilling experience building a modernist beauty in Jasper Place, turned his attention to "that little Carnegie library at the top of the hill" that he found just a little bit humiliating, as a librarian and as an Edmontonian.

Director Morton Coburn and Associate Director Aleta Vikse 1962. [EPL]

20

Sex

BEFORE HE COULD BUILD ANY MORE LIBRARIES, Coburn addressed a more central concern: books. Books—the quality of books—was a problem in his adopted hometown. The chief librarian wanted statistical proof he was improving the intellectual and cultural lives of Edmontonians. This was rather difficult when, in his opinion, few books on the "new releases" stacks were worth reading.

Once the staff had grown accustomed to him, Coburn began asking about the ordering system in the main library and in the branches. There were gaps. The latest and many of the greatest books were missing.

"To my inquiry as to why we were not selecting materials in this or that area the staff response was the same: 'no one asks for such books.' My response was that our public already knew how meagre our coverage was in so many areas that they no longer asked for books treating such subjects."[1]

Besides, librarians were leaders. The reading public does not always know what it wants until someone tells them. All the great marketers do one thing very well: they make you want something you did not know you wanted.

Coburn established a book selection committee. He could already tell that the librarians and assistants under his command were prone to disputes with management. His early successes were not universally celebrated. The union was strong. So instead of imperiously taking over the book ordering functions at the library, he formed a committee. Aleta Vikse, the interim chief, and James Pilton, the brilliant Torontonian, joined him as revolving chairs of the committee. He made sure all librarians participated.

In the late 1950s and early 1960s, popular literature was changing. Writers after the Second World War were altogether different from the writers who had followed the First World War. Jack Kerouac, who published *On the Road* in 1957, was no Ernest Hemingway or F. Scott Fitzgerald. Norman Mailer and others were publishing a new subjective sort of journalism that echoed a sense of aimlessness and alienation, of distrust. In London, Colin Wilson had published *The Outsider* in 1956, initiating a British version of French existentialism. Tom Wolfe and Hunter Thompson, the assassination of John F. Kennedy, the Vietnam War and the coming-of-age of the baby boomers inspired a profound cultural transformation. Canada was, as always, some years behind all of this. But Coburn wanted to make sure Edmontonians had the reading list.

Growing up in Edmonton at the time, Nicholas Spillios was interested in books on various subjects. One subject was particularly interesting: sex. And under Coburn, sex was more likely than ever to be on the shelves.

"I attended McKay Avenue School, which was only six blocks away from the library, so I was there a lot," he says, on a hot summer day in a west-end coffee shop. From the café we can hear construction at the new Jasper Place Branch.

"In those days, there were R-rated books but they were under lock and key. I was in high school and I wanted a book on sex. I had to go to this very imposing librarian, to me she was six feet tall, and somehow gather the courage to ask permission. She had to open the collection to get me the book. I was scared to death of her. But I *needed information*. It was a question of literary perseverance."[2]

Spillios was sufficiently moved to fall in love with libraries. By the early 1990s, he was chair of the board of the Edmonton Public Library and one of the founders of Friends of the Edmonton Public Library in 1993. At a time of rather dispiriting funding for the library system, this not-for-profit society of volunteers started to build support and awareness for the library in Edmonton, to defend it publicly, and to raise money for activities the library might not be able to afford on its own. Spillios has served as president of the Friends of the Edmonton Public Library and today he sits on the board.[3]

She was not tall and imposing, but one of the librarians with the key to the R-rated shelf was Heather-Belle Dowling. "We were just as embarrassed as those kids, I'll tell you," she says, with a sustained laugh. "We dreaded it whenever someone would ask us to open it up. Oh it was such a lively time to be a librarian, in that wonderful Carnegie building. We would go across the street, to the Hotel Macdonald, for coffee. Sometimes, because of split shifts, we would have a two-hour lunch break. We would drink wine, plenty of wine, and come back on the job. I don't know why someone didn't talk to us about that. No one ever did!"[4]

It was a question of relevance. Coburn wanted contemporary books, contemporary architecture, contemporary librarians, and a contemporary system. One of the least contemporary aspects of the Edmonton Public Library was the building on Macdonald Drive, with its obstructive pillars and its old-fashioned layout. It was too small and could not be sufficiently expanded to handle the needs of a population that had more than doubled since the end of the war and promised to double again.

Inspired by Andrew Carnegie, Edmonton businessman and political aspirant Stanley A. Milner has devoted time, energy, money and passion to supporting the Edmonton Public Library since the 1960s. [EPL]

21 The Carnegie of Edmonton

STANLEY MILNER was born in Calgary in 1930 and grew up in Turner Valley. Before Leduc supplanted it after the Second World War, this town was known as the birthplace of Alberta oil. Milner's family didn't stay in any one place for long, as his father was in the Canadian Forces. By the time he was ready to graduate from high school in Winnipeg he had lived all over the west.

Few of these places were terribly peaceful for little boys.

"It was pretty much a given," says Milner, on a warm March day at the Mayfair Golf and Country Club. "If you were a kid anywhere near an oilfield back then, you were going to be beaten up. I moved around a lot and didn't have a lot of friends, a lot of protection. I realized the safest place to be, during a recess or after school, was in a classroom. I did a lot of reading. I came to love books."[1]

Even so, Milner did not grow up to avoid confrontation. In his summer jobs as a young man, he developed a reputation for counting bags of concrete at building sites and walking around with a tape measure. Unethical property developers, at the time, would skimp on concrete and add too much gravel—raising their profits but also ensuring weak foundations. Some people were in on these schemes and some people weren't. When Milner called them on it, the people who were in on it were often displeased. He was a troublemaker who, quite soon, gained the confidence of genuine leaders. His bosses knew what they had in Milner, and gave him a lot of responsibility at a young age.

Milner earned a science degree at the University of Alberta and graduated into an oil boom. All of that reading in his youth had helped create an uncommonly good mind for business. He went into oil and gas and, in 1964, he founded what would become a spectacularly successful corporation—Chieftain Development. By then, his energy and the quality of his thinking were already well known.

By the end of the 1950s, Mayor Hawrelak had achieved two feats. He had led Edmonton through a period of stunning growth and he had also become fabulously rich. His personal business involvement in land deals did not strike everyone as fair. "He had the ambition, energy and ability to become a wealthy businessman and an effective mayor," wrote a *Journal* city hall columnist, Olive Elliott, who covered Hawrelak. But, she said, "he never understood that serving his own interests didn't necessarily serve the city's interests."[2]

Ed Leger, one of the aldermen who watched Hawrelak give contracts and positions to his friends, family members, and allies, began scrutinizing the mayor's real estate transactions. In 1958, he presented a bold petition to city council claiming that Hawrelak had used the office of mayor to enrich himself. According to Justice Marshall Porter, the alderman was entirely correct. He found Hawrelak guilty of gross misconduct and the mayor resigned in September 1959—claiming his political opponents had attacked him unfairly.[3]

One of these political opponents was that young counter of concrete bags. When an election was called to replace Hawrelak, the man who won the election—Elmer Roper—was an admirer of Milner's. In 1961, he helped to convince Milner to run for city council, which was then a part-time position for leaders in other spheres.

An alderman's life is busy. Milner was on four boards and running a successful business on the side when Mayor Roper asked him to sit on the library board. He didn't have the time for it and didn't feel he knew enough about libraries but he agreed—because of one man.

"We all grew up with this idea that Carnegie was a robber baron," says Milner, handsome and spry and well-spoken in his early eighties. "Then you see he had this whole other side to him. He had come from nothing and he built libraries to help other people do the same. You have to remember, in the early 1960s, and before that, libraries were the poor cousin. My plan, once I was put on the board, was to borrow Carnegie's philosophy—to get libraries linked to the education system."[4]

In 1963, Milner's first year as chair of the Edmonton Public Library board, outgoing Mayor Roper and others convinced Milner to run against Hawrelak, who had already grown tired of life outside the spotlight. To become eligible to run for mayor again, Hawrelak paid more than $100,000 to settle a lawsuit with the city.

In true Hawrelak fashion, it would turn out to be one of the wildest and most upsetting municipal elections in Edmonton history. Horrified that Hawrelak could become mayor again, student protesters clashed with hundreds of Hawrelak supporters in Market Square, punching and shoving and spitting. The same supporters, some might say thugs, travelled from debate to debate to shout down Hawrelak's opponents. There were death threats against Milner, so—at the suggestion of the police—he sent his family out of town for the mayoral race and carried a gun. These threats didn't stop until Milner confronted Hawrelak personally. On the eve of the election, in a community hall that was supposed to be the site of the final debate, hundreds of fiery Hawrelak supporters threatened to transform from merely belligerent to violent. A police officer helped Milner escape through a window.[5]

Hawrelak, ever-fascinating to the people of Edmonton, won the close race and ended Milner's political career. His public service did not end, however, as he remained chair of the Edmonton Public Library board.

Milner's first job on the board, after a dirty election, was to clean up a mess. One of the trustees, Philip Cox, the head of the Alberta Teachers' Association, was not keen on Coburn's leadership. Coburn was still a young man at the time, learning how to manage people. He made errors, as any leader would. Cox did not like him. It was not standard behaviour for a board member to seek information and rumours from staff inside the library, finding his own inner networks, but that is precisely how Cox operated. He found staff members in the Civic Service Union 52 who were not at all enamoured with Coburn and his second-in-command Aleta Vikse. The fact that Coburn was an American, an import from another culture, often came up. Coburn and Cox argued, sometimes in person and sometimes through the newspapers. Cox went to the *Journal* from time to time, with stories about Coburn and about the library. Who was really in charge? The young, American chief librarian? Or the board of trustees?

One of the ways Milner solved this problem was to distract everyone. For years, Coburn and others had been talking about a new building to honour Canada's 100th birthday in 1967.

"I realized the centennial was coming up and I knew, as a former alderman, that the city was thinking of ways to commemorate it in some way. So as chair of the board I decided we'd make a big push to get a new library. I spent a lot of time trying to get everyone on side. I had to convince them it would be a good gift to the city—as Carnegie would have done. The chair of the board is always in the business of finding money. But even then, Edmonton was a bit of a cultural centre compared to other cities of its size. If we really want to prove we're made of something, that we're unique, art and culture is the way to do it. And libraries are a big part of that. There was a bit of a boom in the city back then and we had quite a few head offices. We kept them until the city decided it didn't want them anymore but that's another story. What we had to do, back then, was tap into this new spirit."[6]

And find some land. The real estate on Macdonald Drive was not vast enough to support the kind of building the board envisioned. What the city wanted to do, at the time, was develop all of that land at the top of the hill—to build what are now the Telus Towers. Milner found himself in the middle of negotiations, knowing that if it went poorly the city would not only lose its Carnegie Library, but end up with no library at all. As much as Coburn disliked the building, he lacked the power to knock it down and build something new.

The City of Edmonton desperately wanted to knock it down and build something new—an office tower and a concrete pedestal. The question was whether or not Edmonton would get a new library.

At $1.5 million of municipal taxes, the library didn't have the money to buy its own land—even if in some way it were to sell the real estate on Macdonald Drive.

There was a feeling, in city hall, that the city was moving in two directions at once. One was perhaps more dangerous than the other. Elmer Roper, the mayor from 1959 to 1963, was already concerned about urban sprawl, the push deeper and deeper into the farmland surrounding the city. It was expensive to service these areas and it was bad for business, which demanded the collaboration and concentration of a busy downtown.

"He had a vision for the city," says Milner. "He was maybe our first mayor who did. He knew that if your downtown starts to go, you lose your tax base. You lose a lot. He was the first mayor to hire a town planner. There was a feeling, in that moment, that we had to protect the downtown."[7]

Roper and Milner were out of public office by 1964 when the strong lobbying for a new downtown library approached a decisive moment. Milner had found a lot of support but it was still entirely possible the city would choose another project as its centennial legacy. As we now know, downtown boosters in Edmonton were about to begin losing the argument, and would continue losing for forty consecutive years. Libraries weren't popular with everyone. The short history of Edmonton has been a test case for what is, and is not, considered a waste of taxpayers' dollars. Infrastructure for cars is nearly always considered prudent. The mind and heart require tougher arguments.

One thing was certain: the library on Macdonald Drive was coming down. The civic centre, which would be called Sir Winston Churchill Square in 1965, required an anchor institution and it required a lot of parking. The provincial and federal governments offered money for centennial projects. Milner didn't have much leverage but he had a little.

"My argument was that the biggest investment in that building was by Carnegie," says Milner. "It wasn't ours to sell or give away, not in the normal sense. The city really wanted me to sign over a land transfer, giving them the property. By then we knew we could build a library [on Sir Winston Churchill Square] but we had no real way to raise funds. It wasn't at all a sure thing. I can't remember the deal we worked out exactly but I wouldn't sign the papers to transfer the land until it was in writing that the proceeds from the land deal would go to our new building, the centennial project. Then we had them. They were stuck."[8]

The Calder Branch of the Edmonton Public Library opened in 1966 in a former Department of Transport building. [EPL]

22

The dominion of the mall

TWO BRANCHES OPENED IN 1966—Calder and Capilano.

In August, Calder opened close to a strip mall, the Kensington Shopping Centre, on 127 Street and 133 Avenue. It was a temporary location in a converted Department of Transport building. The "temporary" aspect would last some time—almost thirty years. Today, the most handsome building on 127 Street—otherwise concerned with industrial and chain-store strip malls—is a medical spa called External Affairs. It is dark brick with white accents. Inside, men and women undergo Botox and laser treatments where they once read books. Since 1992 the Calder Branch has been a few blocks away in another strip mall on busy 132 Avenue.

If you walk directly north of the Woodcroft Branch through the community of Dovercourt, with the transforming City Centre Airport on your right, you will cross Yellowhead Trail and enter a marriage of light industrial buildings and bungalows. This is Athlone, another neighbourhood label borrowed from the United Kingdom. Veer right and you enter Calder, a mid-century rectangle of houses bordered on all sides by

The Capilano Branch launched in 1966. It was the first Edmonton library to open in a mall. [EPL]

car commerce. The library is on the northern border of Calder, where it meets Kensington.

Many cities in Canada have a Kensington market, inspired by the tony high street in London. Unlike others, Edmonton's is not a pedestrian district. It is designed for parking and walking to Liquor Lake or H&W Produce, Kensington Flowers, Sofalair, Giant Tiger, Kensington Bingo or—best of all—the Calder Branch of the Edmonton Public Library. The space is bright and spacious, like all current EPL strip mall branches, much larger if less memorable than the old Department of Transport building.

The recent evolution of libraries in Edmonton, and in the rest of the continent's suburban cities, is simple to track. Library specialists first suggested building close to shopping malls, with buildings such as Woodcroft and Calder. Then libraries arrived in mall parking lots, like Idylwylde. This was close, but not close enough. In October 1966, Edmonton's first library to open inside a mall—like a small department store—launched in the three-year-old Capilano Shopping Centre at 50 Street and 98 Avenue. In Capilano, as in the modern Calder Branch, the library attracts clients by looking and acting like a shopping destination.

Of the two openings in 1966, Capilano was the media event. Like the new building going up on what had once been Market Square, this library was designed for the future. Librarians will debate anything, of course, but there doesn't seem to be any snobbery around slotting a library in the same complex as a bingo hall, liquor store, and sofa emporium.

"Branches in shopping malls help build community by attracting new patrons to the library," a journalist wrote in a library journal, not in 1966 but in 2005. "They help libraries offer exciting new venues with a retail-like approach and raise awareness of the work libraries are doing."[1]

The definition of "build community" will change from person to person, community to community, and this openness would come to define the most recent building boom of the Edmonton Public Library. But in 1966, as in many corners of Edmonton today, there was no larger community than the one at the mall.

The loveliest route to the Capilano Branch from downtown Edmonton is on the walking trail through Riverdale and along the North Saskatchewan. Don't climb up the hill until after you pass under the Capilano Bridge, and Wayne Gretzky Drive. The Capilano neighbourhood, in between the river valley and Refinery Row, is a pleasant and diverse place—the best neighbourhood in the city if you happen to be a cross-country skier.

Capilano Shopping Centre, at the southern limit of the neighbourhood, is both an indoor and an outdoor mall. It hasn't aged as well as some of its peers, and today the stores aren't terrific attractions: Your Dollar Store with More, Liquor Barn and Liquor Depot, Ricki's and Payless ShoeSource, Winner's and Vo's Nails. In 1966, the Capilano Branch of the Edmonton Public Library was keen to profit from the heavy traffic moving into and out of the mall. The owners of the mall are planning a renovation in 2013, but for the moment the library is the main attraction.

Phase two of the Highlands Branch, in 1963: "the Little House Library." [EPL]

You’re our expert. Build the library.

THERE WAS A BIT OF TIME, between saying yes to the project and designing it, to think about the right kind of library for downtown Edmonton. Coburn had worked with an architect to design the Jasper Place building, but he was still a young man and no expert.

Normally in these situations a city would hire an expensive consultant—a globally recognized authority on the latest and greatest new libraries. Mayor William Hawrelak looked at the proposal to hire such a person out of New York or London. He summoned Coburn.

The mayor went over the reasons to hire a library consultant. Then he sat back and fixed his gaze on Coburn.

“So we need an expert, a consultant on building a library.”

“Yes,” said Coburn.

“You’re our chief librarian,” said Hawrelak.

“Yes.”

“All right, then. You’re also our expert. Build the library.”

And that was that. Coburn laughs when he recalls his conversations and his dealings with Hawrelak. “He was a funny man.”[1]

Coburn went on a fourteen-city tour of libraries in North America and the United Kingdom. Milner accompanied him on a few of the visits. At the time, expensive consultants felt that even a little bit of sunlight aged and damaged books. The miracles of fluorescence could not be overstated. The dominant architectural style of the 1960s and early 1970s, enthusiastically endorsed by designers and builders in Edmonton, was an evolution of modernism called brutalism. The word is not pejorative, or at least its origin wasn't. Le Corbusier, the celebrated French architect, liked the look and the utility of raw concrete or *béton brut*. This evolution of modernism was cheap and handy. Today, when critics complain about Edmonton architecture they complain about many things. It was a quirk of timing more than anything else: from the end of the Second World War until relatively recently, preserving and protecting heritage buildings was an odd notion. Edmonton identified itself as a city of progress, a city of the future, and in the early 1960s the city of the future was made of concrete—not extravagances like limestone and imported tile and panes of glass.

Like CEO Linda Cook today, in 1964 Morton Coburn was concerned with the library of the future.

"We knew, back then, that in a few years everything would be computerized," says Coburn. "Even though we didn't have the technology at the time we knew it was coming, and we listened to the best experts about how to prepare for it."[2]

In Edmonton today, it is rather common to hear leaders complain about the downtown branch of the library. Mayor Stephen Mandel, one of the strongest advocates for the library system in the city's history, is not vague about it: "It's a huge gap on the square," he says. "It's an ugly building and we're going to do something about it. I want to get it re-skinned and to fix the problems in front of the building. The entrance ought to be in the back. Linda [Cook] and I don't agree about that. She wants to keep the entrance in the front. And, as you know, she's a very strong negotiator."[3]

I mentioned to Coburn that the City of Edmonton had plans to re-skin the library, to poke holes for windows and to drape it in curtains of mirrors or thick glass, to avoid chunks of falling concrete and to make it more beautiful, more welcoming, and more energy efficient.

"Well, the main floor is all glass," he said. "I visited Edmonton two years ago and I think the building has held up beautifully."

Stanley Milner was also a great lobbyist for the library. He might have been Mayor Hawrelak's least favourite Edmontonian, but he found support on council, with the provincial and federal governments, and with the business community. In 1965, a new downtown library was officially announced as Edmonton's centennial celebration project. The site of the library would be Market Square—the city's public market. The budget was set at $4.5 million. The design, by Rensea, Minsos & Holland Architects, was for a six-storey building with space for 800 cars in an underground parking lot.

Even though he was one of the most successful businessmen in Edmonton, Milner was still counting bags of concrete in 1965. He was on the job site with a tape measure.

"A contract is a contract, but you have to watch those extras," says Milner. "My big concern was that we get a solid proper building with no corners cut. The city said, as part of the deal, that they were building the library and the board was to stay out of it. The architects were a respectable firm but still...they were pretty close to Bill [Hawrelak]."[4]

Many Edmontonians had come to love Hawrelak. Others had come to expect he would be personally involved in major projects, skimming a little bit or a lot for himself and for his associates. Sure enough, Hawrelak was kicked out of office yet again. In March 1965, another judge found him guilty of violating conflict of interest laws while in office; he had owned forty per cent of a property development company that had sold land—very profitably—to the city.[5]

While the library's major project downtown was underway, some other relatively minor ones were evolving. The library completed an expansion of the Woodcroft Branch—tripling its size. Idylwylde was one of the busiest branch libraries on the continent and the old streetcar library project continued to evolve. In 1962, the first diesel bookmobile, designed and built in Edmonton, had hit the streets. And an old one came back into service. "To meet the demand from the suburbs for bookmobile service, a retired bookmobile was renovated and incorporated into an expanded schedule in November," wrote Coburn.[6]

One of the most important thinkers of the 1960s, Marshall McLuhan, had been born in Edmonton in 1911 and spent his childhood in a two-storey home in Highlands, east of downtown. As a boy, McLuhan had wandered to the river and watched a horse on the opposite shore. He always remembered thinking how the horse could fit into his nursery—a memory that informed the media theorist's thoughts on perspective.

The Highlands Branch of the Edmonton Public Library opened temporarily in a storefront on 118 Avenue. The following year it opened at 11818 67 Street, in what everyone called the "Little House Library."[7]

This location was altogether too far west to serve the core of Highlands and other east-end neighbourhoods such as Beverly Heights. And it was a compromise. "Our sixth branch, the Highlands, opened to the public mid-June in a small renovated bungalow," Coburn wrote in the 1962 Annual Report. "The lack of space limits service to the circulation of books. Hand-charging is used. The popularity of the branch indicated the need for proper quarters and in October the City Council granted monies for a new building."[8]

In August 1964, that new building—700 square metres on the main floor and 325 square metres in the basement—opened at 6710 118 Avenue. It was another rectangle, with a glass front and a flat roof. The Highlands Branch, unlike many other library branches built in the same period, sidestepped significant renovations until 2011. When you walked into the Highlands Branch you were, more or less, walking into 1964.

The best route from the downtown branch to Highlands is to walk straight south toward the riverbank and turn left on Jasper Avenue. You

The original Highlands storefront location on Alberta Avenue in 1962. [EPL]

will pass the Shaw Conference Centre and see, down below, a re-imagined Louise McKinney Park. In the warm months, the riverboat—the Edmonton Queen—might be floating down or struggling up the North Saskatchewan. When you take a canoe ride on the river through the city, from west to east, here is where you would begin to imagine what this place looked like in the late eighteenth century. Of course, you'll pass kayakers and dragon boat racers in training instead of voyageurs.

Walk east on Jasper Avenue, above the river valley, south of Chinatown on the downtown east side. The Quarters is beginning its slow transformation from parking lot neglect to something altogether different. Here, the Singhmar Group is building a Hilton hotel designed by Gene Dub. The company's founder, Prem Singhmar, arrived from India with relatively little in 1985, and since then his successful firm has built three hotels in the capital region. Further along Jasper Avenue, the development along the river slows and transforms into something more natural; the road veers away from the river at the pretty corner of 82 Street and you walk north.

Top: In 1964, the purpose-built Highlands Branch opened at 6710 118 Avenue. [Provincial Archives of Alberta PA 451/1]

Left: Kids want to get out of that sunshine and into a good book. Highlands Branch. [EPL]

A rendering of the new and improved Highlands Branch, opening in 2013. [EPL]

A few blocks along 82 Street, you will see Commonwealth Stadium, another concrete monument—this one to track and field and football instead of books. At the 112 Avenue strip mall, turn right and, the moment you can, cross northeast through Borden Park and Northlands. What we once called Northlands Coliseum and now call Rexall Place, for the moment the home of the Edmonton Oilers, is in the distance. If you're lucky it will be late July and Edmonton's oldest party—the ever-transforming exhibition and midway—will be bringing in the crowds. You'll have to pay admission but it will be worth it. Watch a horse race and climb on a midway ride to bring back memories of thrills, first loves, and nausea. Edmonton's traditional agricultural exhibition transformed into Klondike Days in 1962 to celebrate our rather thin connection to the gold rush to Dawson City, Yukon, at the end of the nineteenth century. Klondike Days was, for some time, a marvellous success. Capital Ex, a more recent incarnation, was a failure. In a 2012 contest, Edmontonians chose to call the summer fair K-Days. The K? Yours to decipher. The city without a mythology is, in 2013, searching for an enduring new theme for its annual fair. If an answer is anywhere, it is probably in a library.

The Highlands Branch, like the Jasper Place Branch, is moving into a new architectural era. The 1964 rectangle was closed in November 2011 and torn down to make way for a two-storey structure with more natural light that pays homage to the original building's roots in modernism while hinting at what comes next for libraries. It is part of a broader civic streetscaping project for 118 Avenue; the idea, proven around the world, is that building something beautiful instead of another hunk of functional concrete will help create a spirit of joy and dignity in a neighbourhood that has suffered from a beauty deficit. Like all of the new buildings going up in this library centennial boom season, Highlands Branch will operate as a community centre and an arena of ideas as much as a lovely place to borrow a book.

CEO Linda Cook's philosophy is woven into the design. "One of the things I see as I look down the road are libraries turning from places of information to places of culture. It is and will be a place to find contentment, but it will also be a place to develop your own: to self-publish a book, to learn how to make a film, to share ideas, to develop a project with others. I don't think books are going to go away but print books will move toward e-books. We have to be ready for that, provide space for it, and develop a business model that works for us."[9]

In 1965 and 1966, as Edmonton prepared to enter a new era in libraries, there was a sense of pride, anticipation and fear in the city. Again, the conversations were about more than the printed word.

Stanley A. Milner used all of his political skills and business acumen to ensure that Edmonton's 1967 centennial project would be a spectacular new library. Then he made sure construction went well. [EPL]

Big Brother in Edmonton

THIS WAS AN ERA OF RECORD-BREAKING CONSTRUCTION in downtown Edmonton as entire blocks of old buildings were destroyed and new ones conceived. Stone came down and concrete went up. But the plans for the city's centennial project went beyond six storeys of bare concrete.

In 1964, the Edmonton Public Library controlled the movement of two and a half million books. The circulation department completed an audit of the system in July and discovered a loss of $50,000 worth of books in one year—just at the downtown branch. And that was after the downtown branch had hired its first security guards, in 1963, to prevent theft. For the entire system, the figure was $70,000. Circulation control manager G.F. Smythe wrote a response to the *Edmonton Journal* after a library patron complained in a letter to the editor about having her overdue book fines referred to the Credit Bureau.

These books belonged to Edmonton's taxpayers, wrote Smythe, and the losses were serious business. "Library books have been found in garbage pail [*sic*], laneways, department stores, schools, hospitals, abandoned railway cars in northern Alberta, in foreign countries such as Mexico, Australia, Africa, and France. One was even kindly returned by an English lady who found it on the beach at Bournemouth."[1]

Heather-Belle Dowling often caught thieves even if she didn't physically tackle them. "I do remember coming into the rare book area, and a man was putting a book in his pants. I said, 'Get out!' and Morton was angry with me. He had wanted me to hold on to him and call the police. How was I supposed to do that? Oh, and it wasn't just theft. When we put in the mezzanine there was a bit of a catwalk, see-through. The girls would be up walking on it and some of the old men, the drifters, would look up under their skirts. Yes, that became an issue. One particular time I did grab a man, actually grab him, and shout at him for that."[2]

In 1966, Philip Cox, the trustee who had battled with Coburn, was not reappointed. He went straight to the *Journal*. Many of his complaints were personal and staff-related but the newspaper sensed the story in Cox's dismissal from the board.

"Controversy also resulted from his opposition to a proposal that patrons be searched on leaving the library, Mr. Cox said."[3]

The newspaper began editorializing about the draconian new measures to prevent theft and recover lost books. If a child lost a book and her parents were unable to replace it, the entire family would lose borrowing privileges. Case after case appeared in the *Journal* of the library's aggressive new tactics to prevent more lost and stolen books. Then, even worse, as the plans for the new library became more detailed, the newspaper reported that closed-circuit televisions and video cameras were to be installed to prevent theft. As the Centennial Library neared completion in 1967, several articles mentioning "Big Brother" and *1984* appeared in the newspaper—a reference to the George Orwell novel and its Ministry of Truth.

This narrative would dominate the remainder of Coburn's years in Edmonton, at least in the *Journal*. The newspaper had no trouble finding sources within the library—a few angry and disgruntled staff members who were keen to have the chief librarian replaced.

As the opening approached, Milner spoke to the media about stories of video surveillance.

"The device will not only curtail book thefts, but it will also protect the public from undesirables," the board chair said. "I think most people will accept it graciously."[4]

If most people were prepared to accept it graciously, they weren't being published in the *Journal*. Stories about the surveillance system continued to run with the usual references to George Orwell. After several articles and letters, a patron named Shirley Hunter wrote a response. "The critics seem to be conjuring up some horrifying possibilities. Will the camera's eye invade the biffy to make sure we wash our hands? Will it snoop over our shoulders to see whether we're reading Karl Marx or Flopsy, Mopsy, Cottontail and Peter?"[5]

The problem wasn't just book theft. From January to April 1967, in the run-up to the grand opening of the Centennial Library, there were eight incidents of indecent exposure in the Carnegie building. "I hope, too, that the cameras will deter those perverts who sometimes haunt public places, waiting for opportunities to shock the young and innocent without getting caught."[6]

When the library opened, another philosophical patron named D.G. Turnbull offered a counter-argument in the letters pages of the *Journal*:

> *I, of course, noticed the television cameras and receivers and was quite intrigued. As I browsed through the shelves, I was struck by the heightened feeling of being watched, and became mildly apprehensive, particularly when looking at specific volumes in the political sciences section.*
>
> *Gradually, the novelty of TV cameras began to evolve into something much more sinister than was the intended purpose, and I became acutely aware of the fact that wherever I went, and whichever way I turned, I was being observed. The answer was to simply leave the library and not return.*
>
> *However, I became very distressed when I noticed there were many younger people in the library, relaxing in some of the excellent facilities, and*

> *apparently completely oblivious to the fact that they were being observed. It occurred to me that this type of conditioning in the younger people would leave them wide open to further intrusions of privacy with* TV *cameras installed in the art gallery, in railway stations, bus depots and airports. Then a camera could be installed in every city block.*
>
> *From this stage it would not be far from installing a camera in each home. Lo and behold, we would have arrived at* 1984.[7]

Turnbull was both correct and incorrect. Today, few of us notice cameras. We expect and, for the most part, ignore video surveillance. Guarding our privacy is little more than an intellectual preoccupation. On the first and second floors of the Edmonton Public Library, and in the branches, the majority of computers connected to the Internet are busy. Most customers are using Facebook.

Facebook is a free product. A common saying, in the year of the 100th anniversary of the Edmonton Public Library, is that if the product is free, you're the product. George Orwell was right about many things: we are more or less accustomed to constant surveillance, if not government surveillance, then corporate surveillance. The data business is one of the fastest-growing sectors of the economy. Social networks like Facebook exist because other companies are enormously interested in where we live and where we work, what we like and dislike, and how we spend money. We give this information away for free and call it leisure. Many of us do it at a library.

Her Royal Highness Princess Alexandra of Kent dedicated the new library on Edmonton's central square in 1967. [EPL]

25

That brilliant, sunny Saturday afternoon

PRINCESS ALEXANDRA OF KENT and her husband Sir Angus Ogilvy arrived in Edmonton on a sunny day at the end of May 1967. Edmonton's business and political leaders dressed up in Klondike outfits and gathered at the Hotel Macdonald to meet the young couple with a Cheechako breakfast and a rousing rendition of *Won't You Come Home, Bill Bailey.* The royal couple visited the Glenrose Rehabilitation Hospital and, due to bomb threats inside the school, attended an outdoor concert and dance performance at Victoria Composite High. Mayor Vincent Dantzer presented the couple with white okalig fur parkas and bone carvings for their two children. And, on the afternoon of May 27, the princess arrived at Sir Winston Churchill Square.

In his Edmonton Public Library News Notes, Coburn described the "blare of band music and the crackle of fireworks."

> *They were all here that brilliant, sunny Saturday afternoon when Princess Alexandra dedicated the Edmonton Centennial Library—marching bands, majorettes, City Police Honour Guard, Highland dancers, Gerry Smythe*

> *of Circulation Control coordinating the program with a walkie-talkie, the Centennial Voyageurs, Premier E.C. Manning, Bishop Burch, the mayors of Anchorage and Hull, Mr. John Holgerson—the Executive Director of the Edmonton Civic Centennial Committee, Mr. S. Milner—Chairman of the Library Board, and hundreds of excited spectators. The guest list of Federal, Provincial, and Civic Officials and dignitaries resembled a chapter from* The Canadian Who's Who.[1]

Published estimates of the cost of the building varied from $3.7 million to $4.5 million. It was decorated with furnishings that appear straight out of a Stanley Kubrick film, *A Clockwork Orange* or *2001: A Space Odyssey*, with rounded chairs, pod tables, whimsical globe lighting, and a lot of sharp corners and empty space. The chairs in the children's library downstairs were red, orange, and gold toadstools. There were sculptures and art on the walls, and the already-infamous security apparatus near the front doors. Proceedings began with a concert in the basement theatre and then Coburn led the princess on a tour of the library.

"Keenly interested and delighted with her surroundings, Her Royal Highness requested to see 'all of it,' much to the consternation of Gerry Smythe and his staff who had worked for days coordinating security with City Police and the RCMP. However, with obvious pride, they arranged that she see the entire building."[2]

There were a few problems. The Carnegie Library on Macdonald Drive remained open, as the library staff slowly transferred books from one location to another. Odd chemicals dripped into the parkade under the new library and stripped paint from cars. The plaque that went up on May 27, 1967, had an error: the French word "erigée" was misspelled. It had to be redone. Still, the as-yet-unnamed downtown library—Centennial Library?—was a marvel. Delegations from other cities arrived to study it for their own projects and renovations.

"I saw elevators, escalators, television cameras to screen patron activity," wrote an enthusiastic journalist, stunned by all there was in

Top: The central branch in the year of its birth, 1967, in evening wear. [EPL] *Bottom: Before and after the central branch opened, the "Big Brother" aspect of its surveillance system was a topic of conversation and newspaper opinion pieces.* [EPL]

Top: The fantastical children's theatre in the basement of the new central library in Edmonton. [EPL]

Bottom: The entrance of the central branch featured a mural by the Quebec artist Jordi Bonet. [EPL]

Top: The second floor of the central library was designed and furnished like the set of a Stanley Kubrik film. [EPL] *Bottom: The artwork rental service at the central branch.* [EPL]

a library of the future *besides books:* "a theatre, kitchens, a classroom for budding librarians—all there in what promises to be the cultural centre of the city."[3]

A two-year children's library card, on opening day, cost five cents. Upstairs in the adult section, the same card was a quarter. Futuristic gadgets abounded: a Xerox 914 copier and IBM punch cards for circulation. There was a Wollensak four-track tape recorder, Kodak and Zeiss projectors and cameras, Recordak Magnaprint Readers and Starmac Readers, a Se-Lin labelling machine. For a while, at least, the negative press about Orwellian security dissipated—replaced by a feeling of progress and big city boosterism. Edmonton had arrived, again.

Coburn wrote that "1967 was the year when Edmonton's new central library building was completed and because of the almost superhuman effort put forward by the staff, library patrons were not deprived of service for even a single day during the move. Like London's old Windmill Theatre, during the Second World War, their slogan can now be, 'We Never Closed!'"[4]

Staff morale was high. Colleagues had accomplished something amazing together, and the library—not just a sports team or a discovery of oil—was again a symbol of the city's pride and ambition. Every branch in the library participated in that summer's Klondike Days parade. The staff members dressed up in 1890s clothes, walked "*mit beer tankards,*" and wrote and performed a song, to the tune of *There is a Tavern*:

There is a library in our town, in our town
Where friends and workers sat them down, sat them down
To eat pancakes, 'mid laughter free
And that's the place we had to be.

The petting zoo in the children's library at the central branch would end in controversy. [EPL]

26

Then the Sixties happened

OUTSIDE THE DOWNTOWN BRANCH of the Edmonton Public Library, in the culture at large, what we have come to call "the sixties" were happening. Young men and women were talking differently, dressing differently, reading differently.

Coburn and board chair Milner were young men. The downtown branch was designed with youth in mind. At the end of the 1960s, there were few places in the city as delightful, for a kid, as the children's library in the basement—with its theatre, its 22,000 books, and its mini zoo.

"It's gaily coloured," wrote *Journal* columnist John J. Barr, "with racks, tables and chairs scaled down to kid-size. Along one wall is a line of cages, with budgies, rabbits, Abyssinian guinea pigs, gerbils, garter snakes, hamsters and white mice. Along another wall, there's a wading pool with live turtles. Any parent who doesn't take his children there ought to be shot."[1]

Outside the library, there were protests against the Vietnam War and other gaily coloured events in the square. Inside the library, staff members began to resent the extra work and to twitch under the extra stress and bad publicity. Stories that had circulated years earlier, about book theft and strategies to combat it, transformed in the *Edmonton Journal* to The Man coming down with unnecessary toughness on non-violent people hungry for a good time. The video cameras, the security guards, the searches, the extra rules. To some journalists, the library was the "least sixties" institution in the city.

In 1968 Milner convened a press conference to put the story to rest. No one likes to be searched by a security guard. No one likes video cameras, even though they weren't able to see books anyone is reading. Security measures were necessary because of more-or-less rampant indecent exposure, drinking parties in the downstairs washroom, vandalism and theft.

"We must provide the proper atmosphere and protection for patrons from undesirable elements," said Milner, at the news conference. "In any large public building, this is a problem."[2]

The solution was not in tune with the culture. In a piece of stunt journalism, an *Edmonton Journal* reporter planned to steal a book—to see if he'd be roughed up by security on his way out. Milner received a tip about the plan and the reporter was gently charged with theft. The mini-war between the newspaper and the library was harder on Coburn than Milner. The chief librarian was prone to excessive anxiety about the issue. Milner, the oil executive and occasional politician, was accustomed to battles.

Ever since Philip Cox had been removed from the board, some staff waited for opportunities to speak to new board members about Coburn's management style. "I'm not sure what it was, exactly," says Coburn. "It went back to that idea that I didn't like librarians."[3]

Apart from the ongoing security issues, which lived mostly in the pages in the *Edmonton Journal*, the transition from an old library to a new one was a sparkling success. Activity in the central building was lively, and the rhythm was becoming regular. The eight branches and three bookmobiles were busier than ever. In 1969 Edmontonians borrowed a total of 2,281,980 books, magazines, pamphlets, pictures, phonograph records and tapes—5.4 items per capita.[4]

Not everyone was happy, internally, but with 134 staff members some discontent is inevitable.

"By the end of the year it could be said that the new central building, opened in the summer of 1967, had completed its breaking-in period and was beginning to feel comfortable," wrote Coburn in the 1969 annual report. "At peak hours, especially on Sunday afternoons, the 'standing-room only' sign was usually up. During the year, despite the longest cold spell on record and the transportation strike during the summer, it is recorded that there were 940,492 admissions to the adult floors and 398,354 to the Children's Library."[5]

The final year of the 1960s contributed to Edmonton Public Library lore, producing one of the stories every director tells. The animals that had been part of the children's library since the opening of the new building didn't always bring delight to the kids. Every year the library celebrated a book week, an invitation to every child in the city to participate in a theme. The end-of-the-week party was in the basement theatre attached to the children's library. With his typical dry humour, Coburn writes, "there was some excitement on this occasion when one of the monkeys brought to entertain the children climbed the curtains on the stage of the theatre and disappeared into the ceiling. Four days later he was lured out with a dish of fruit salad."[6]

In the end, shenanigans in the children's library wouldn't turn out to be terribly funny for Coburn. But no one in Edmonton could tell the monkey story without a smile.

The Carnegie Library was demolished by PCL Construction, an Edmonton firm whose first local project was its construction. [EPL]

27

Phantom Edmonton

NO ONE MENTIONED, in the 1969 annual report, that the Carnegie Library had come down to make way for the AGT Towers. There are photos of the demolition, completed in part by the same company, Poole Construction Limited (PCL), that had built the library back in 1923 as its first local job. That gentle, rounded place on Macdonald Drive was gone—replaced by a concrete plaza that was, and is, a great place to drop off or pick up an office worker. The *Edmonton Journal*, which seemed intent on attacking the library and its management at any opportunity, did not mourn the loss of a heritage building.

"I don't remember anyone complaining at the time," says local historian Tony Cashman. "People were quite excited about the new library in the square. It certainly wasn't controversial."[1]

Today, of course, the demolition is a test of one's sanity in Edmonton. Look at a photograph of the Carnegie Library, with its Doric columns and red tile roof, its big moulded windows and the pocket park before it: a wonderful place to lie down with a book or make a snowman. Now stand in Sir Winston Churchill Square and look south, at the downtown branch

The demolition of the Carnegie Library was, curiously, not controversial. [EPL]

of the Edmonton Public Library and to the southwest the concrete towers that replaced the original downtown branch. The Carnegie building is one of the icons of a lost Edmonton, a phantom Edmonton, a victim of the boom-and-bust psychology that has defined the city since its earliest days.

The 1969 annual report was Coburn's last. He would remain at the library for another couple of years, but now that Milner and other supporters had fulfilled their mandates on the board he knew his time in Edmonton was growing short. The Canadian Union of Public Employees, in the late 1960s and early 1970s, was feisty and powerful.

Grievances were common. Negotiations between the library and the union, over contracts, were so unpleasant they required a provincial government mediator. The library board, weak after the departure of

Milner, did not know how to respond politically or publicly. The mayor at the time, Ivor Dent, had run federally for the New Democrats. He said, in the press, that he supported the union and the employees in the labour battles—not the board or management.

Three employees were dismissed and the union supported them. One, who had been accused of uttering a racist comment, was reinstated against the wishes of the board chair and Coburn. City council called for a drastic reorganization of the library.

"Some people never liked that an outsider, an American, was in the position," Coburn recalls. "When the board changed there were, unfortunately, trustees who felt that way. You put the trustees and the union together...with a few nasty people on the staff, well, it doesn't matter that the vast majority was happy. There was a dirty plot to get rid of me.

"Near the end, if a story was coming out, the paper wouldn't talk to me," he adds. "They certainly wouldn't listen to me. They spoke to the disgruntled staff, union representatives. I knew I wouldn't be in Edmonton much longer. It became impossible to run the library system. Sooner or later my allies were off the board entirely and the new ones didn't like Mr. Coburn. I had no choice."

An iguana escaped from the children's library zoo and spent some time on a very hot electric heating duct. This is not healthy for cold-blooded creatures. He went a little nutty. The *Journal* and others called for the zoo to be phased out. Someone new asked to be in charge of the animals in the children's library. Coburn said he granted her wish.

"The final absurdity was she claimed, to the board, that I had forced her to put her hands in a snake pit," says Coburn.

Norbert Berkowitz, the board chair, resigned in exasperation. Coburn held on a little longer and then he resigned as well, along with his closest protégés and collaborators Aleta Vikse and James Pilton.

"The appointment of Mr. Coburn as Director gave our library a new lease on life," Vikse wrote, in her letter of resignation, "for it has been through his guidance and leadership that the Edmonton Public Library has become known as one of the finest in Canada and has achieved international fame. No small part of this achievement was due to the expertise of Mr. Pilton and his assistance in the transition from a mediocre library to one of note."[2]

Heather-Belle Dowling, who moved on to start the library system in Strathcona County, remembers it as a sad and confusing time. "Every staff has disagreements," she says, "but what they did to Morton and the others was cruel. It was very hard on the three of them. I sometimes wonder if the charges against him weren't trumped-up. It was wrong. You don't destroy people."[3]

Sad and a little bit humiliated, Coburn moved to Vancouver for two years. He knew that, despite the geographical vastness of the country, the library community could fit into a gymnasium.

"I would never find another job in Canada," he said. "I would always be known as the man who was fired from the Edmonton Public Library."

The advantage of a damaged reputation in Canada is that few other places in the world are overly concerned with Canada. A job opened up for Coburn in his hometown, as director of building programs at the Chicago Public Library.

"I had rare experiences in Edmonton, building the Jasper Place Library and then the downtown branch," he says. "When they kicked me out of town, they kind of kicked me upstairs."

Coburn has worked with architects on the design of libraries in Chicago for thirty-eight years. He has had a hand in the central library and most of the system's seventy-eight branches. He is still an employee of the Chicago Public Library and he remains obsessed with libraries and what they ought to be.

Three years ago he visited Edmonton. "It's changed so much," he says. "But you still have that river valley and those wonderful cultural programs."

He visited the library, of course—his library. "That which remained from my time is the exterior of the building's façade, the escalator to the second floor and the auditorium. Otherwise, the entire interior has been completely changed, and all for the good."

Our conversation, Coburn said, awakened his memories of his time in Edmonton, "things I have not thought of in forty years." He asked me to give his kindest regards to his old friend Stanley Milner. On his last visit to the city, he noticed the plaque that had adorned the outside of the building was missing.

Milner had given me a photograph of the plaque: "THE EDMONTON PUBLIC LIBRARY, A CENTENNIAL GIFT TO ALL SEEKING KNOWLEDGE, INSPIRATION OR RECREATION." Mayor Vincent M. Dantzer's name was on it, along with members of the board, including Milner, the city commissioners and aldermen. On the bottom right it said, "M. Coburn: Director of Libraries."

Coburn wrote to me after we spoke.

"Can you discover what has happened to the building's original plaque on which appeared my name? Edmonton gave me too much to be pleased and happy about to be disturbed by the disappearance of a piece of metal!"[4]

Lieutenant-Governor of Alberta Lois Hole, second from the left, helps cut the ribbon at the Whitemud Crossing Branch in 2002. Her love of learning and support for libraries was inspirational. [EPL]

28 All it needed was a lava lamp

IN THE EARLY 1970S, two new branches opened in malls: Southgate in 1971 and Dickinsfield in 1973. The library system itself was in so much turmoil it was difficult, for the board and for the city, to properly celebrate the extensions.

South Edmonton represented, in 1971, some of the city's most rapid growth. Queen Alexandra School, on 106 Street south of Whyte Avenue, had opened in 1906 as Duggan Street School. Moving south from Edmonton's oldest continually operating school, down 106 Street, the city becomes newer and newer, into post–Second World War suburban communities like Allendale and Pleasantview.

The Southgate Branch opened below ground, without any unfashionable natural light.

"It's just inside the southeast mall entrance," wrote an *Edmonton Journal* reporter in March 1971. "As you come down the stairs your eye first rests on high black leather chairs on a red shag carpet grouped around a record rack. Further away, on a grey carpet, green, yellow, blue and orange free form chairs perch about coffee tables."[1]

Top: The architectural rendering of the Dickinsfield Branch (the small storefront on the left) featured some futuristic images of cars. [EPL] *Bottom: The Dickinsfield Branch in less colourful reality.* [EPL]

The very busy Southgate Branch of the Edmonton Public Library opened in the shopping mall in 1971. [EPL]

Given its basement setting, the Southgate Branch sounded like it started off as a great place to put on some headphones, close your eyes, and freak out. All it needed was a lava lamp.

Mary Rendell, the head librarian at Southgate, was "a soft spoken woman with salt-and-pepper coloured hair, brown eyes and a conservative taste in dress. She seem[ed] an odd choice for a head librarian, having a degree in theology from Trinity College in Toronto."[2]

The reporter never elaborates on why librarians and theologians seem incompatible. In 2002, the library branch in the dark mall location moved across the freeway to a strip mall, anchored by a Red Robin and a vast skateboard shop. The new Whitemud Crossing Branch is twice the size of the former Southgate Branch and much brighter, filling a former cinema multiplex destroyed by the invention of stadium seating. There is an air of business-like efficiency about the clean and open branch.

Inside the Whitemud Branch, a former movie theatre taken over by books. [EPL]

Nothing of its hippie roots remain. Every weekday morning at 9:45, the anteroom between the doors fills with people keen for a computer station or something new to read.

Dickinsfield Shopping Centre, at 144 Avenue and 92 Street, forty blocks north of downtown, is now called Capital Centre. There is a Shell service station and a food mart, a barber shop and a drug store, a daycare and a car wash that could use its own refreshing splash of water. The branch opened in October 1973 in a less-than-imaginative white-washed space after a long and occasionally frustrating search for a northern location. Dickinsfield was a new neighbourhood, with a new mall, so the library building fit the feeling of progress and geographical expansion in the city. No one complained, in 1973, about urban sprawl. Still, by the time the branch was opened, city budgets and library budgets were constrained: growth, it turns out, is expensive. It felt like someone had fit a library into a space designed for cereal and canned vegetables, with cold white floors and fluorescent lights and supermarket aisles. There was, for a time, the head of a shark protruding from the upper limits of the circulation desk, but this was not an era of goofiness.

The north side of the city would continue to grow, through the seventies and into the eighties. In 1984, a time of recession in Edmonton, the busy Dickinsfield Branch reached its limits and hopped to a larger space in Londonderry. The Londonderry Mall location was lovingly renovated and expanded in 1997. Today it is a bright, 1,400-square-metre branch serving a massive area and many thousands of Edmontonians—the expanding, culturally diverse north by northeast quadrant of the city.

In the early 1970s, to solve several problems at once and to maintain a sense of control, Mayor Ivor Dent appointed his executive assistant, Allen Rowe, as acting director of the library system. Rowe knew a lot about bureaucracy and politics. Managing a divided staff of librarians in a hostile union environment, with a deteriorating fiscal situation, and keeping the system out of the papers for a while, would be an entirely new challenge. The city sent Rowe on a couple of training courses to prepare: *Principles of Supervisory Management* and *Developing Leadership Skills, Part Two*. All of this would come in handy as Rowe made the transition from interim director to administrator.

In 1973, the library board hired its fifth official director, Brian Dale, who had served as head librarian in Kitchener, Ontario. After several dramatic years of political battles, buildings and demolitions, errant monkeys and reptiles, Orwellian hyperbole and union stand-offs, the board and the city were interested in an altogether calmer library system.

Brian Dale was the fifth director of the Edmonton Public Library. [EPL]

29 Something called "Alberta culture"

NO ONE MOURNED the demolition of the Carnegie Library on Macdonald Drive because the past, in the late 1960s and early 1970s, was for forgetting. If a building, no matter how beautiful or historic, was in the way of progress, it could not remain. It's easy to look back on this era and call it ridiculous but it's also unfair. A modern city was a city of concrete towers in its core and kilometre after kilometre of single-family bungalows extending out into the periphery. Edmonton was a modern city.

Of course, none of this was cheap. Remaking a city, in only a few years, meant ending a period of growth for the library system. Director Brian Dale's four years in Edmonton were not nearly as exciting as any two of Coburn's years. The transcendental meditation courses in the library downtown matched the atmosphere in board meetings, except when someone brought up the stinginess of the provincial government.

The new Progressive Conservative government, under the dynamic young premier Peter Lougheed, was slow to support libraries despite a natural inclination toward building something called "Alberta culture." The minister of the new Alberta Culture department, Horst Schmid, was actively involved in events at the library even if he couldn't convince the provincial treasurer to throw any new money its way.

"Drinking beer by the lake in the summer and sprawling before our TV set in the winter," warned Schmid, at a German book exhibition in the main branch in January 1973, would slowly destroy our heritage. He quoted author Gilbert Highet: "It is perfectly possible that by the year 2000 the civilized world will have grown so rich and so comfortable, so deeply devoted to simple asinine pleasures...that real education, once available to us through the world of books, will be lacking."[1]

Dale, forty when he arrived, worked to have more art and entertainment in and around the library—with modest success. The *Edmonton Journal* published a glowing profile of him, to introduce him to the community. He said he abhorred libraries that are "dead" and wanted to make the library into a place for local artists and thinkers to come together with average citizens.

Not that there was any money.

"The library budget in Edmonton is one of the first city services to be pruned and one of the last to be expanded," wrote Dona Harvey in the *Journal*, shortly after Dale set up his office. "The situation is typical of that in most North American cities...and Brian Dale is worried about the trends he sees. 'The public libraries in many large cities in the United States are going belly-up,' he declares. 'If we don't learn from their mistakes, we're going to be in similar trouble here.'"[2]

Dale concentrated on activities and outreach, to compete with the dreaded television set. He created the first Community Programs Division of the library, which focused on everything but books: theatre and films and public lectures in the downtown branch, exhibitions, dance performances, and concerts. For people who couldn't leave their homes because of illness or handicap, Dale launched "shut-in service," bringing books from the library to them.

One day two brothers with hearing impairments came into the downtown branch of the Edmonton Public Library, looking for library cards. They were in Edmonton on a mission for the Church of Jesus Christ of

Latter-day Saints, the first two deaf missionaries in the history of the church. There was some confusion over whether they could have cards: they were Americans, after all, and their documentation was unclear.

Bernice Briggs, a library clerk at the time, decided they were Edmontonian enough to become members. It wasn't until later that Briggs and everyone else realized Thomas and Virl Osmond were not just any Osmonds: they were Donny and Marie's brothers.[3]

It was a time of study and reflection, not investment, in the library system. The provincial government wanted an Alberta-wide framework, a network for libraries. It commissioned reports and recommendations while the actual brick-and-mortar buildings and staff and books in Edmonton demanded money. The building on Sir Winston Churchill Square, despite all its newness, was leaking. Skylights dripped and windows developed buckets of condensation. The heating system was disastrously inefficient. To save money, a system that had been bent on expansion now tried to figure out what to reduce, what to close.

There were problems with a building on the other side of the river as well. It was too small, too old. "The ideal solution to the 'Strathcona Problem,'" the management and board reasoned, "would be to shut this branch down."[4]

But this new trend was happening in Canada: the protection of heritage buildings. The arguments against knocking down the old building and putting up something new were singularly annoying to everyone. Minister Schmid, of the Alberta government, was opposed to the idea of knocking down old buildings. At the same time, he wasn't able to help with extra funding to keep an underperforming library open.

The *Edmonton Journal*, no longer attacking the library board and administration, now reported on what funding cuts and budget problems meant for the future of the library system: reduced hours and, possibly, fewer branches.

Patti Meekison, the vice-president of an organization called Friends of the Strathcona Branch Library, presented a long letter to the board in response to comments by director Brian Dale in the *Edmonton Journal*.

Dale's comments, printed January 31, 1976, hinted that the old building would have to close sooner than later.

"Has the library done as much as possible to inform its users of the levels of support it obtains from city and province? As evidenced by our appearance here, your patrons will become concerned about their libraries only when they are directly and personally involved in their future operation or when they are faced with the prospect of losing part or all of the library service they value. Perhaps only then will they become a force strong and united enough to exert pressure on governments for an increase in funding."[5]

As Schmid hinted in his speech, and as the city and province were proving with car-oriented growth, walking to a library of an afternoon to choose and borrow a book seemed an old-fashioned activity. Investing in progress was something else altogether. As though to prove it, Brian Dale submitted a letter of resignation to the board on October 27, 1976.

"The reason for terminating my employment at this time is because I have accepted a position with a commercial enterprise engaged in computer technology," he wrote. "I enjoy new challenges and feel the time is right for me to make a change."[6]

It's not as though every aspect of 1970s progress in Alberta was detrimental to libraries. There were displays about banned books, instead of banned books. This was not the case everywhere. In South American countries such as Argentina and Chile in the 1970s, owning or carrying a book that contained subversive or revolutionary or counter-revolutionary content could mean arrest, detainment, even murder.[7]

In Alberta, challenged books have been less likely to be politically subversive. From time to time, we are upset by nudity, violence, or blasphemy. In the 1920s, the Edmonton Public Library board was often petitioned to remove *The Life of Mary Baker G. Eddy and the History of Christian Science* from the shelves. Karl Marx didn't always fare well. But compared to Nazi book burnings, thought control and murder in the Soviet Union under Stalin, Fidel Castro, North Korea, the Taliban, even Canada Customs, the suppression of free expression in Alberta was relatively mild. Since 1963 the Edmonton Public Library had posted a statement of intellectual freedom on the walls of every building in the system.

Several books are challenged every year in Alberta. In the late 1980s and early 1990s, Jewish groups in Edmonton challenged anti-Semitic tracts and books of Holocaust denial on the shelves such as *The International Jew: The World's Foremost Problem* and *The Protocols of the Learned Elders of Zion*. Incoming head librarian Penny McKee agreed the books were despicable but refused to remove them. The most famous instance wasn't in Edmonton but it was close. In the middle of the 1990s, then Alberta cabinet minister and future candidate for the prime minister's office, Stockwell Day, supported removing *Of Mice and Men*, by John Steinbeck, from classrooms in Red Deer. "It bothers Christians," Day said, "when the name of Jesus Christ is used in a blasphemous way."[8]

While this is probably true, it also strikes me as irrelevant. But we're never far from this sort of thinking. After the terrorist attacks in New York and Washington, D.C. on September 11, 2001, the U.S. government passed the Patriot Act, allowing agents to obtain records of books borrowed at public libraries.[9]

In the Edmonton Public Library, in the 1970s, teenagers gathered to talk frankly with doctors and police officers about whether it was wrong or merely an ill-advised idea to try heroin. And, more importantly, the library was becoming one of the centres of a growing literary culture.

Robert Kroetsch published *The Studhorse Man* in 1969, which brought the city to literary life. The Edmonton of *The Studhorse Man* is a city of lust and snow and magic. Hazard, the unforgettable hero of the novel, explores an exotic yet familiar Edmonton, hunting for his stallion, visiting the taverns and bedding a curator in the legislature building. It's a boozy, chaotic city of mysteries, a place where a cowboy, a poet or a curator could have a lot of fun.

Carolina Jakeway Roemmich (left) and longtime Edmonton Public Library collaborator Linda Goyette published Edmonton In Our Own Words *to help mark the city's centennial in 2005.* [EPL]

"It has been argued," Kroetsch wrote, in *The Studhorse Man*, "that to this day a few wild horses survive in the coulees and ravines of the North Saskatchewan River, there in the heart of the City of Edmonton."[10]

Henry Kreisel, a legendary professor at the University of Alberta, had published *The Betrayal*, set in Edmonton, in 1964. But it was concerned with a man who had escaped from the Nazis and his frightening European memories, rather than the here and now of the city. *The Studhorse Man* was something else, an attempt to capture the spirit and the mythology of the place.

Today at the U of A, in the humanities building, you'll find the Salter Reading Room. Every year there is a Salter Tea and the F.M. Salter Memorial Prize has been awarded since 1962. Salter arrived as assistant professor of English Literature in 1939 and set the tone of the department, offering the first creative writing class in Canada and pushing students like Rudy Wiebe to write and publish stories set on the prairies—not New York City and London, cities that merely *seemed* more literary.

The longest-running Writer in Residence program of its kind launched at the University of Alberta in 1975. Matt Cohen, Elizabeth Smart, David Adams Richards, Trevor Ferguson and others were lured to Edmonton for a semester or two, and often inspired to write a poem or a story set on the banks of the mighty North Saskatchewan. Rudy Wiebe, whose writing career flourished along with that of his friend Kroetsch, lived and still writes near the Strathcona Branch. Margaret Atwood lived and worked in Edmonton. Leonard Cohen wrote a song, *The Sisters of Mercy*, about women who lived just off-campus.

Today, there are enough books about Edmonton that Heather Zwicker, a professor of English Literature at the U of A, can run a class about it—from *The Studhorse Man* to the poems of Alice Major, the African-Canadian comic book mashups of Minister Faust and a growing number of crime novels set in Edmonton by writers like Janice MacDonald and Wayne Arthurson. A city staple, *Edmonton In Our Own Words* by Linda Goyette and researcher Carolina Roemmich, was written in a third-floor office of the Edmonton Public Library.

By 1975, the bookmobile shared the streets with the booktrailer. [EPL]

An off-season Santa Claus

THE EDMONTON PUBLIC LIBRARY decommissioned its old bookmobiles and found the third incarnation of its long-ago innovation, the streetcar library: the booktrailer. Three of them, crafted in Mond, Ontario, arrived in the mid-1970s to reach far-off neighbourhoods unlikely to have their own libraries for some time.

Sprucewood and Strathcona Branches came close to disappearing as the provincial government continued to study the situation. Neighbours in both communities fought to keep the libraries open, though public and media support was not always with them. Coverage in the *Edmonton Journal*, about keeping the Strathcona Branch open, verged on the incredulous. Why would anyone want to keep such an old, drafty building?

One of the newspaper's most popular columnists at the time, Frank Hutton, was not a subtle operator.

"Let's be realistic!" he wrote in February 1977. "There's a possibility that the Sprucewood Library, serving the Spruce Avenue and Norwood districts, may have to close. And if it does, who cares?"[1]

Closures were not so much possible as imminent when, in spring 1977, a month after a provincial budget speech with no good news for city libraries, a bit of money showed up—and a plan. When Schmid made the surprise announcement, which raised library grants from $1 per capita to $1.50, Edmonton and Calgary reached the same level as rural Albertans.

"Schmid, long criticised for ignoring the financial plight of Alberta libraries, will be able to act as an off-season Santa Claus by announcing further funding for library services for Albertans, including long-sought grants for the establishment of province-wide regional library systems."[2]

Even after the bump, Edmonton was ranked 27th in Canada for provincial support of the library system. Still, librarians and supporters of the library celebrated. For a few days.

Mayor Terry Cavanagh and others on city council had other ideas. If the City of Edmonton were to receive an extra $436,000 in funding for the library system, then the City of Edmonton would decrease its grant to the Edmonton Public Library by the same amount. The only way the library could advocate for its own money was to propose something new—automation.

"Library officials describe the current mechanization as in the 'horse and buggy' or, at best, the 'Model-T' league," the *Journal* reported. "It is constantly breaking down and requires a high degree of manpower. Automation will reduce the circulation division staff from 54 to 42, allow much greater control of the books in circulation and provide inter-library loans so fewer duplicates of books will be needed."[3]

Vince Richards, a calm Englishman with twenty-seven years of experience as a librarian in England and in Canada, was appointed the sixth director of the Edmonton Public Library in the spring of 1977. He did not have to move far. Richards was, at the time, head librarian at Red Deer College. He declared his intention to computerize the circulation system within a year or two.

In an interview with the *Saint John's Edmonton Report*, the precursor to the *Alberta Report*, the new library director said he was prepared to deal with financial challenges—he was even a little excited about it.

"The soft-spoken Englishman has unconventional views about the future of libraries. 'Libraries have been reticent about beating the drums. But a recent survey shows more people use libraries in the U.S. than attend all sports and entertainment functions.' And he sees the libraries as a defense against the imposition of the values of secular humanism which are stressed in the school system. 'Here, at least, people have a choice,' he said."[4]

It wasn't choice over books, or even funding, that put the library back in the media again after several years of calm—even neglect. Every now and then Frank Hutton, the *Journal* columnist, would call out the library for allowing ne'er do wells to warm up on cold days. But the Edmonton Public Library had become such a neutral institution in the city that unless there was a funding crisis or a call to close one of the branches, there was little to say—or think—about the library.

This suited city council just fine.

Cec Purves, a former alderman, won the mayoral election in October 1978. He had been on council when the library had gone through its union battles in the early 1970s, and board minutes suggest he found the whole thing tiresome. The library itself was not a priority for Purves or for the council; they weren't interested in increasing funding but they weren't bent on cutting budgets either.

Earlier that year, in March, the central branch of the Edmonton Public Library became one of the biggest stories in a year that was supposed to be all about the Commonwealth Games.

The sixth director of the Edmonton Public Library, Vince Richards, endured a miserable economic situation, baffling technological change, and one of the busiest library systems on the continent. [EPL]

31 Freedom of expression

EDMONTON ARTIST ROBERT DMYTRUK worked with the library in 1978 to display some of his recent work: twenty nudes. Edmonton architect Gene Dub, then an alderman, described them: "Basically," he told the *Saint John's Edmonton Report*, "they are conventional paintings reminiscent of the turn-of-the-century Matisse style, not very earth-shaking."[1]

This was the view of Vince Richards, the library director, his staff and most of the board. Then, three weeks into the exhibition, acting board chair Terry Laing received complaints from unexpected sources. Letters of complaint had arrived from Alderman Olivia Butti and Mayor Cec Purves.

Purves demanded the board remove the "gross and vulgar" paintings immediately. At his weekly press conference, Purves told the *Journal* he had the power to replace the library board, if necessary.

"If that's what they call art, we're in trouble," said Purves, declaring that he would have no trouble censoring art if it were in the interest of the city.[2]

Laing agreed and called a special board meeting. She moved to take the paintings down by noon the following day. One board member,

Frank Perry, supported her. The others voted to keep the exhibition up, against the wishes of the mayor, even if it meant he replaced them all.

For weeks the story ran, and not just in Edmonton. The *Journal* did so well with the story it ran essays on censorship and freedom of expression, by authors and essayists like Myrna Kostash, for the next two months. Vince Richards and others were able to plug the issue back into the reason we have libraries—not to push the boundaries of expression, necessarily, but certainly to start and sustain debates.

"Here's a young guy trying to get started," said Alderman Gene Dub. "The mayor's being a little too strict and is cutting off his freedom of expression. These paintings are not even bordering on the obscene. We're too narrow in our moral view, and we may be doing more harm than good calling them pornographic."[3]

Business was brisk in the library as long as the nudes were up, and by the end of March Dmytruk had sold several of them.

There were other experiments and bold changes in the late 1970s, but none so colourful. Richards and his team completed the computerization project; in 1979, Edmonton became the first city in Canada with a fully integrated computerized circulation system and catalogue. For the first time in Alberta's history, the boards of the Edmonton Public Library and the Calgary Public Library met in person to share ideas and cook up a way to pitch the province for more money. The library set up a "speaker's corner," an opportunity for citizens to stand atop a soapbox in the core of downtown and argue, shout, debate, or practise the lost art of oratory. Few people used it, outside the Toastmasters and tabloid newspaper reporters looking for whimsical first-person accounts of failed ideas in action, and it closed. The smoking room in the downtown library shut down, to the delight of newspaper columnists who had complained about the clientele it attracted.

The decision wasn't popular with everyone.

Richards told the newspaper it was the direction all libraries were moving—not because smoking rooms were unhealthy, but because they needed more space for books. The people who used the smoking room felt they understood why it was shut down: to get rid of them. One woman, who withheld her name, told the *Journal* it was the only place she could go.

"'I can't stare at the four walls of my room all day,' she said, 'I wish there was someplace else to go but if they shut this place down where will people go to meet other people?'"[4]

The role of a library in a city was as debatable as ever: educational institution, lecture hall, arts and recreation facility, shelter, meeting place, idea incubator, smoking room and, of course, that place with books.

The Edmonton Public Library commemorated the province's 75th anniversary in 1980 with a collection of children's writing and art. [EPL]

32

Lougheed, Trudeau and the busiest library on the continent

ALBERTA TURNED SEVENTY-FIVE IN 1980, and the Edmonton Public Library wanted to celebrate. They might have thrown a cocktail party. The board might have instituted an Alberta writing prize. It seemed natural, at the time, to publish a book.

Who might write such a thing? Grant MacEwan had retired as Lieutenant-Governor and was actively writing histories. Robert Kroetsch always seemed game for a wacky assignment. Métis author Phyllis Webb was Writer in Residence at the University of Alberta in 1979 and 1980; perhaps she could blend the province's deep and more recent history.

In the end, they decided to ask some of the city's most creative writers—kids—to contribute to a book. It was both arduous and wonderful for library staff to commission art and stories by Edmonton children. The book, called *75 and Growing*, had a print run of 2,000.

On October 9, the board launched "Library Lovers' Day," part of a public relations campaign to convince all three levels of government and citizens to support one of the city's most important institutions. Kids wore pins with a cartoon bookworm and the words "certified library lover." The campaign was sweet, goofy, and utterly successful, the first in a continuing series of imaginative public relations strategies for the Edmonton Public Library, right up to the cheeky campaign in the run-up to the library's centennial. On the purple library card I used to borrow many of the materials to write this book, it says, "Chicks dig big brains."

In his 1980 annual report, Richards wrote about a just-published Statistics Canada readership survey showing that "contrary to popular stereotyping, Edmonton is a very literate city, using its bookstores and public libraries at a much higher rate than Alberta or Canada as a whole."[1]

While Edmonton has suffered from a reputation problem in the last twenty-five years, illiteracy is not among the negative stereotypes about the city. Something has changed, at least in the imaginations of Edmontonians, since 1980.

The Lougheed government's celebration of the province's 75th anniversary year was a high point for cultural investment in Alberta, and all of that scheming and arguing by library boards in Edmonton and Calgary paid off. The per capita provincial grant climbed from $1.50 per Edmontonian to $3 per capita. Two new branches, after waiting patiently for years to launch, moved from idea to genuine planning: Mill Woods and Castle Downs.

Today, the site of Castle Downs Town Square is a rather unglamorous strip mall, indistinguishable from others in the city. Nothing remains of the 1981 retail experience, but since the launch of the subdivision this has been a crossroads and meeting place—with shopping on one corner and a park on the other side. The library was built several blocks north of Blatchford Field, which in 1929 became the first airfield licensed in Canada. In 2013 it is on the verge of transformation, from a small airport to an experiment in northern living; a super energy-efficient home to 30,000 people. Edmontonians are trying to decide whether to name this new community after former mayor Kenny Blatchford or to give it a new moniker altogether, with or without a nod to the area's aviation history.

Top: The famous, and famously leaky, bubbles of the Castle Downs Branch. [EPL] *Bottom: Dikes could not prevent periodic flooding.* [EPL]

Top: The literary knights of Castle Downs have an invitation for you. [EPL]
Bottom: Castle Downs Branch was relocated to Lakeside Landing in 2002. [EPL]

In true Edmonton fashion, much of the conversation around this has been lovingly sarcastic.

"Lovingly sarcastic" sums up the opening of the Castle Downs Branch of the Edmonton Public Library in 1981. The posters, inviting Edmontonians to the celebration featured three and a half identical knights in armour, each one carrying a sword and a lollipop. The building itself featured large front windows leaning into a sloped and bubbled glass roof. It was bright, which was lovely, and permeable: not so lovely. The building would endure constant leaks, mould and parking lot floods over its twenty-year history.

Mill Woods was the 1970s version of what is currently happening at the City Centre Airport as it is transformed into a residential community. One hundred years earlier, this land was part of the surveyed Papaschase Indian Reserve; arguments continue to this day over the legality of the land transfer to the federal government, and private land speculators.

Constructed in the southeast corner of the city, Mill Woods represented the newest and best thinking in residential master planning, with looping roads that defied Edmonton's grid system when it was approved in 1971. Legends abound about families driving in and never coming out again. The community was built around a town centre and the Grey Nuns Hospital. The Mill Woods Branch of the Edmonton Public Library, which opened in September 1982, was not originally at the centre of the town centre.

The Mill Woods Recreation Centre, with its signature wave pool, was another destination. The library board debated the issue. Ever since the Second World War they had bet on shopping mall traffic to inject life and relevance into branch libraries. This was altogether different, to package swimming and lifting weights with lifting a book. The recreation centre, like everything else built in Edmonton since the 1960s, was a bunker—short on windows.

Once, the Mill Creek flowed uninterrupted into the community that took its name. Today if you walk through the ravine as far as it will go you will come up at the border of a light industrial park. Walk south and southeast through the park, past car detailing shops and oil sands service businesses, and you will reach 75 Street. At the border of 75 Street and Whitemud Freeway, if the season is right, you can play a bit of mini golf, hit a few balls in the batting cage, or zip around a go-kart track a few times.

Then, in one of the city's great transportation mysteries, you cross the bridge over the freeway and 75 Street becomes 66 Street. Enter Mill Woods. There is, on the left, an area that would seem like the extension of Mill Creek if it had been allowed to flow naturally. It is a golf course. In the summer, the route down 66 Street past the Grey Nuns Hospital and the vast Mill Woods Town Centre is a meeting place of the natural and the artificial, the tree and the strip mall. The recreation centre, in the midst of its own re-imagining today, is at 28 Avenue.

New library branches in recreation centres work well today. But in the 1980s the relationship between fitness and books was not nearly as powerful as the relationship between buying things and borrowing books.

The decision to locate the library at the recreation centre didn't have a terribly detrimental effect on overall circulation figures for the Edmonton Public Library at the time—especially after the recession hit in late 1981. Albertans have not created many enduring mythologies about themselves but they do love a good story. We like to blame the global economic shocks of the early 1980s, which resulted in low oil prices for much of the decade, on one man: Pierre Elliott Trudeau. The National Energy Program, which lasted from 1980 until its cancellation in 1986, certainly didn't help matters. I was a kid at the time and I remember the delight in spelling out "PETRO Canada as Pierre Elliott Trudeau Rips Off Canada."

No matter who was responsible for the recession, there was a recession—a vicious one in an economy that ran on oil. Inevitably, the high point of Alberta cultural investment ended up being just that. Edmonton Public Library Director Vince Richards, and everyone else in the sector, was soon climbing down.

Top: The children's area of the original Mill Woods Branch. [EPL] *Bottom: The Mill Woods Branch at the Mill Woods Recreation Centre.* [EPL]

The Strathcona Branch was nearly demolished several times. This is what it looked like in the 1980s. [EPL]

Still, he had a lot to boast about. "Traditionally, heavy demand is placed on libraries in times of economic hardship," Richards wrote, in the 1982 annual report.[2] As we saw during the Depression of the 1930s, this isn't always true. But it was certainly true in the 1980s, especially after the city annexed enough land to double the geographical size of the city and increase the population by 9,000. The Centennial Library, in this era, was the single busiest library building in North America.[3] Edmontonians borrowed massively, setting a system-wide record in 1982 of 5,362,614 circulated items for a population of just over half a million. Records continued until 1984, when the city topped 7.5 million in circulated items.

"The panic and depression of 1912 gripped Edmonton in 1913," Richards wrote, about global economics, a growing city, and the library. "Downtown Edmonton was dying following an annexation of over fifteen square miles outside of the united Edmonton-Strathcona. This pattern seemed to be repeated in 1983, even in the Library.... Nonetheless the Centennial Library remained the busiest single library building in North America, with a circulation of 2.6 million."[4]

Of course, the trouble with all of this was that Richards, as library director, was the leading advocate for more funding from the municipal and provincial governments. If the library were successful despite severe budget cuts, what was the substance of his argument for operational increases? The abstract pitch, that libraries were brilliant educational institutions that transformed the city, meeting places, keepers of mythology...it didn't work so well if city council or the provincial treasurer simply shrugged and said, "Yes, we agree, keep those circulation numbers climbing!"

There is little to remember of financial success in the early 1980s, in the library system or anywhere else. The Oilers helped the city through those years, winning multiple Stanley Cups and building a sense of pride in Edmonton that would prove to be splendid, superficial, and unsustainable.

Some other pieces of more enduring civic pride were saved. After years of arguments that look charmingly absurd from 2013, the City of Edmonton and the Alberta government committed to enhancing one of its architectural successes: that dark little Strathcona Branch on Calgary Trail. The branch reopened in 1985 as a protected heritage building.

Almost every spare dollar, in the 1980s, went to upgrading every system in the library. Computers were no longer a clever time-saving tool. They were essential, making the difference between a dying library, a functioning library, and a thriving library. Despite the financial challenges, and pesky new systems coming out every few months, the Edmonton Public Library was able to stay near or close to the top of automation in North America.

But like the municipal and provincial governments themselves, the library decided it could not rely on the direct and indirect effects of oil prices on the economy and government revenue.

Back to the mall: the Mill Woods Branch in Mill Woods Town Centre, 1988. [EPL]

33

Public libraries are going to die

THE BOARD OF THE EDMONTON PUBLIC LIBRARY, growing weary of fluctuating public fortunes, launched an endowment fund so corporations and citizens could contribute. When the provincial grant actually declined, in 1987, this strategy transformed from a lovely idea to an emergency. In 1988 the library would be seventy-five years old, and closing down two branches, laying off staff, and decreasing services to the public didn't seem a correct way to celebrate.

Edmonton's capital development program helped with funds to renovate the Jasper Place Branch. The book sale brought in some money and a few foundations helped out with program grants. Late fines increased. Friends of the Sprucewood Library, in the Norwood and Alberta Avenue neighbourhoods, rallied to keep their library open and wrote stinging letters to the *Edmonton Journal* about Premier Don Getty's government.

The letters worked as well as they ever do, and the celebrations started anyway. With 314,000 cardholders, more than half the population of the city, and the busiest main library in North America, there was plenty to cheer. In March 1988, the party started with a homecoming tea for current and past employees and board members. A magical mystery tour in May was a public party with celebrity guests and an exotic, storybook adventure featuring ethnic foods. A special anniversary library card went out to 35,000 people who registered as members and the library launched its first Writer in Residence program, welcoming prolific children's author Monica Hughes. Edmontonians weren't ready for a library in a recreation centre; the library moved into Mill Woods Town Centre, a shopping mall down the street. Soviet poets and novelists arrived in the city as part of a cultural exchange called "East West Passage," which may or may not have contributed to glasnost and perestroika all around. Another idea, at the time, was to create a comprehensive and easy-to-access "image bank" that would document every aspect of the library system since its inception in 1913. This way, whoever compiled material for a centennial book, for example, in 2013, would have an easy time of it. Would that it had happened.

Vince Richards, director for eleven years and overseer of a dramatic technological revolution in the system, sat back and predicted the future for an *Edmonton Journal* arts reporter. Edmontonians should expect books in more languages as more people from around the world move to the city.

"Don't, however, anticipate the library will start stocking and lending CDs (compact discs)," wrote James Adams, now an arts reporter with the *Globe and Mail*. "It's sitting tight on the matter right now; although the demise of the LP seems imminent, Richards believes CDs, themselves, will soon be superseded by DAT (digital audio tape) just as videocassettes superseded videodiscs. Ironically, the library made a heavy investment in videodiscs in the early 80s and now has a collection of 8,000!"[1]

Nearing the end of his time as director, Richards was not afraid to provide a few statistics to the reporter: a bit of public shame for the library's anniversary year.

"Last year, for instance, the province reduced its assistance to libraries by $300,000, while in terms of per capita expenditure, Edmonton aldermen have allocated 'only' $18.48—a statistic that puts Canada's fifth-largest city 24th among the country's 32 major libraries."[2]

Keith Turnbull, a local man who had worked for Edmonton Public Library before taking off for Saskatchewan, was lured back to Edmonton in the anniversary year. He became the head of the main branch, and a liaison between the head office and the thirteen community branches. His title, in those days, was deputy director of public services.

"It was a tough time for libraries, the eighties and nineties," he says. "People were always saying, 'Public libraries are going to die.' We'd hear it from politicians and bureaucrats, the people we had to rely on, 'You don't need a library! You can put a whole library on a disc. Who needs books?'"[3]

Turnbull remembers the system at that time as, not surprisingly, progressive and conservative at once. The library was progressive with technology. Maybe, in matters like videodiscs, it was too progressive. Yet the system was not embracing the changing role of libraries in our communities. Not enough, anyway.

"A lot of the people who were there had been there a long time," he says. "You can't blame them. And it was discouraging."[4]

The shelves needed replacing. So did the floors, carpets, roofs, ceilings and lights. But there was little money to do it. The budget for building maintenance was eight per cent less than it had been at the height of the recession. Municipal funding to the library had decreased thirteen per cent from 1981 to 1989. Provincial funding declined twenty-seven per cent. At the same time, use of the system increased eighty-one per cent.[5]

In the summer of 1989, after twelve years as director, Vince Richards retired.

Penny McKee arrived from Ontario to take over as director of the Edmonton Public Library in 1990. She brought with her a change in tone for the library in Edmonton. The Penny McKee Branch was named in her honour. [EPL]

34

Someone fabulous

THE TRUSTEES OF THE EDMONTON PUBLIC LIBRARY had two important jobs in late 1989 and early 1990: to find a new director and to find more money.

Doug Ross, the chair of board at the time, decided to take a risk. A new director would arrive at a library with a miserably low budget and an overall state summed up by Richards as "shabby." How could they recruit someone fabulous? Even worse, if they did recruit someone fabulous, would they expect this person to begin lobbying the government on day one?

They had frankly given up on the provincial government at the time, as provincial governments across the country had frozen their library budgets. Municipal funding statistics were bleak—even embarrassing. The *Edmonton Journal* launched the story.

"Ross said between 1982 and 1988 library funding from the City of Edmonton has increased by only 7.2 per cent compared to increases of 61 per cent in Calgary, 118 per cent in Winnipeg, 38 per cent in Regina and 39 per cent in Saskatoon. Across Alberta municipal funding for libraries increased by 42 per cent."[1] Edmonton was at the bottom of the list.

The strategy worked. It didn't raise Edmonton terribly far up the list but it helped a little bit, raising the budget 8.8 per cent for 1990, or an extra $360,000.[2]

Job two, the fabulous new director: Penny McKee, chief executive officer of the Peterborough Library, arrived in Edmonton in June 1990. Immediately, she set about doing precisely what leaders like Keith Turnbull had been calling for: redefining the library and preparing for its future. If funders were apt to question its relevance, McKee and the Edmonton Public Library had to set about redefining relevance.

The new vision didn't even use the word "books."

"The purpose of the Edmonton Public Library is to help the people of Edmonton meet the challenges of the future by providing the widest access to the collective knowledge and culture of the world. The Edmonton Public Library will achieve this by collecting and organizing resources, by cooperating with other institutions and community groups, and through the aggressive use of technology."[3]

McKee was a bright, and bright-faced, manager. It's difficult to find a photograph of her in the informal Edmonton Public Library "image bank" where she isn't smiling. Before her four years as CEO in Peterborough, she had been chief librarian in Aurora and a branch head in Toronto. She had served as president of the Ontario Library Association and arrived in Edmonton with an air of fate about her. In a small library in Lakefield, Ontario, she had bought a raffle ticket to support the place and won a painting of Wayne Gretzky.

An original, in oils.

"I guess that was the sign that I'd be coming to this city," she told *Ministream* magazine, a couple of months after her arrival. Her plan was to hang The Great One in her office, as a bit of a good luck charm in the fundraising game before her.[4]

The library appointed a director of development, a full-time fundraiser to increase the annual budget of $16 million. McKee's initial attempts at lobbying the municipal government were not terribly successful. Reluctantly, she retired the bookmobile—a continental movement that started in Edmonton in 1941 with the streetcar library—when city council decided it wasn't worth a seven per cent budget increase to keep the service running.

"You know, that's the first memory that pops into my mind, when I think about the library," says Bill Smith, Edmonton's mayor from 1995 to 2004. "That old bookmobile rumbling through the neighbourhood. It was a diesel bus and blew this terrible black, smelly smoke everywhere. But you knew it was coming and you wanted to get in there. It got a lot of us kids hooked on books at an early age."[5]

The failure to secure more money from city council did, however, inspire some creativity. In December 1990, Alderman Ken Kozak suggested that if McKee and the library were in such a terrible financial position they ought to start charging user fees: say, 25 cents per item.

"Free to All" had been the slogan carved over the front door of the Edmonton Public Library. Within a year of arriving in the city, McKee had to defend a sacred principle. The argument, once it started, was difficult to stop. Certain aldermen wanted a better answer than "it's always been this way" or "it wouldn't be right."

Doug Main, Alberta's culture minister at the time, even threatened to pull back funding as long as libraries bought books simply for entertainment and recreation purposes, such as soft cover romance novels.

McKee read the Alberta government's own vision statement back to it: that libraries "provide culture, recreation, research opportunities and a bridge between the people of the community and the resources of that community and beyond." She wondered aloud about Minister Main's ability to discern between information and entertainment.

"Who's to judge what is entertainment to one and intellectual stimulation to another?" McKee said to the *Edmonton Journal*. "Shakespeare was popular in his day, and if he was living today he'd probably be one of those authors not acceptable to Doug Main."[6]

The 25-cent suggestion would not go away quite so easily. Petitions went up in the main branch and in other branches across the city, opposing Kozak's suggestion. Kozak demanded they come down. When he asked who had drafted the petition, McKee said she had done it when a patron had called in and suggested it. *Journal* columnist John Geiger described the city councillor's fury:

"What's more, Kozak said, the drive for signatures was helped by library staff who, 'in the absence of a neon sign' were encouraging patrons to 'at least head in that direction.' For McKee to go and actually promote a petition 'in total opposition to what I was doing I found somewhat offensive, in bad taste, and possibly over exerting one's authority as an administrator.'"[7]

All of this may have been true but it made McKee an extremely popular boss in an extremely short time, a courageous defender of readers' interests above all else. She was a new sort of manager, an activist and a director and a colleague at once.

The circulation manager during the McKee years said she was also a tough leader—demanding a lot. "She changed our culture in that we [became] a much more forward-thinking and positive organization," Val Solash told the *Edmonton Journal*. "I had sixty staff. She knew all of their names inside of the first two weeks that she was here. She was the kind of leader who stopped and talked to the kids who were putting books on the shelves."[8]

The Kozak and Main episodes revealed that McKee's ambitions, to expand the library system and make sure it kept up with technological innovations, were impossible to achieve without more money. Not annual book sale money but real, sustainable money.

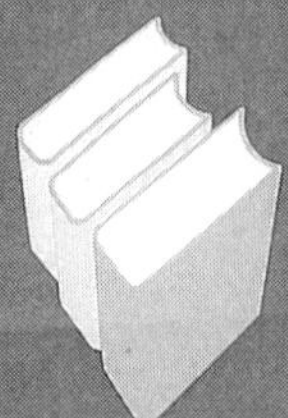

The Penny McKee Branch of the Edmonton Public Library was in the Abbottsfield Mall in the city's northeast. [EPL]

35

Free to all

IN 1993, Edmonton was the last city in the province without a user fee in its libraries. It had given up the practice in 1972, when patrons paid $2 per year for the right to borrow. The problem with Kozak's 25-cent suggestion was that it added up. Not everyone, and certainly not poor users, carried money. The beauty of a library, as an agent of change, is that it works for everyone, rich or poor. As he often noted, Carnegie would not have become Carnegie if he had not been invited into a free library at a crucial moment in his education.

The mayor in the early 1990s, Jan Reimer, confided in director Penny McKee and then stated publicly that it was unlikely the library would receive the sort of increase it needed, at least from city council. Ralph Klein, the new premier, was certainly not voted in on a "spend more public money on cultural institutions" ticket.

To find an extra $1.4 million a year, McKee and the library board decided to roll out a user fee. Edmontonians on social assistance, or those who claimed to have a low income, could sign a declaration to exempt themselves; and children under the age of eighteen could borrow for free. Everyone else would pay a $12 annual fee.

"We know our customers very well," McKee said at the time, "and they tell us what they want. They want more services and they're willing to pay for them. Considering what you get at the library, $12 is a bargain."[1]

Not everyone liked the idea. There was some debate in city council and the *Edmonton Journal* editorial board suggested closing down a branch or two—Strathcona, again—or maybe cutting out video rentals instead.

But it was a prescient move. The Friends of the Edmonton Public Library launched in 1993 as an independent, not-for-profit group to advocate for more money or even abstract political and philanthropic support. But new money was not on its way. The Klein government tried to remove libraries from "core services" into a cultural industry portfolio, like a theatre or an arts festival. Provincial funding, from this point, would come from lottery money instead of general revenue. McKee joined the president of the Alberta Library Association at the time, Linda Cook, to denounce the changes.

The Klein Revolution was both popular and unstoppable, but the lobbying worked. Gary Mar, then the minister of community development, made a successful pitch to his colleagues to keep libraries as core services.

"Thanks to Penny, we survived the worst of the Klein years," says Keith Turnbull, deputy director of the library in the 1990s, and the one in charge of finding money. "We did a review when Gary Mar was minister, and he was certainly supportive—morally supportive. But it was hard to go any farther. The funding was relatively poor compared to other libraries in Canada. Jan Reimer and Bill Smith were both supportive, but they were unable to do much. And even though there weren't massive cuts there certainly weren't any increases, provincially."[2]

This battle to improve or even lead, in an atmosphere of stagnant revenue, defined McKee's time as director. Many of her expansion plans would not come to life until the turn of the century.

Politicians and children mingled at the opening ceremony for the Lessard Branch in 1996. [EPL]

Still, somehow, she found ways to expand. The last branch library the city had constructed was in 1982 in Mill Woods. Constructing a new branch, in the mid-1990s, seemed an impossible dream.

But in 1996, a new branch opened in the west end of the city—at the Lessard Shopping Mall at 6104 172 Street. It had long been an under served part of the city, the expanding western suburbs that now bump against Enoch Cree Nation on the far side of Anthony Henday Drive. Again, the library decided their best bet was a location in a mall—this time a strip mall. It shared space, at the time, with a Chinese restaurant and a convenience store. Today, the branch and the Chinese restaurant and the convenience store are gone. The property is now one of the largest mosques in the city, the MAC Islamic Centre, a block away from Talmud Torah, Edmonton's 101-year-old Jewish public school, and across the street from a Ukrainian Orthodox church.

The best route to the former Lessard Branch is on foot, through the river valley and up a steep set of stairs into the neighbourhood of Wolf

Willow. The houses are large in Wolf Willow, many of them mansions. You pass the orthodox Beth Israel synagogue and turn left on 170 Street, past a strip mall with a Starbucks, a Sorrentino's Restaurant, a Husky gas station, and a bright kosher food store that bounces with Israeli pop music. Walk south along the sidewalk and turn right at the end of the street.

Today, a food store and deli is the entry point to what was once the home of the Lessard Branch. Some of the best Lebanese sandwiches in the city are made in this building but the new west-end branch—the Lois Hole Library—is several blocks north of here, in a stunning location that Penny McKee could not have imagined in her era of financial restraint.

Stanley Milner, one of the greatest champions in the history of the Edmonton Public Library, took McKee and the board up on an offer in 1996. The library he helped build had been called the Main Branch, the Downtown Branch, and the Centennial Library but none of these names were definitive. In a hunt for funds, McKee and the board researched other library systems in North America and hit upon naming rights. The practice had been standard behaviour for years in sports facilities and entertainment complexes—see the Winspear Centre on the corner—but it was relatively new to libraries.

The eventual decision to name the downtown branch after Stanley Milner was about far more than a cheque for $250,000. The oil executive was just as well known, in the community, for his philanthropy. The tales of his fights with Hawrelak were legendary, and the library was one of their battlefields. He grew up with libraries and, as his success in business grew, he chose the library as one of his beneficiaries. If not for Milner, the pretty old Carnegie Library on Macdonald Drive would have been torn down for the sake of progress and it would have been replaced by a 1960s version of the room above a liquor store, where the downtown branch began.

Today, a few variations remain but most Edmontonians call it the "Stanley Milner Branch" or the "Milner Library," one of the two. My kids just call it "the Stanley Milner."

Milner wrote the first cheque and headed up the committee to find $1.5 million to build three new branches. Despite supporters on city council like Michael Phair and Brian Mason, municipal funding of the Edmonton Public Library had dropped about $700,000 in two years. The population of the city had grown fifteen per cent since the Mill Woods Branch opened, and library use in the city had grown forty-four per cent. McKee said, in 1996, that the fourth busiest library system in Canada ran on twenty to thirty per cent less money than any other system of similar size.[3]

Enough money came in to build one branch, maybe two, beginning with a new Woodcroft Branch. And it came with plenty of controversy, as residents argued with the library board and city council about whether or not to relocate from the Westmount Mall area to the Edmonton Space and Science Centre.

It was, in short, a tough time to be the director of the Edmonton Public Library. For this reason and others, Penny McKee decided to step down. A columnist at the *Edmonton Journal* at the time, Susan Ruttan, summed up the atmosphere in November 1996:

> *Last week I went looking for a copy of Robert Graves' 1929 book,* Goodbye to All That. *I expected to find this classic in the public library, not a bookstore.*
>
> *In fact, it wasn't in the downtown library (a branch library has a copy). It was in Audrey's Books.*
>
> *Maybe Edmonton has great bookstores because it has a threadbare public library. Which is fine for those with money to buy books; those who don't have it need a good library.*
>
> *To give you a picture of how we rate, the City of Edmonton ranks 30th out of 35 among Canadian cities in its spending on public libraries. In money spent on reading materials per capita, Edmonton Public Library ranks 28th out of 36 cities. That ranking is unlikely to improve, since the freeze in the library's 1997 grant proposed in the draft city budget will mean a new cut in books and magazines bought.*

A sunny day in Abbottsfield. [EPL]

Edmonton's public library is relatively well-used—it ranks 13th in books circulating per capita—but it's 27th in average salary and benefits.

We are in a time when grand old institutions are being battered. The public library, one of the grandest, is not immune.

Edmonton's public library system has had it rougher than most. Being in a less-than-rich city and a penny-pinching province, it's had cuts in city grants and an unending freeze in provincial grants. Meanwhile, the cost of books and magazines goes up and up.

Think of what a public library is. It's a place where anyone—six-year-old child, immigrant, homeless person—can learn about thousands of things, for free. The creation of public libraries in the last century meant knowledge ceased to be a privilege of the higher-ups and became a right of every citizen.

Now, bit by bit, it's being chipped away.

Edmonton's public library was never one of the fat cats, even before the 1990s cutbacks hit.

Penny McKee, the outgoing director of the library, thinks that gives us an advantage. Edmonton Public Library has long experience with doing with less, she argues, so it's handled the budget cuts of recent years with greater ease than some more used to big budgets.

I'm not so sure. As a relative newcomer to Edmonton I'm shocked by the $12 annual membership fee being charged.

That's a whopping amount, twice the fee in Calgary. And frankly, any fee is objectionable. Reading and learning are a public good, not something which should be taxed.[4]

The future was looking miserable for the Edmonton Public Library, and everyone seemed to be admitting it. Policy-makers, dizzy with excitement over information technology and the Internet, publicly questioned the relevance of the institution—and not only in Edmonton.

Keith Turnbull still builds up an uncommon growl in his voice when he remembers making the counter-argument, on an almost daily basis, to someone declaring the impending death of the library.

"It's not dying! It's a living, breathing entity and it's always changing. It's one of the last public spaces we have left. It's not a mall. Go to the Milner library at lunch and you'll see a lawyer next to a homeless person. It's a commons."[5]

Penny McKee, the leader who had encouraged a feisty culture in the Edmonton Public Library, retired at the end of 1996. Six years earlier, McKee had survived a bout of breast cancer. When the cancer returned, shortly after her retirement, it was a devastating blow to her friends and colleagues in the library system. She died in the palliative care ward of the Grey Nun's Hospital in May 1997.

"She really was a woman of vision in terms of library service for Edmonton," Jim Campbell, chair of the library board, said at the time. "She was very strong, very forceful in doing the right thing for the library."[6] The second branch she helped to build, in the expanding community of Abbottsfield opened in September 1997 with her name on it: the Penny McKee Branch of the Edmonton Public Library.

McKee's successor was a friend and collaborator, and just as feisty.

Linda Cook, the CEO *of the Edmonton Public Library, grew up on the south side of the city—borrowing books from the bookmobile.* [EPL]

36

The girl from Bonnie Doon

AT ABOUT THE TIME Linda Cook was graduating from high school, in Edmonton's Bonnie Doon neighbourhood, she won a short story contest. It was prestigious enough that the newspaper covered it. Cook remembers the headline in the *Edmonton Journal*: "Girl wins fiction prize."[1]

She wasn't one of those young people who travel the world aimlessly after graduation, trying to figure out what to do with her life. She entered the University of Alberta for a BA in English literature. From there she took a library science degree and entered the workforce as a librarian: first at the Misericordia Hospital library and then with the Government of Alberta.

Librarians in the 1970s were moving out of the traditional library and into government and the corporate world. It was a fascinating time to come of age as a librarian, as institutions—Cook remembers—"were beginning to realize how important it was to have somebody who knew how to process and dispense information."[2]

She moved out of government to lead the library system for the Yellowhead region, and studied for her master's degree. She had worked with Penny McKee and other librarian-administrators in the province, to build a united voice for more government funding and to seek more modern solutions to the old funding problem.

Ask anyone who knows Cook and you hear the same thing: she is and has always been a diplomat in the Canadian tradition, a practitioner of "soft power."

In her introductory interview with the *Edmonton Journal*, after taking the leadership job at EPL in January 1997, Cook said, "I don't have [children], so I was never juggling that type of thing, and I was really able to concentrate on my career."[3]

Her career, since that interview, has been astonishing.

While the Edmonton Public Library could look back and talk about innovations and moments of leadership and success—the streetcar library, technological innovation, heavy circulation in otherwise troubling years—the system was in miserable shape in 1997. McKee had done a marvellous job, setting up a plan and a vision for the future, but it was difficult then for anyone to imagine that any of these plans could make it out of the realm of fairy tale. The system had grown, modestly, even as funding levels had fallen. If the Edmonton Public Library had an advantage in 1997, as McKee had noted in her interview with Susan Ruttan, it was in its culture of doing more with less—hardly something to brag about.

Cook had already heard, by 1997, that the Internet was going to make libraries irrelevant. She didn't agree. Early on, she hinted at what she saw public libraries becoming in the next fifteen years.

"They are such a viable part of the community, and not just because of the entertainment value and going to the library with your children. I think they are viable economically as well. So many people say: how can they compare to the fire department or to the police department? But if you really look at it and you have a public library and people have access to it, the trite expression is that it's the university of the people. Anybody can use it. I think it provides people with a place they can go and learn about anything they want to. I think it keeps people off the streets; kids, they have a place they can go."[4]

Keith Turnbull remembers the late 1990s, the time of Cook's arrival, as turbulent and hopeful at once.

"Linda came in at a time of radical change," he says. "We really needed someone to consolidate things. Linda wanted to know what was really going on, as soon as she arrived. She didn't want me to be a yes man. Well, that's hard for me anyway."[5]

It had been some time since Cook had acted, on a day-by-day basis, as a librarian. So she taught at the University of Alberta and at Grant MacEwan Community College to "keep herself grounded," to stay in touch with up-and-coming librarians and the latest thinking. A librarian who grew up with Cook, Pat Cavill, who now lives in Calgary, speaks frankly about her.

"Well, just look at the library when she came in," says Cavill, whose father—an immigrant from England—dropped out of school when he was twelve and educated himself in the Idylwylde Branch of the Edmonton Public Library. "It wasn't in the best shape, financially. But Linda is so smart: smart about funding, smart about politics, a smart manager. She basically turned it into the best library system in the country. It has to be! Ask anyone! She's such a good leader, and humble. Of course, it doesn't hurt that she's a beautiful woman."[6]

Despite all of her talents, little of the Edmonton Public Library's twenty-first century successes seemed possible in early 1997—when most of us had to agree that the library was "threadbare."

The Riverbend Branch of the Edmonton Public Library was a $3-million project. A third of the money came from donations. At the grand opening in 2000. [EPL]

What is the opposite of threadbare?

IN 2000, Cook celebrated her first major success: the Riverbend Branch of the Edmonton Public Library. Of the $3 million raised for the project, an unprecedented and fairly astonishing $500,000 came from the public—from fundraising outside of government sources.

The library opened in May, with an air of hopefulness. Michael Phair was an eloquent supporter on city council, and Mayor Bill Smith was moved by public support for the library whenever budget cuts were coming down, but Cook hadn't yet made any breakthroughs with the city. By the time the Riverbend Branch opened, Edmonton still ranked 31 out of 35 major public libraries in Canada in support from the municipal government.

"That's been a bit of an issue in the last few elections," City Councillor Larry Langley admitted, at the opening of the library. "But the fact remains that there are only a few dollars to go around."[1]

After fourteen stagnant years the three newest branches, in Lessard, in Abbottsfield in the northeast, and now in Riverbend in the southwest, extended the reach of the Edmonton Public Library into the ever-expanding

The Riverbend Branch in the centenary year. [EPL]

The grand opening of the Riverbend Branch wasn't just about books. [EPL]

city. More and more Edmontonians were buying new houses, not yet built, in new neighbourhoods. While schools and other public institutions were difficult to manage, as these communities went up, a new sort of strip mall arrived with them. The new branch was tucked into Riverbend Square, indistinguishable at first from the commercial buildings—a sushi restaurant, a lingerie boutique, cafés, Booster Juice, Safeway and some banks. Its immediate neighbour was Blockbuster Video; at a time when politicians were predicting the demise of the public library, no one foresaw the end of the video store. I walked to the Riverbend Branch inefficiently, by way of the High Level Bridge and across the University of Alberta campus, down into Hawrelak Park, over a footbridge and the Quesnell Bridge, and down into the Whitemud Ravine. There are many transitions, from city to forest to park and city and forest, ending in a neighbourhood built for cars. With all of the generous cul de sacs, I found myself lost several times. Reaching the library was glorious—as it should be. On a late weekday afternoon it was busy and pleasant inside, somehow quiet and loud at once.

Riverbend is a wealthy subdivision. Much of what Cook discussed, when she took the job in early 1997, was about community. In Riverbend, we define community much differently than we do on Sir Winston Churchill Square, where Cook's office is on the third floor.

Part of Cook's success, as an administrator and as a community leader, is that she perfectly understands the culture of the city. She grew up here. She knows that, based on the context, she will shake someone's hand one day, hug her the next day, and address her formally on the third day. Edmonton is strange.

In 2001, Cook went quietly public with a plea for libraries. The last major cut to libraries from the provincial government was in 1994, the same year Edmonton Public Library introduced its $12 annual fee. Since that time, the average price of books had gone up significantly—twenty-seven per cent just since 1999. As much as the library tried to put a happy face on the annual fee, memberships had declined since its introduction.

Anyone who asked for a free membership received it, but that almost never happened.

"People are proud," Cook told *Edmonton Journal* columnist Ron Chalmers. Some people who might have borrowed in the past, with a library card, only looked at material in the branches. When the Banff Public Library did away with their fees, membership jumped forty per cent.

"Edmonton could eliminate fees," Chalmers wrote in February 2001, "update its collection, increase programming and expand its hours—if the provincial government would budget just $12 million to double its library funding across Alberta."[2]

At the time, the government of Premier Ralph Klein was working toward retiring the debt. Not the infrastructure debt but the dollars-and-cents debt. The phrase "just $12 million" might have inspired some chuckling around the table at the next cabinet meeting. The beauty of Cook's strategy, in 2001, was that a *Journal* columnist asked for the money on behalf of the community—not Linda Cook.

Things started to improve, but not quickly. Cook convinced the city to slowly increase its budget from the tax levy, if only according to inflation. Still, by city budget season in 2002, the Edmonton Public Library was looking at shutting down one of the branches. The city manager had proposed an increase of 4.1 per cent for 2003.

It wasn't enough. The library board debated the issue and made an announcement. With a four per cent increase, a branch would have to close: Sprucewood, Abbottsfield, Calder or Strathcona. Leaders in those communities mobilized. "I remember vividly what happened anytime we talked about cutting funding or closing a branch," says Bill Smith, who was mayor at the time. "You just couldn't do it. Not when Linda was in charge."[3]

Cook made her arguments. City council, presented with the option of putting a bit more money in the pot or closing a branch, added $224,000 to the 2003 library budget.

"We looked at everything," Cook said at the time, utterly relieved. "We looked at raising membership fees. We looked at reducing library materials, closing for a small period of time, but the problem is we need to make the work go away. When you close for a day or a couple of days, (people) just come back in droves on the day that you're open."[4]

Her pitch, the plea she had made, resonated with council. Keith Turnbull, who worked with her then, said Cook began to succeed in this realm beyond anyone's imagining. "She really excels in dealing with political bodies, particularly with city council. She's great at understanding and explaining what the library does for the community. It's hard to say no to her!"[5]

A few months later, it happened again. The provincial government increased its library funding by almost a million dollars, bringing the level back to where it had been in 1993—before the cuts.

"If you're feeling curmudgeonly, you could point out that in real, adjusted-for-inflation dollars, libraries are still farther behind than they were a decade ago," wrote Paula Simons, who had become city columnist at the *Journal*. "But Linda Cook, Edmonton's director of libraries, isn't feeling churlish. Delighted would be closer to it...she and her board are still figuring out where the money will go."

"'This is good news, and quite frankly we weren't expecting it,' [Cook] says. 'We've been lobbying for 10 years for an increase in the provincial library grant. We're very pleased the government is going in the right direction now.'"[6]

Simons, who has charted the city's growth and ambitions in the *Edmonton Journal* in the last ten years, had noted the fragrance of change in the air. Edmonton was still below the other major Canadian cities in library funding, but not for long. The notion that library spending, cultural spending, was at the bottom of a list of other more important priorities was beginning to crumble. There would be another increase for the library in the 2005 budget, under a new mayor—Stephen Mandel.

When Mandel was elected in October 2004, he assigned portfolios to the councillors—areas of specialization. One was missing: culture. Arts leader Fil Fraser was horrified that Mandel, who had spoken of culture during his campaign, had forgotten to include it. I was a journalist at the time, and I walked over to city hall to ask Mayor Mandel about arts and culture, and Fraser's exasperated letter to the editor. How could he have forgotten culture?

"Forgotten it?" he said. "I kept that one for myself."[7]

Mayor Stephen Mandel took office in 2004 and immediately began agitating for a stronger library system in Edmonton. [EPL]

The mayor who changed everything

STEPHEN MANDEL, who grew up in Windsor, Ontario, doesn't pretend he was the world's biggest reader as a kid. He was a maniac for sports. But his mother was a reader, and instilled in him a deep respect for literature and for the arts. He met his future wife, Lynn Mandel, a former professional dancer, at the University of Windsor in the early 1970s. When they moved to Edmonton she taught dance at Grant MacEwan Community College for ten years. Her husband was a developer but she never let him stray terribly far from her world—from those lessons he had learned from his mother—and the sports maniac and entrepreneur would become a determined political champion for arts and culture in Edmonton.

When you talk to people close to the Edmonton Public Library, or almost any other cultural institution in the city, they tend to use a variation of the phrase, "Mandel changed everything." Of course, he didn't work alone. Edmontonians were ready for this change, for a conversation about potholes *and* culture.

"I'll admit it, when I came into office I was quite a bit more conservative about all this stuff," Mandel says. "And I remain conservative. But supporting arts and culture, supporting libraries, it's never a waste of resources. It makes us money: we're a more attractive city, a destination for investment and for people. And the library: we're bringing in people from around the world every day. It makes our city great. The library is the place where they can learn what we're all about, where they can become Canadians and Edmontonians."[1]

Of course, even with a supportive mayor and city council, if the library doesn't have an eloquent and passionate spokesperson any increases would be unjustifiable.

"Here's the thing," says Mandel. "When Linda comes in, we say: hide your wallets! She is so good at making the case for the library, and she's done such a great job there. It really is a source of pride for the city."[2]

The front of the Stanley A. Milner Branch of the Edmonton Public Library at night. [EPL]

How to be an Edmontonian

IN THE SUMMER OF 2009 my family moved to France for a year. A year is just long enough to begin feeling like an immigrant instead of a tourist. There are rules and customs to learn. There is paperwork. My wife and I had grown up in a country of newcomers with very little understanding what the experience was like. We could have isolated ourselves in France, or spent time with British and American ex-pats, but we decided instead to live like immigrants. We have two daughters, and they were three and one at the time. In France, school starts at two. Avia, our oldest daughter, was obliged to go to school.

It took her a month and a half to learn French, to develop friendships. While we had spent time at the library in Edmonton, both our local Strathcona Branch and at Stanley Milner downtown, it was nearly always to find books. In France, we understood what a library does—or can do. It was different from a high street or a market or a café. It was different from a museum.

The library, in our French city, was a magnet for *les étrangers*. The library was a public institution that turned foreigners into French people: it gave us the language, the resources, the activities, the cultural cues we needed to feel at home in a new city, a new country. Best of all, it was the only place in Douarnenez where I could ask someone an elemental question about French life without feeling stupid.

Librarians, in France and in Edmonton, long to help people change their lives in some way. Carnegie was right.

Mayor Stephen Mandel goes back to this as the library's most important mission—a cultural gateway. Assimilation isn't the right word. It's more an invitation. The Edmonton Public Library is the best place in the city to learn how to be an Edmontonian.

The 2004 municipal election coincided with a global building and renovation boom, for libraries. It seems strange, considering the number of people who had been questioning their relevance since the early 1990s that architectural marvels are going up all over the world with the word "library" on their signs. Inside and out, few of these buildings resemble what Antonio Panizzi had in mind in 1836 when he spoke of the "emphatically British library." Books are only part of the equation. With nearly every one of these projects, certainly the successful ones, it seems cities and countries are building public institutions that sum up or represent their culture.

The little Library and Culture House in Vennesla, Norway, population 12,000, looks and feels like its land and history, the character of its people. The new central branch of the Vancouver Public Library feels like Vancouver's modern aspirations and its glassy, royal sense of self. Its sister city, Seattle, attempts something similar—with a more playful design. The Royal Danish Library in Copenhagen, another city of rain and water, tilts and undulates. The Stuttgart City Library is clean and cool, a representation of a modern German man or woman. The National Library in Belarus comes closest to Edmonton's northern spirit. Four young people in Villaneuva, Colombia, all in their twenties, won a competition to design a small city library by using local wood and stones. The building sings of its place.

The New York Public Library, which is the image that comes to mind when we think of iconic North American libraries, with its lions out front, is one of the best representations of that city and its ambitions. Today it feels like a museum, with gallery space on the main floor and a constant flow of tourists with cameras. It's not nearly the most beautiful space in a city crammed with them, but if feels like a mini-version of the city—its past and its present and its future. Bryant Park, behind the library, is a leafy sanctuary from the metropolis—a giant outdoor reading room. There is a curated space in Bryant Park, operated by the library, to sit and take a coffee, to browse from a selection of newspapers, magazines, and books. In the 1970s Bryant Park was one of the darkest, dingiest, and most dangerous corners of the city. Today it's an extension of the library—of library-ness. It is open, calm, civilized, yet still essentially New York.

Whatever a library is, today, it is of its place. It cannot be duplicated.

Still, we wonder why. Why go to all the trouble if books—and therefore libraries—are doomed?

Because they aren't doomed.

"The mayor and council understand this is a way to build the city," says Linda Cook, in her office at the Stanley Milner Branch. "That said, we can't rely on traditional arguments, on what's been done in the past, to support the work we're doing today and in the future."

Since Cook took over the leadership of the Edmonton Public Library, its annual budget has more than doubled—less than $20 million to more than $50 million per year. From her first day on the job, she says her focus has been on customer service. That's the quasi-literary trick of empathy: figuring out the customers and what they want. Giving them what they want before they know they want it.

I have spoken to hundreds of people about the library, putting this book together. We all come to life when someone asks, "What is the role of the library in the age of the Internet?" Almost no one, today, several years into the Internet age, thinks it's an irrelevant institution.

What Linda Cook and her staff have been doing, since 1997, is redefining customer service as community service. Access to books changed Andrew Carnegie's life. Books remain one of our culture's most essential and enduring resources, but if they aren't central to the lives of most Edmontonians, we have to be honest and adapt. If we set aside nostalgia, how can the modern library continue to change lives?

The outgoing chair of the Edmonton Public Library board of trustees says community service is flexible. Every branch serves its community differently.

"We have been, in the last ten years at least, cutting-edge in Canada," says Brent McDonough. "One example is RFID [radio frequency identification]. The self check-out. It's freed up our staff, who would otherwise check out books, to spend time with our customers."

Today, when you walk into the Stanley Milner Branch, at least one librarian stands in the central hall on the main floor. It is usually a woman and she is always smiling.

"Can I help you?" she says.

And you are tempted to tell her yes. You are worried about the economy, about your company, your children and the progress of their education, about the environment, the architectural possibilities for this building, about your new novel's prospects, about growing old. She would, with scant hesitation, direct you to the correct reference material—in book or online form—to answer or at least help you explore the question.

Cook remembers the day she presented the idea of RFID to city council. It would require a $6 million investment, half from the City of Edmonton and half from the Government of Alberta. Someone had to commit first. She had made her presentation and it looked like the councillors were unconvinced by this community service idea. What would librarians do, if they weren't checking books in and out? Councillors finished their debate and Cook walked across the square to her office. It was evening by now, dark outside. She continued to listen to the debate by radio even as she put on her coat and turned off the light. And then one of the councillors sighed and said, "Can we have one last look at the library proposal?"[1]

The idea bloomed.

I've told the story of how Jared Tkachuk, an outreach worker in the library, helps the homeless Edmontonians who congregate in the building. He isn't alone. Colin Inglis is a retired teacher in Edmonton, roaming downtown to help homeless people off the street. I see him nearly every day in the library, helping someone get identification or just listening.

"Library experts from across the world are watching what we are doing," says Councillor Don Iveson, who has served on the board of trustees, in our conversation at the Sugarbowl café. "It's absolutely something we should be proud of."[2]

There isn't another public space in the city quite like the library. We have city hall, and community leagues, but they're simply spaces. No one stops you with a smile and asks how they can help. The community-led services philosophy pioneered at the Edmonton Public Library operates inside and outside the walls of the branches; more and more of the librarians aren't in the library at all. As for the building itself, what it is today is not necessarily what it will be tomorrow. McDonough calls it "thinkering," allowing the Edmonton Public Library to experiment with its role in the lives of citizens.

"It's a community hub that reinvents itself all the time, and it's active, adaptable," says Iveson. "At three in the afternoon it can be a place for the Cambodian community coming in to do a workshop on financial literacy—led by a reference librarian who's an expert in that. Then at four a group can come in to reconnect with their Cree language roots. It's versatile, an open space, and it's often a partnership."[3]

Both McDonough and Iveson talk about growing up in Edmonton and the role of the library in their early lives. McDonough remembers the futuristic chairs of the Stanley Milner Branch, when it first opened,

The grand opening of the jolly children's library at the Stanley A. Milner Branch on Sir Winston Churchill Square. [EPL]

and the smell of the bookmobile when it came through his neighbourhood. Iveson's local library was the Southgate Branch, when it was still in the mall's basement. They would go as a family, and not just to take out books. It was a once-a-week destination.

"I took out the space shuttle operator's manual thirty or forty times," he says. "I thought I would be an astronaut. And today, my son goes to Milner once a week, for the programming. Then he stays for the books and the literacy games on the computer. He never wants to leave."

Some of us are counted more than once, of course, but there were fourteen million total visits to the Edmonton Public Library in 2011. With a metro population of one million, it's a clear sign of the library's continued—if evolving—relevance.

"I was enormously lucky," says Iveson. "My parents valued books and education, literacy. That isn't the case for everyone. One in six children in Edmonton grows up in poverty. Where literacy fits into the equation, for some of these families, I don't know. Think about early literacy, pre-kindergarten. There's almost no judgment in libraries and I can imagine any kind of Edmontonian having the same kinds of experiences I had as a kid. Where there is no encouragement at home, or worse, when there is abuse at home: the library is a refuge. An outlet, a surrogate, a safe space."[4]

Iveson talks about libraries as analogous to health care: with us from birth to death. We never outgrow our need for libraries, or we shouldn't. Keeping the institution relevant, as a community service and as a repository for a shifting but authentic local culture, is always about changing lives. For Andrew Carnegie and Charles Dickens and Thomas Hardy, whose novel *Jude the Obscure* is about a working-class boy who longs to be a scholar, the library transported them from one social realm to another. Today the methods may have changed but the dreams have not. Libraries are in the business of making us better people, elevating our possibilities and—through literature—our spirits.

The Edmonton Public Library launches Edmontonians.

A statue of Lois Hole, reader and gardener and leader, in the Lois Hole Library in Callingwood. [EPL]

40

A terrible shame to lose a reader

THE STRATHCONA BRANCH, after surviving innumerable attempts on its life, expanded in 2006. Its gardens were restored and its upstairs auditorium became a Fringe venue, often devoted to historical plays set in Edmonton. On a summer or winter Saturday, the spirit of the place extends into the farmer's market and it is a resonant place year round, attached to McIntyre Park with its well-used gazebo and the theatre district beyond.

In 2008, the Lessard Branch closed and the lovely Lois Hole Library opened in Callingwood. It is the most aesthetically pleasing branch to be built since the Carnegie building, the most thoughtful, the most authentically Edmonton: a model for future projects. Honouring the late Alberta Lieutenant-Governor, author, and super-gardener went beyond name recognition. There is a bronze statue of Lois Hole, set into one of the benches where she liked to read. Hole was an early environmentalist and the building is fittingly LEED certified for energy efficiency.

Linda Goyette redefined the phrase "writer in residence" in 2007, bringing back the position after years of budgetary constraints, and the

Milner library exploded with workshops, readings, and outreach activities. Every Writer in Residence since then has taken the position in new, sometimes strange, and always marvellous directions. Also in 2007, Edmonton's first Writer-in-Exile, Jalal Barzanji, a former Kurdish refugee, set up an office on the third floor of the library and began working on his prison memoirs. The library launched the Alberta Readers' Choice Award, at $10,000 the richest literary prize in the province.

"I do like the idea of the library as a place to make things as well," says Cook. "Reading actively, of course, but also building things—creative and intellectual projects."

The seventeenth branch of the Edmonton Public Library, called eplGO, opened on the University of Alberta campus, in the Cameron Library, in March 2009. Ernie Ingles, the vice-provost and chief librarian of the U of A, had been collaborating on ideas and projects with Linda Cook for years. They worked on the Alberta Library together and reignited a spirit of collaboration between the Edmonton Public Library and the U of A that had begun almost a century earlier. Their relationship began in an untraditional fashion. Shortly after Ingles arrived in Edmonton, in 1990, he nearly hired Cook to lead the Rutherford Library at the university.

"I to'd and fro'd but in the end I hired someone else," he said in his book-filled office on the third floor of the historic Rutherford South. Postcards with photographs of the old Carnegie Library on Macdonald Drive were propped on his shelf. "I often say it's the best thing I ever did. EPL is the best damn library in Canada, and it all goes back to one reason: Linda. She's an effective manager, which is important, and politically she is very astute—which is even more important. People disbelieve me when I say this but Linda is quite shy. Yet she can work a room like few others I know. No institution just happens. It's leadership. It makes or breaks an organization."[1]

There is an uncommonly healthy relationship between the city and its major university in 2013, a relationship that has had its highs and

The new ambitions of the Edmonton Public Library, architectural and spiritual, launched with the opening of the Lois Hole Library in 2008. [EPL]

Inside eplGO on the University of Alberta campus. [EPL]

lows in the past. Ingles hopes it transcends the personalities of its current leaders: mayors and presidents, chief librarians and CEOs.

We talk on a rainy and windy fall day on the administrative level of the School of Library and Information Studies, an Edmonton institution because Morton Coburn and Bruce Peel had plotted together to make it happen here instead of Calgary or Winnipeg or Saskatoon. Ingles retired in 2013, the centennial year of the Edmonton Public Library. He will continue working, in some adventurous fashion, but he's looking forward to reading—a lot. He grew up in rural Manitoba, near the Saskatchewan border, borrowing books from the Women's Institute collection in tiny Roblin. His success in Edmonton has come from studying and adopting the school's and the city's cultures, he says, "bleeding green and gold." This came naturally to Cook, he says, because she is "of the city. Her roots are in Bonnie Doon. She grew up with Edmonton and the city grew up with her. You can't fake that. It comes across in your character and it comes out in the decisions you make."[2]

Ingles and Cook didn't borrow the model for eplGO, a physical collaboration between a university and its city's public library system, from any other place. It felt normal here, even obvious.

"This university is a small city in itself, with 12,000 staff and 40,000 students and various others on any given day," says Ingles. "The convenience of a small EPL branch makes a lot of sense, and its focus on popular books gives people a bit of a break from what they might be researching. Just as importantly, studies show we lose readers when they graduate from high school. They go off and train and start their careers and, frankly, they stop reading for pleasure until they're a bit older and they're starting families. Then they come back. Linda and I thought eplGO might be a way to bridge that gap. Once you stop something it's not always easy to start back up again. It's a terrible shame to lose a reader."[3]

As the full decade of the 2000s ended, the Edmonton Public Library began to receive national and international recognition for its community-led service philosophy.

Linda Cook is a little embarrassed by the good reviews she receives from city leaders and librarians across the country.

"There are a lot of factors in our success," she says. "We've been blessed with a supportive mayor and council, a new spirit in the city. But it all comes down to the reason a public library exists in the first place. No one does it to become rich. Library staff members have such a feeling of well-being and accomplishment when they can help someone. They want to help people live better lives. It takes a special kind of person to work in a public library and, at the moment, we have a lot of extraordinary people. That's the most important reason we've been successful."[4]

Growth and expansion, in the library system and the city, hasn't always been elegant.

The economic boom in the mid-2000s brought more people and more pressures than the city was prepared to handle. Some of the steam was released in front of the Stanley Milner Branch of the library, one of the busiest spots in downtown Edmonton. The atmosphere in front of the building is occasionally unpleasant and very occasionally scary. Either way, it has to change.

The mayor wanted to move the entrance to Centennial Plaza, on the south side of the building. Linda Cook argued publicly, light-heartedly, and passionately with him. Wouldn't that mean turning our back on Sir Winston Churchill Square?

They both agreed the building needed help, inside and out.

"We want to take this building from the poor cousin on the block to one of the family," says Cook.

Rather than tear the building down, the library and the city are looking at a renovation to replace its inefficient mechanical systems, bring in more natural light and give it a more appealing exterior. The crucial question of "those front doors," physically and imaginatively, making sure the library is as safe, as welcoming, and as beautiful as it can be will be answered this centennial year. People in Edmonton are talking about a new feeling in the city, a sense of honesty about our history, our

An architectural rendering of the new Clareview Branch of the Edmonton Public Library, set to open in 2013. [EPL]

geography, and our civic personality; all of this will be part of the design.

Talking creatively about design was not something Linda Cook had imagined in 1997, when there was barely enough money to buy books and keep the lights on. In 2008, the board of the Edmonton Public Library launched a ten-year capital plan worth $330 million, for repairs and renovations to the branches. City council didn't reject the idea. Instead, it directed administrators to come up with a funding strategy. "I dare say, if we funded more libraries, we wouldn't need as many police officers or social workers," said Councillor Linda Sloan, at the time.

By 2012, the EPL had produced a set of stunning architectural renderings of what the reimagined Jasper Place and Highlands Branches will look like when they are finished. The Edmonton Public Library is partnering with other organizations and agencies to be joint tenants of new buildings in Clareview, Mill Woods and, farther south, The Meadows, which will mix new library space with recreation, seniors' services, and multicultural centres.

If we look back to the first downtown branch, we will remember the words carved above its front doors: "Free to All." We can define free in as many ways as we like. The library represents free access to information and freedom of expression. We are still arguing about whether or not the library is sufficiently free.

The Meadows, opening in 2014, will meld a recreation centre and a new Edmonton Public Library branch. [EPL]

The new Mill Woods Branch, opening in 2014, will blend a library with a seniors' and multicultural centre. [EPL]

Anyone who asks to have a library card without paying a $12 yearly membership fee will receive one. Librarians don't ask to see anyone's tax returns. Perhaps we would be better off making it free and asking for a donation—whatever we can afford. Or perhaps that is more awkward and intrusive than asking people whether or not they can afford $12. Either way, despite an enormous jump in population since 1994, and philosophical certainty that the services of the Edmonton Public Library are well worth $12, we still haven't returned to the record numbers of members we had before the fee.

Alberta and Quebec are the only two provinces that have library fees.

"How do other provinces, struggling with deficits and bigger tax loads, manage to avoid library user fees?" asked an editorialist in 2005. "They subscribe to the widely accepted theory that reading and access to books and computers are a basic necessity for citizens in a democracy."[5]

There is, of course, a good counter-argument. The library always has another program, another innovation, another department, a new set of books, or films, or computers or renovations to fulfill its mandate of launching Edmontonians into a better life.

The children's library in the Stanley A. Milner Branch. [EPL]

41 To launch a new generation of readers

ON AN UNUSUALLY HOT DAY in the summer of 2012, parents and their children moved freely from the cold water fountain in front of city hall, through the silliness of the Street Performers' Festival, and into the Stanley Milner Branch of the Edmonton Public Library. I was one of those parents and my two daughters, six and four, were with me.

Like Don Iveson's son Dexter, my children are drawn to the computers in the children's library. It's difficult to imagine now, in our litigious time, a petting zoo or monkeys swinging from curtains or even an iguana. The library doesn't need a zoo to be thrilling for a child. That day in July it was bright and cool in the library, and my daughters scrutinized the stacks: one book per week is our limit right now, for no good reason.

I like to pretend I understand my children but I have no idea what they're thinking as they move past the books, pulling one out and examining it and putting it back. Normally, this library visit takes between ten and twenty minutes, finding the right book. They will occasionally please me by seeking my counsel. As often as possible, I am either ignorant or I feign ignorance, which gives me an opportunity to introduce one of my daughters to a librarian. Then I back away and watch. My shy daughter asks a question and the librarian either answers it or seeks elaboration. The librarians always seem careful to preserve a sense of magic in the transaction, to let my daughters make their choice—a better choice, surely, than if they had done it on their own or with me.

My grandfather and grandmother, standing in front of the Carnegie Library on Macdonald Drive one evening, novels in their hands. My daughter, asking for a book about Amsterdam on the hottest or the coldest day of the year. They are among the millions of memories about the Edmonton Public Library, some real, some imagined, and all of them—taken together—are the birth of some new idea about what this place is, has been, will be.

Happy birthday, EPL. Here's to another hundred years of reading Edmonton.

A Timeline of the Edmonton Public Library

1904 | Edmonton is incorporated as a city. Population 7,000.

1905 | Alberta becomes a province of Canada. Edmonton is made the capital.

1907 | The Alberta Legislature passes An Act to Provide for the Establishment of Public Libraries (Public Librairies Act).

1909 | The first Edmonton Public Library board consists of Mayor Robert Lee, Alderman J. E. Lundy, C. Ross Palmer, K.W. McKenzie, Judge N. D. Beck, Prof. Riddell, and L. Madore.

1910 | The Edmonton Public Library purchases a site, known as the Wilson property, on Macdonald Drive, known then as College Avenue. This is the site where Telus Plaza now stands at 100 Avenue and 100 Street.

1912 | The library boards in the cities of Strathcona and Edmonton meet to consider the establishment of two libraries—one for each side of the river. Mr. E.L. Hill is appointed librarian for both libraries.

1913 | Strathcona Library opens to the public at 8331 104 Street. Edmonton Public Library starts operations in its temporary quarters at the corner of Jasper Avenue and 104 Street, on the second floor of the Chisholm Block, above a meat shop and a liquor store.

1914 | The Edmonton Public Library moves to the Roberts Block, on 102 Street and 102 Avenue.

1915 | The number of borrowers increases by nearly thirty per cent. Circulation averages five volumes per borrower, with fewer than 30,000 circulating books.

1917 | The Edmonton Public Library moves again, to the Civic Block at 99 Street and 102 Avenue, today the address of the Winspear Centre.

1918 | Owing to the Spanish Influenza epidemic in Edmonton, the circulation of books is suspended from October 18 to December 2. The Young People's Department does not resume full operation until after the end of the year.

1919 | The board approves the creation of the position of children's librarian.

1920 | The board moves that: "it is expedient and in the interests of the people of this City that a suitable building be erected for the purposes of the Central Library..." Negotiations resume with the Carnegie Corporation, which offers a grant of $75,000.

1922 | In January the board receives a reply from the Carnegie Corporation stating they cannot increase the grant from $75,000 to $150,000. The Board decides to send the chairman to New York, and to request a meeting in February with Mr. Bertram, the Carnegie Corporation's secretary. The Carnegie Corporation agrees to a grant of $112,500.

1923 | Local architects H.A. Magoon and G.H. MacDonald complete the Carnegie Library building on Macdonald Drive. It opens formally on August 30th. Carved above the front door: FREE TO ALL.

1924 | A Ukrainian section is launched with the purchase of some fifty volumes and the acceptance of about one hundred books collected by the Ukrainian population.

1925 | The board refuses a request to have the book on the life of Mary Baker Eddy, by Willa Cather and Georgine Milmine, removed from the shelf.

1926 | The chief librarian's report for 1926 recommends "the desirability of library extension in the Province, particularly in view of the fact that no department of the Government was directly concerned in Library matters."

1927 | In November the artist, Mr. William Johnstone, writes to offer to sell a portrait of the Prince of Wales to the Board for $500. The board responds by saying that it could not see its way clear to purchase the painting but is willing to care for the picture. It hangs in the library.

1929 | The Strathcona Branch wins a second prize for landscaping in the competition for public buildings arranged by the Horticultural

Society. The Edmonton Public Library's central branch receives commendation from the judges.

1931 | The chief librarian's report shows the circulation of books in January is twenty per cent greater than that in January 1929. The same increase is noted in April and May.

1932 | According to the annual report, "the vast increase in service rendered has not been accompanied by any increase in numbers or remuneration of staff..."

1933 | The borrowers' register, containing some 20,000 names, reveals the general and extensive use of the library and "coincided pretty well with a cross-section of the City Directory as regards occupation."

1936 | In September Chief Librarian E.L. Hill resigns. Grace Dobie is appointed acting librarian.

1937 | In January the board passes a motion to city council not recommending the payment of a retirement allowance to Mr. Hill.

1938 | Edmonton's population reaches 60,000. In October the board adopts the pension scheme accepted by the city council for civic employees, commencing November 1.

1939 | The board resolves to offer the position of chief librarian of the Edmonton Public Library to Mr. Hugh C. Gourlay at a salary of $3,000 per annum.

1941 | The Streetcar Branch of the Edmonton Public Library is approved on a trial basis for one year, starting in September.

1942 | The annual report states that the library is affected by the war in every phase of its work—from the difficulties in obtaining materials to the many adjustments necessary in keeping the library adequately staffed.

1943 | The finance committee studies the establishment of a music room.

1944 | The board purchases a grand piano from Woodwards for $895. Then the library returns it and buys an upright Heintzman for $1,796.

1947 | The first bookmobile, a retired Edmonton Transit bus, is added to serve areas in Edmonton that the streetcar library can't reach.

1949 | The Strathcona Branch opens a children's room.

1953 | The Sprucewood Branch starts operations at 11824 85 Street in St. Alphonsus Church.

1955 | The second director of the Edmonton Public Library, Mr. Hugh Gourlay, retires.

1956 | Morton Coburn becomes the third director.

1957 | The annual book circulation at the Edmonton Public Library exceeds one million for the first time.

1958 | The new Sprucewood Branch opens at 11555 95 Street. The new building is constructed by R.H. Rae and Sons.

1959 | Mr. V.C. Strong of Edmonton Truck Body Ltd. designs the first purpose-built bookmobile. The board agrees to the proposal for a price of $11,300.

1960 | Idylwylde Branch opens on June 1, in a combined health and library building at 8310 88 Avenue, in the Bonnie Doon area.

1961 | Three bookmobiles manned by four crews make fifty weekly stops and operate a twelve-hour schedule, five days a week.

1962 | The children's library in the downtown branch has a new home in an annex to the main building.

1963 | Young Edmontonians borrow more books in 1963 than in any other period during the Edmonton Public Library's first fifty years.

1964 | City council approves the construction of a new library building as the 1967 Centennial project, and a special committee is established to oversee the plan.

1966 | The Calder Branch and the Capilano Branch open to the public.

1967 | The new Centennial Library opens on May 27. Her Royal Highness Princess Alexandra of Kent unveils the commemorative plaque, assisted by Mayor Vincent Dantzer.

1971 | Southgate Branch opens in the Southgate Shopping Mall.

1972 | Morton Coburn resigns as the third director of the Edmonton Public Library. Allen W. Rowe, then Executive Assistant to Mayor Ivor Dent, is appointed acting director.

1973 | Mr. Brian Dale is appointed the library's fifth director, with Mr. Allen W. Rowe as administrator. Dickinsfield Branch opens in the Dickinsfield Shopping Mall at 144 Avenue and 92 Street.

1975 | The first booktrailer arrives in Edmonton.

1976 | Mr. Brian Dale resigns.

1977 | Mr. Vincent Richards is appointed the library's sixth director. Detailed planning begins to introduce computers to various library operations, and the first equipment is installed.

1979 | The Edmonton Public Library becomes the first public library in Canada to use a fully integrated computerized circulation system.

1980 | The Edmonton Public Library publishes a collection of children's writing and art, *75 and Growing*, to commemorate Alberta's 75th Anniversary.

1981 | The EPL receives an international award for its Library Lovers' Day campaign. Castle Downs Branch opens.

1982 | The Mill Woods Branch opens in the Mill Woods Recreation Centre.

1983 | The Edmonton Public Library celebrates its seventieth anniversary. Library materials circulation reach 6.6 million, the highest recorded in a Canadian library.

1984 | For the second consecutive year the EPL is the busiest library in Canada, with circulation topping 7.5 million. A new Alberta

Libraries Act takes effect on April 1. Dickinsfield Branch relocates to the Londonderry Mall and is renamed the Londonderry Branch.

1986 | In a dire financial situation, the EPL board forms a committee to solicit donations from corporate and private sectors for a library endowment fund. More than 2,000 people attend a series of sixteen authors' readings, including Alice Munro, René Lévesque, and Timothy Findlay.

1987 | For the fifth straight year, EPL achieves the highest circulation of materials, at the lowest cost per item circulated, of any public library in Canada. The Southgate Branch has been the busiest branch library in Canada since 1984, with a circulation of 1,405,066. The tragedy of the tornado, which hits Edmonton in late July, brings losses to the library in damaged and missing materials. Overdue fines are waived and lost items written off.

1988 | With funding from the Alberta Foundation for the Literary Arts, the Edmonton Public Library initiates a Writer in Residence program in September 1988 to celebrate its 75th anniversary. The Library's first Writer in Residence is Monica Hughes, a renowned Edmonton author who writes for young adults.

1989 | The Edmonton Public Library and the Writers' Guild of Alberta host a cultural exchange between Canada and the USSR. A reading entitled "East West Passage" is held for several Soviet poets and novelists. Director Vincent Richards retires in the summer of 1989 after twelve years of service.

1990 | Penelope McKee is the seventh director. Attendance at the Edmonton Public Library is 3,130,214, outdrawing the Edmonton

Oilers by a ratio of five to one. The Board decides to discontinue the bookmobile.

1991 | In January, the Friends of the Edmonton Public Library is formed as a support organization with Jeffrey Moore, a law student, elected chair.

1993 | The Library Access Division coordinates 164 volunteers to bring library materials to 3,000 people in their homes or institutions because they are unable to use regular libraries.

1994 | The EPL re-introduces a $12 adult membership fee, with household discounts. Children under 18 do not have to pay. Adults with limited income can have their fee waived.

1995 | Plans begin for a new capital campaign, Foundations of Learning, to raise funds for the Library Development Plan, including three new libraries in Edmonton.

1996 | In a ceremony on August 22, the EPL renames the Centennial Library after Stanley A. Milner to honour his many contributions. Milner spearheaded the construction of the main library as Edmonton's project to celebrate Canada's centennial in 1967, and served as the chair of library board between 1963 and 1968. Penny McKee, director, retires.

1997 | Linda C. Cook joins the Edmonton Public Library as its eighth director. The new branch in Abbottsfield is named after Penny McKee, who dies of cancer in May.

1998 | The EPL provides computer stations for all fifteen branches. These computers give customers access to the Internet and various electronic databases, and the capability to check the online catalogue and their own accounts.

1999 | The EPL updates its mission statement: "Edmonton Public Library connects the people of Edmonton to the knowledge and cultures of the world."

2000 | The Riverbend Branch opens on May 18 with Scottish pipes and Chinese lion dances. The Bill and Melinda Gates Foundation and Microsoft Canada donate $1.8 million to help libraries in Alberta expand public access to the Internet. The EPL receives fifty-four computers under this program.

2001 | The new Heritage Room opens on the second floor of the Stanley A. Milner Branch, housing a special, non-circulating collection of 10,000 titles, with a focus on the history and development of Edmonton, along with northern Alberta and western Canada.

2002 | "Edmonton: A City Called Home" is a multimedia project that engages Edmontonians in the preparation of a new, comprehensive historical resource about the city's history and culture. Comprising two books by Linda Goyette—a collection of first-person narratives and a book for children—and the creation of a website, this is the City of Edmonton's education project to celebrate its centennial in 2004.

2003 | The EPL celebrates its ninetieth anniversary with a kick-off celebration at Strathcona Branch on March 13. Staff from the library and Fort Edmonton Park dress in period costumes.

2004 | A task force explores library services to Aboriginal peoples. Library staff and members of the Aboriginal community work together on a report to the library board. There are more than 8.5 million visits to the EPL. Almost 140,000 people attend 4,000 programs.

2005 | Strathcona Branch moves to temporary quarters in preparation for a major expansion and restoration. Milner Library celebrates the completion of the third phase of the renovation and expansion. Castle Downs Branch adds 2,700 square feet to accommodate the increased demand for service for 250,000 visitors per year.

2006 | In September the EPL begins radio frequency identification tagging of materials. RFID allows customers to check out their own library materials. Linda Cook becomes the president of the Canadian Library Association.

2007 | Federal census shows that Edmonton is growing faster than any other Canadian city. Writer in Residence Linda Goyette creates a support group at the library for writers who have arrived in Edmonton from other countries, and edits an anthology of their work called *The Story That Brought Me Here*. Jalal Barzanji begins a one-year term as Edmonton's Writer-in-Exile, working at both the Edmonton Public Library and the University of Alberta, Faculty of Arts.

2008 | The Lois Hole Library opens at 17650 69 Avenue. It is named in honour of the fifteenth Lieutenant-Governor of Alberta who was a champion of public libraries.

2009 | The eplGO Branch at the University of Alberta opens in March. Introductory Cree language conversation classes are offered for the first time at EPL, free of charge.

2010 | EPL receives national and international recognition for its Community-Led Service Philosophy with nineteen community librarians taking library services beyond the walls of the buildings and into the community—meeting with hundreds of agencies and groups in the neighbourhoods served by each branch. Chris Craddock becomes EPL's Writer in Residence, and in September, Goran Simic becomes Edmonton's fourth Writer-in-Exile.

2011 | EPL begins lending services at the Edmonton Institute for Women, and book clubs start at the Edmonton Young Offenders Centre. Marty Chan becomes the 2011 Writer in Residence, initiating several new approaches using social media. Design and construction begins on the new buildings to replace Jasper Place, Highlands and Mill Woods Branches and the new Clareview and Meadows Branches. Through its Safe Communities Initiative Fund, the Province of Alberta awards EPL a three-year $605,000 grant in support of the "Building a Safer Community Through Inclusive Learning" collaborative project with Boyle Street Community Services.

2012 | EPL is presented with the Alberta Municipal Affairs Minister's Award for Excellence and Innovation in Public Library Service for services for Aboriginal peoples. Jocelyn Brown becomes the 2012 Writer in Residence. eReader lending is initiated system-wide. Tenders are awarded for the construction of a new Mill Woods Branch and a schematic design of a new Calder Branch. Linda Cook, Chief Executive Officer of EPL since 1997, is awarded the Queen Elizabeth II Diamond Jubilee Medal at a ceremony celebrating the outstanding service of Capital Region leaders.

2013 | EPL joins other metro Edmonton library systems to sponsor two Writers in Residence, Omar Mouallem and Natasha Deen, as part of the Metro Edmonton Federation of Libraries Writers in Residence program. The Library welcomes its first customers to the new Jasper Place Branch. On March 13, the City celebrates "Edmonton Public Library Day." EPL marks its centennial with a year of free library cards for all city residents, birthday BBQS, and guest speakers. An ambitious pilot "Makerspace" program is launched at Milner Library.

Notes

Foreword

1. Omar Mouallem, "Top 40 Under 40," *Avenue* Edmonton, November, 2011: http://avenueedmonton.com/top-40-under-40/todd-babiak.

1 Without a library, is a city a city?

1. Lewis Cardinal, *Spirit of Edmonton: Reclaiming Monto: A Collective Vision Connecting the River and the People* (Edmonton: Indigenous Peoples' Arts and Culture Coalition, 2011).
2. Pierre Berton, *Klondike: The Last Great Gold Rush, 1896–1899* (Toronto: Anchor Canada, 2001), 216.

2 Permanence and maturity and pride

1. Alberto Manguel, *The Library at Night* (Toronto: Knopf Canada, 2006), 26.
2. City of Edmonton, "City of Edmonton Population, Historical," 2005.
3. John E. Lundy, *Draft Historical Script* (Edmonton: Edmonton Public Library, 1988).

4. John Blue, *Alberta, Past and Present: Historical and Biographical, Volume III* (Chicago: Pioneer Historical Publishing, 1924), 16–17.
5. Anne Newall, "Historical Sketch," *Annual Report of the Edmonton Public Library and the Strathcona Public Library,* 1913.
6. Tony Cashman, in conversation, April 19, 2012.

3 The richest man in the world

1. Peter Krass, *Carnegie* (Hoboken: John Wiley and Sons, 2011), 43.
2. Joseph Frazier Wall, *Andrew Carnegie* (Pittsburgh: University of Pittsburgh Press, 1989), 108.
3. Manguel, *The Library at Night,* 101.
4. Patricia Dalrymple et al., *Strathcona Public Library* (NAIT: Edmonton, 2001), 13.
5. Edmonton Public Library, Minutes of Meetings of the Board, July 19, 2012.
6. George M. Hall, "Edmonton: Capital of Alberta," *Annual Report of the Edmonton Public Library and Strathcona Public Library,* 1913.
7. Newall, "Historical Sketch."
8. E.L. Hill, *Annual Report of the Edmonton Public Library and the Strathcona Public Library*, 1913.

4 A repository for Edmonton-ness?

1. Antonio Panizzi, *Report from the Select Committee on the British Museum together with the Minutes of Evidence, appendix and index*, 1836.

5 A big city negotiation

1. Thomas Carlyle, *On Heroes, Hero-Worship, and the Heroic in History* [1888] (Project Gutenberg, 2008), http://www.gutenberg.org/files/1091/1091-h/1091-h.htm.
2. Philip Rowland Harris, *The Reading Room* (London: British Library, 1979), 9.
3. Heather McIntyre, "Library—a place to rebuild your life," *Metro Edmonton,* March 14, 2012.
4. McIntyre, "Library—a place to rebuild your life."
5. Panizzi, *Report from the Select Committee.*

6 Above the liquor store and meat shop

1. Lawrence Herzog, "'Sweet Memories of the Palace of Sweets," *Real Estate Weekly* 26, no. 21 (May 29, 2008): http://www.rewedmonton.ca/content—view—rew?CONTENT—ID=2221.
2. Herzog, "'Sweet Memories of the Palace of Sweets."
3. Lawrence Herzog, "Vanished Buildings of the 1913 Boom," *Real Estate Weekly* 25, no. 36 (September 6, 2007): http://www.rewedmonton.ca/content—view—rew?CONTENT—ID=1965.
4. Edmonton Public Library, Minutes of Meetings of the Board, May 28, 1915.
5. Jac Mcdonald, "Civic Block demolition OKd by City Council," *Edmonton Journal,* June 28, 1989.
6. E.L. Hill, *Annual Report of the Edmonton Public Library,* 1918.
7. David Howell, "A deadly path tore through city," *Edmonton Journal,* December 2, 2005.

7 Edmonton's acropolis

1. Linda Goyette and Carolina Roemmich, *Edmonton In Our Own Words,* (Edmonton: The University of Alberta Press, 2004), 235.
2. Goyette and Roemmich, *Edmonton In Our Own Words,* 235.
3. Goyette and Roemmich, *Edmonton In Our Own Words,* 235.
4. Goyette and Roemmich, *Edmonton In Our Own Words,* 235.
5. Edmonton Public Library, Minutes of Meetings of the Board, Meeting of April 13, 1922.
6. Lawrence Herzog, "The Legacy of Magoon and MacDonald," *Real Estate Weekly* 21, no. 50 (December 18, 2003): http://www.rewedmonton.ca/content—view2?CONTENT—ID=583.
7. Percy Johnson, "The Edmonton Public Library: An Architectural History of a Carnegie Library Building," (master's thesis, Concordia University, 1994), 58.
8. Johnson, "The Edmonton Public Library," 64.
9. Johnson, "The Edmonton Public Library," 65.
10. Edmonton Economic Development Corporation. "Account of CJCA's first broadcast," n.d.
11. *Edmonton Public Library Grand Opening Program,* Edmonton Public Library Archives, August 23, 1923.
12. Cashman, in conversation, April 19, 2012.

8 "We're bigger than our buildings"

1. E.L. Hill, *Annual Report of the Edmonton Public Library,* 1924.
2. Hill, *Annual Report,* 1924.
3. Hill, *Annual Report,* 1924.
4. Lawrence Herzog, "Industry on the River," *Real Estate Weekly* 25, no. 12 (March 22, 2007): http://www.rewedmonton.ca/content—view—rew?CONTENT—ID=1785.
5. Herzog, "Industry on the River."
6. E.L. Hill, *Annual Report of the Edmonton Public Library and Strathcona Public Library,* 1913.
7. "90 Years of Photos," Edmonton Public Library, https://www.epl.ca/edmonton-history/90-years-of-photos.
8. E.L. Hill, *Annual Report of the Edmonton Public Library,* 1927.
9. E.L. Hill, *Annual Report of the Edmonton Public Library,* 1929.
10. Edmonton Public Library, Minutes of Meetings of the Board, 1929.

9 Tough times in the "Rome of the West"

1. Lawrence Herzog, "Oliver Gets Through the Depression" *Real Estate Weekly* 26, no. 2 (January 17, 2008): http://www.rewedmonton.ca/content—view—rew?CONTENT—ID=2089.
2. E.L. Hill, *Annual Report of the Edmonton Public Library,* 1930.
3. *Edmonton Public Library: draft historical script,* May 25, 1988.
4. The Applied History Research Group, "The National Association of Canada and the Ku Klux Klan," University of Calgary, 1997.
5. Goyette and Roemmich, *Edmonton In Our Own Words,* 274.
6. Raymond J.A. Huel, "J.J. Maloney: How the West Was Saved from Rome, Quebec and the Liberals," in John E. Foster, ed., *The Developing West: Essays on Canadian History in Honour of Lewis H. Thomas* (Edmonton: University of Alberta Press, 1983), 233.
7. Huel, "J.J. Maloney," 234.

10 From the library to the street—and the legislature

1. E.L. Hill, *Annual Report to the Edmonton Public Library,* 1932.
2. Goyette and Roemmich, *Edmonton In Our Own Words,* 281.
3. Goyette and Roemmich, *Edmonton In Our Own Words,* 281.

4. Goyette and Roemmich, *Edmonton In Our Own Words*, 289.
5. Editorial. "Historical Information," *Edmonton Journal*, centennial celebration supplement, 2002.
6. Grace Dobie, *Annual Report of the Edmonton Public Library*, 1937.
7. Unnamed U.S. state governor, quoted in E.L. Hill, *Annual Report to the Edmonton Public Library*, 1934 and 1935.

11 A firecracker of a man

1. Brian Brennan, *The Calgary Public Library: Inspiring Life Stories since 1912* (Calgary: Calgary Public Library, 2012), 41.
2. Alexander Calhoun, *Report to the Board of the Edmonton Public Library*, February 21, 1939.
3. Calhoun, *Report to the Board*, 1939.
4. James W. Pilton, *Hugh Cameron Gourlay, 1903–1971*, (Edmonton: Edmonton Public Library, 1971), 3, 22.
5. Pilton, *Hugh Cameron Gourlay*, 1.
6. Hugh Gourlay, *Annual Report of the Edmonton Public Library*, 1939.
7. Pilton, *Hugh Cameron Gourlay*, 5.
8. Pilton, *Hugh Cameron Gourlay*, 6.
9. "A Surprised Old Tramcar Finds Itself a Traveling Library," *Christian Science Monitor*, January 24, 1942.
10. Pilton, *Hugh Cameron Gourlay*, 14.
11. Hugh Gourlay, *Annual Report of the Edmonton Public Library*, 1941.
12. Hugh Gourlay, *Annual Report of the Edmonton Public Library*, 1945.
13. Gourlay, *Annual Report*, 1941.
14. Pilton, *Hugh Cameron Gourlay*, 9.

12 The violinist with a broom

1. Hugh Gourlay, *Annual Report of the Edmonton Public Library*, 1943.
2. "Played Two Roles," *Edmonton Journal*, September 4, 1948.
3. Pilton, *Hugh Cameron Gourlay*, 9.

13 A centre of culture

1. Gourlay, *Annual Report*, 1943.
2. Gourlay, *Annual Report*, 1945.

3. "City Library Music Centre Has Plans for Full Season," *Edmonton Journal,* August 31, 1946.

14 Gourlay's error

1. "Seek Amendment to Libraries Act," *Edmonton Journal,* October 11, 1947.
2. Pilton, *Hugh Cameron Gourlay,* 17.
3. "Library to ask for a City Grant," *Edmonton Journal,* September 14, 1948.
4. Pilton, *Hugh Cameron Gourlay,* 17.
5. "Board Seeking $5,000 Grant to Carry Library through Year," *Edmonton Journal,* September 25, 1948.
6. "Board Seeking $5,000 Grant to Carry Library through Year," *Edmonton Journal,* September 25, 1948.
7. "Grant of $5,000 Made to Library," *Edmonton Journal,* September 28, 1948.
8. "Demands Inquiry into Operations of Public Libarary," *Edmonton Journal,* April 26, 1949.
9. "Public Library Policies Defended," *Edmonton Journal,* May 20, 1949.
10. Pilton, *Hugh Cameron Gourlay,* 20.
11. City of Edmonton, "City of Edmonton Population, Historical," 2005.
12. "Library Staff Honors A. Alexeeff," *Edmonton Journal,* December 5, 1953.

15 Call me Bill

1. Brian Brennan, "Mayor's hallmark was success against all odds," *Business Edge,* vol. 2, no. 5, February 28, 2002. www.businessedge.ca/archives/article.cfm/mayorshallmark-was-success-against-all-odds-1156.
2. Goyette and Roemmich, *Edmonton in Our Own Words,* 314.
3. Brennan, "Mayor's hallmark."
4. Quoted in Brennan, "Mayor's hallmark."

16 The first branch

1. Brennan, "Mayor's hallmark."
2. Elise Slotte, "Does Chinatown actually exist in the Quarters?" *Edmonton Journal,* March 15, 2012.
3. Cashman, in conversation, April 19, 2012.
4. Stephen Mandel, in conversation, May 11, 2012.
5. Pilton, *Hugh Cameron Gourlay*, 22.

17 That tiny Carnegie library on the hill

1. Cashman, in conversation, April 19, 2012.
2. Morton Corburn, in conversation, June 4, 2012.
3. Corburn, in conversation, June 4, 2012.

18 The fight against the fleshpots

1. University of Alberta Faculty of Education. "Faculty Profile: School of Library and Information Studies." http://www.ualberta.ca/ALUMNI/history/faculties/81maylib.htm.
2. Coburn, in conversation, June 4, 2012.
3. Heather-Belle Dowling, in conversation, May 19, 2012.
4. Dowling, in conversation, May 19, 2012.
5. Dowling, in conversation, May 19, 2012.
6. Morton Coburn, *Annual Report of the Edmonton Public Library,* 1963.
7. Lawrence Herzog, "Westmount Mall at 50," *Real Estate Weekly,* vol. 23, no. 35 (September 1, 2005). http://www.rewedmonton.ca/content—view—rew?CONTENT—ID=1147.
8. Brenda Bouw, "Debate still on over location of new library; Three sites under consideration." *Edmonton Journal,* October 22, 1996.
9. Editorial, "Library wisely listened to people who use it." *Edmonton Journal,* January 11, 1997.

19 Mid-century modern

1. Lawrence Herzog, "When Jasper Place joined Edmonton" *Real Estate Weekly,* vol. 20, no. 40 (October 3, 2002). http://www.rewedmonton.ca/content—view2?CONTENT—ID=216.
2. International Federation of Library Associations and Institutions, IFLANet, Quotations about Libraries and Librarians: http://archive.ifla.org/I/humour/subj.htm#lib.
3. Lawrence Herzog, "A New Library for Jasper Place," *Real Estate Weekly,* vol. 28, no. 42 (October 21, 2010). http://www.rewedmonton.ca/content—view—rew?CONTENT—ID=2959.
4. Quoted in Herzog, "When Jasper Place joined Edmonton."
5. Linda Cook, in conversation, April 4, 2012.

6. Andrea Sands, "New Jasper Place library designed to meet possibly book-free future" *Edmonton Journal.* September 11, 2010.

20 Sex

1. Coburn, in conversation, June 4, 2012.
2. Nicholas Spillios, in conversation, June 9, 2012.
3. Spillios, in conversation, June 9, 2012.
4. Dowling, in conversation, May 19, 2012.

21 The Carnegie of Edmonton

1. Stanley Milner, in conversation, April 7, 2012.
2. Goyette and Roemmich, *Edmonton In Our Own Words,* 323.
3. Goyette and Roemmich, *Edmonton In Our Own Words,* 324.
4. Milner, in conversation, April 7, 2012.
5. Goyette and Roemmich, *Edmonton In Our Own Words,* 326.
6. Milner, in conversation, April 7, 2012.
7. Milner, in conversation, April 7, 2012.
8. Milner, in conversation, April 7, 2012.

22 The dominion of the mall

1. Donna Gordon Blankinship, "Let's Go to the Mall." *Library Journal,* vol 130, no. 2 (February 1, 2005), 44.

23 You're our expert. Build the library.

1. Coburn, in conversation, June 4, 2012.
2. Coburn, in conversation, June 4, 2012.
3. Mandel, in conversation, May 11, 2012.
4. Milner, in conversation, April 17, 2012.
5. Edmonton Public Library, "Biographies of Mayors and Councillors" Online. http://www.epl.ca/edmonton-history/edmonton-elections/biographies-mayors-and-councillors?id=C.
6. Morton Coburn, *Annual Report of the Edmonton Public Library,* 1962.
7. Edmonton Public Library, "Capsule History," Online. http://www.epl.ca/edmonton-history/epl-capsule-history.

8. Coburn, *Annual Report,* 1962.

9. Cook, in conversation, April 4, 2012.

24 Big Brother in Edmonton

1. G.F. Smythe, "When $50,000 in books disappear in a year, you've got to act," *Edmonton Journal,* March 10, 1966.

2. Dowling, in conversation, May 19, 2012.

3. "Former Member Reveals City Library Board Conflict," *Edmonton Journal,* January 12, 1966.

4. "TV Will Watch Library Patrons," *Edmonton Journal,* April 12, 1967.

5. Shirley Hunter, "Who's Afraid of TV Monitors?" *Edmonton Journal,* May 2, 1967.

6. Hunter, "Who's Afraid of TV Monitors?"

7. D.G. Turnbull, "Big brother?" *Edmonton Journal,* July 5, 1967.

25 That brilliant, sunny Saturday afternoon

1. Milton Coburn, "Edmonton Public Library news notes," 12, no. 3, (December 1967).

2. Coburn, "Edmonton Public Library news notes."

3. Elaine Verbicky, "Library meant for People," *The Western Catholic Reporter,* May 25, 1967.

4. Morton Coburn, *Annual Report of the Edmonton Public Library,* 1967.

26 Then the Sixties happened

1. John J. Barr, "The library that turned me on." *Edmonton Journal,* November 17, 1967.

2. "Library Chairman Tells of Incidents," *Edmonton Journal,* February 1, 1968.

3. Coburn, in conversation, June 4, 2012.

4. Morton Coburn, *Annual Report of the Edmonton Public Library,* 1969.

5. Coburn, *Annual Report,* 1969.

6. Coburn, *Annual Report,* 1969.

27 Phantom Edmonton

1. Cashman, in conversation, April 19, 2012.

2. Aleta Vikse, Letter of resignation to the board of the Edmonton Public Library, June 7, 1972.
3. Dowling, in conversation, May 19, 2012.
4. Coburn, in conversation, June 4, 2012.

28 All it needed was a lava lamp

1. "Southgate Mall Library Officially Opens Thursday," *Edmonton Journal,* March 17, 1971.
2. "Southgate Mall Library Officially Opens Thursday," *Edmonton Journal,* March 17, 1971.

29 Something called "Alberta culture"

1. "Schmid warns against drift away from books," *Edmonton Journal,* January 11, 1973.
2. Dona Harvey, "Who says a library's just for books!" *Edmonton Journal,* January 26, 1973.
3. Bernice Briggs, in conversation, June 1, 2012.
4. Board Minutes, Edmonton Public Library Board, April 1, 1974.
5. Patti Meekison, Presentation and letter to the board of the Edmonton Public Library, February 12, 1976.
6. Brian Dale, Letter of resignation, October 27, 1976.
7. Manguel, *The Library at Night,* 115.
8. Darren Lund, "Behind Day poise, narrow views persist," *Edmonton Journal,* July 7, 2000.
9. Manguel, *The Library at Night,* 125.
10. Robert Kroetsch, *The Studhorse Man* (Edmonton: University of Alberta Press, 2004), 29.

30 An off-season Santa Claus

1. Frank Hutton, *Edmonton Journal,* February 16, 1977.
2. Guy Demarino, "Library Aid Big Step Up," *Edmonton Journal,* March 15, 1977.
3. "City libraries to reap benefits of $436,000 gov't grant," *Edmonton Journal,* April 1, 1977.
4. "New library head stimulated by province's money squeeze," *Saint John's Edmonton Report,* April 25, 1977.

31 Freedom of expression

1. "After the great nudes debate, sales are up," *Saint John's Edmonton Report,* March 31, 1978.
2. Jim McNulty, "Library bares all; mayor is miffed," *Edmonton Journal,* March 23, 1978.
3. "After the great nudes debate, sales are up."
4. "Library 'regulars' upset," *Edmonton Journal,* January 23, 1979.

32 Lougheed, Trudeau and the busiest library on the continent

1. Vince Richards, *Annual Report of the Edmonton Public Library,* 1980.
2. Vince Richards, *Annual Report of the Edmonton Public Library,* 1982.
3. Vince Richards, *Annual Report of the Edmonton Public Library,* 1983.
4. Richards, *Annual Report,* 1983.

33 Public libraries are going to die

1. James Adams, "City library system bubbling at 75," *Edmonton Journal,* March 11, 1988.
2. Adams, "City library system bubbling at 75."
3. Keith Turnbull, in conversation, May 28, 2012.
4. Turnbull, in conversation, May 28, 2012.
5. Edmonton Public Library, "Capsule History."

34 Someone fabulous

1. Mike Sadava, "'Have not' libraries plead for city funds," *Edmonton Journal,* November 22, 1989.
2. John Geiger, "Library budget boost a bid to save face," *Edmonton Journal,* November 28, 1989.
3. Edmonton Public Library, "Capsule History."
4. "Library director puts fund raising, staff development at top of her list," *Ministream,* July 20, 1990.
5. Bill Smith, in conversation, June 15, 2012.
6. David Howell, "Alberta policy OKs recreational funding for libraries," *Edmonton Journal,* August 4, 1990.
7. John Geiger, "On Kozak's attrition of library petition," *Edmonton Journal.* February 7, 1991.

8. David Howell, "Public library expanded under former director," *Edmonton Journal*, May 26, 1997.

35 Free to all

1. Stephen Irwin, "Library wants to hit readers with $12 fee," *Edmonton Journal*, September 8, 1993.
2. Turnbull, in conversation, May 28, 2012.
3. James Stevenson, "Library launches fundraiser," *Edmonton Journal*, September 5, 1996.
4. Susan Ruttan, "Public library a treasure worth preserving," *Edmonton Journal*, November 16, 1996.
5. Turnbull, in conversation, May 28, 2012.
6. David Howell, "Public library expanded under former director," May 26, 1997.

36 The girl from Bonnie Doon

1. Jeff Holubitsky, "The book on Cook," *Edmonton Journal*, January 5, 1997.
2. Cook, quoted in "The book on Cook."
3. Cook, quoted in "The book on Cook."
4. Cook, quoted in "The book on Cook."
5. Turnbull, in conversation, May 28, 2012.
6. Pat Cavill, in conversation, March 25, 2012.

37 What is the opposite of threadbare?

1. Tamsin McMahon, "Library patron adds new chapter with Riverbend opening," *Edmonton Journal*, May 19, 2000.
2. Ron Chalmers, "It's time for province to take another read on library funding," *Edmonton Journal*, February 21, 2001.
3. Smith, in conversation, June 15, 2012.
4. Sarah O'Donnell, "Spending boost saves library branch," *Edmonton Journal*, December 19, 2002.
5. Turnbull, in conversation, May 28, 2012.
6. Paula Simons, "Increase in cultural funding small dance step in the right direction," *Edmonton Journal*, April 10, 2003.
7. Mandel, in conversation, May 11, 2012.

38 The mayor who changed everything

1. Mandel, in conversation, May 11, 2012.
2. Mandel, in conversation, May 11, 2012.

39 How to be an Edmontonian

1. Cook, in conversation, April 4, 2012.
2. Don Iveson, in conversation, August 9, 2012.
3. Iveson, in conversation, August 9, 2012.
4. Iveson, in conversation, August 9, 2012.

40 A terrible shame to lose a reader

1. Ernie Ingles, in conversation, September 22, 2012.
2. Ingles, in conversation, September 22, 2012.
3. Ingles, in conversation, September 22, 2012.
4. Cook, in conversation, April 4, 2012.
5. Editorial, "Free reading in Hole's honour," *Edmonton Journal,* January 15, 2005.

Select Bibliography

Berton, Pierre. *Klondike: The Last Great Gold Rush, 1896–1899*. Toronto: Anchor Canada, 2001.

Blue, John. *Alberta, Past and Present: Historical and Biographical, Volume III*. Chicago: Pioneer Historical Publishing, 1924.

Brennan, Brian. *The Calgary Public Library: Inspiring Life Stories Since 1912*. Calgary: Calgary Public Library, 2012.

Cardinal, Lewis. *Spirit of Edmonton: Reclaiming Monto: A Collective Vision Connecting the River and the People*. Edmonton: Indigenous Peoples' Arts and Culture Coalition, 2011.

Carlyle, Thomas. *On Heroes, Hero-Worship, and the Heroic in History*. Project Gutenberg, 2008. http://www.gutenberg.org/files/1091/1091-h/1091-h.htm.

Dalrymple, Patricia et al., *Strathcona Public Library*. NAIT: Edmonton, 2001.

Foster, John E., ed. *The Developing West: Essays on Canadian History in Honour of Lewis H. Thomas*. Edmonton: University of Alberta Press, 1983.

Goyette, Linda and Carolina Roemmich. *Edmonton In Our Own Words*. Edmonton: The University of Alberta Press, 2004.

Harris, Philip Rowland. *The Reading Room*. London: British Library, 1979.

Krass, Peter. *Carnegie*. Hoboken: John Wiley and Sons, 2011.

Kroetsch, Robert. *The Studhorse Man.* Edmonton: University of Alberta Press, 2004.
Manguel, Alberto. *The Library at Night.* Toronto: Knopf Canada, 2006.
Pilton, James W. *Hugh Cameron Gourlay, 1903–1971.* Edmonton: Edmonton Public Library, 1971.
Wall, Joseph Frazier. *Andrew Carnegie.* Pittsburgh: University of Pittsburgh Press, 1989.

Index

The abbreviation EPL *refers to Edmonton Public Library.*

Other Titles from The University of Alberta Press

Edmonton In Our Own Words

LINDA GOYETTE & CAROLINA JAKEWAY ROEMMICH

KEITH TURNBULL, *Foreword*

504 pages | B&W photographs, maps, timeline, notes, bibliography, index; The official publication of the City of Edmonton's Centennial

ISBN-13: 978-0-88864-449-7 | $39.95 (T) paper

Canadian History/Regional Interest

When Edmonton Was Young

TONY CASHMAN

LESLIE LATTA-GUTHRIE, *Foreword*

172 pages | 12 B&W photographs, foreword, index

ISBN-13: 978-0-88864-511-1 | $19.95 (T) paper

Canadian History/Regional Interest

Naming Edmonton

From Ada to Zoie

CITY OF EDMONTON

480 pages | Duotone photographs, 24 pages full-colour locator maps, historic maps, appendices, index

ISBN-13: 978-0-88864-423-7 | $49.95 (T) cloth

Regional History/Toponomy